SURREAL

ALSO BY/
MICHÈLE GERBER KLEIN

Charles James: Portrait of an Unreasonable Man

MICHÈLE GERBER KLEIN

the extraordinary
life of
gala dalí

HARPER

An Imprint of HarperCollins*Publishers*

HarperCollins books may be purchased for educational, business, or sales promotional use. For information, please email the Special Markets Department at SPsales@harpercollins.com.

FIRST EDITION

Designed by Elina Cohen

Library of Congress Cataloging-in-Publication Data
Names: Gerber Klein, Michèle, author.
Title: Surreal : the extraordinary life of Gala Dalí / Michèle Gerber Klein.
Description: First edition. | New York, NY : Harper, [2024] |
Includes bibliographical references and index.
Identifiers: LCCN 2024022948 | ISBN 9780063220577 (hardcover) |
ISBN 9780063220584 (trade paperback) | ISBN 9780063220591 (ebook)
Subjects: LCSH: Dalí, Gala. | Dalí Salvador, 1904-1989—Family. |
Artists' spouses—Spain—Biography. | Artists' models—Spain—Biography.
Classification: LCC N7113.D28 G47 2024 |
DDC 709.2 [B]—dc23/eng/20241212
LC record available at https://lccn.loc.gov/2024022948

25 26 27 28 29 LBC 5 4 3 2 1

TO MICHAEL WARD STOUT, WHOSE IDEA THIS WAS,
AND TO MY FATHER, WHO TAUGHT ME FRENCH

contents

PRINCESS OF THE FOREST

The lion cub curled up in her lap. He started to purr. Gala could hear the reporters and photographers outside the ballroom coughing and shuffling impatiently as they waited to be let in. Salvador carefully adjusted the strap of the unicorn headdress he had spent days making for her. He plumped the enormous red velvet cushions on the bed behind her so she would be more comfortable and tickled her gently under her chin. Gala smiled. The doors opened. Film cameras started to whir.

It was 7:00 p.m., September 2, 1941, in Pebble Beach, California. The ocean breeze smelled of salt and eucalyptus, and the waxing crescent moon hung so low in the warm, clear night sky that it seemed to graze the tops of the trees in the vast pine forest to the land side of the Del Monte, California's most storied hotel. The Dalís' art party was about to begin.

Gala and Salvador Dalí checked into the Pembroke Lodge, on the Hotel Del Monte's grounds, at the beginning of June. They had been in the United States for less than a year. On June 28, 1940, Hitler's troops had invaded Arcachon in the south of France, where they had been working, and the Dalís, like hundreds of thousands of similarly terrified and displaced people from all over Europe, had fled to America as quickly as they could. In their haste, most of their possessions, including valuable canvases later confiscated by the

Germans, had been lost or left behind. With the invasion of France, the art market had imploded. They were homeless, and their future was unsure. Salvador, whose preferred mode of expression was an idiosyncratic mixture of French and Catalan, barely spoke English, and Gala's knowledge of the language was severely limited. Although they were traveling with their patron the Phelps Dodge heir Edward James, for all intents and purposes, they were refugees.

The Dalís were not, however, unknown. Two groundbreaking, provocative films Salvador had made with Luis Buñuel, *Un Chien Andalou* (1929) and *L'Age d'Or* (*The Age of Gold*, 1930), were respected as important milestones in the history of filmmaking by the American movie industry, which, as twenty million Americans went to the movies each week, was enjoying a golden age of its own.

Salvador, who was just thirty-seven, had been at the forefront of the art world for more than ten years. He had had eight one-man shows in four countries—France, England, Spain, and the United States—and had graced the cover of *Time* magazine in 1936. With his signature pomaded black hair and silver-headed cane, he was the avatar of Surrealism in America. Most recently, he and Gala had designed the *Dream of Venus* pavilion for the 1939 World's Fair in Queens, New York, which received forty-four million visitors and was covered by media on both sides of the Atlantic.

Promising that Dalí would be "good for business," Gala, who was the business end of the partnership, had asked the hotel's proprietor, Samuel Morse, for a celebrity discount. Morse was taken with Gala's hypnotic, slanted eyes, described by her first husband, the subversive French poet Paul Éluard, as "the color of old gold." He also respected Gala as "an extraordinary, versatile, and ingenious woman"[1] who understood the value of fame. He gave the Dalís a free suite, with a studio for Salvador.

Samuel Morse was the great-nephew of the Samuel Morse who in 1832 invented the Morse code and the telegraph. As the developer of the Monterey Peninsula, he became the third owner of the Del Monte, originally built by Charles Crocker in 1818. When that gorgeous Spanish-style structure was damaged by fire in 1924, Morse lovingly restored and expanded the compound, which hosted several American presidents, including Herbert Hoover and Teddy Roosevelt. By 1941, the Del Monte was a favorite getaway for European royalty, global millionaires, and Hollywood celebrities.

In addition to the pine forest, which ranged over approximately ten square miles of low hills and shallow valleys, and the eucalyptus-bordered, seventeen-mile-long drive along the Pacific, the immaculate grounds included a racetrack, a lake for boating and fishing, tennis courts, the famous Pebble Beach golf course, an Arizona Cactus Garden, and a Roman Plunge Pool Complex. Here Salvador did the breaststroke every morning with his head out of the water (so as not to damage his long waxed mustache), looking, as the hotel's publicist Herbert Cerwin affectionately remembered, "for all the world like a skinny walrus."

Morse, who believed that publicity was worth a hundred times more than advertising, had gone out of his way to hire the best public-relations person in California. Herb Cerwin "would do anything" for a good story and Cerwin and his wife, Dagmar, made a point of befriending the Dalís, and invited them to neighborly backyard barbecues where Herb grilled steaks, Gala tossed salads, and the two couples got to know each other. "The Dalís," Cerwin wrote in his memoirs, "were so close that they spoke for one another. She was devoted to him. He depended on her."[2]

As soon as the sketches of sets and costumes for the Ballets Russes' *Parade*, which Gala and Salvador had begun working on in the south of France, were finished, Herb approached them with the idea of throwing their version of a "Hollywood" PR party. Salvador, who loved the limelight, was thrilled with the idea. More strategic in view of the optics a lavish festivity might present, Gala demurred.

The United States which was flooded with refugees from all over the Continent had shut off virtually all immigration as it prepared to go to war. It would be better, Gala thought, to host a benefit to help artists still trapped in Europe.

"Gala and I were lucky. Other artists are not. . . . Some have no money. Dalí will assist," Salvador (who often referred to himself in the third person and invariably agreed with his wife) told Herb. Gala had already telephoned Alfred Barr, the director of the Museum of Modern Art in New York. Barr, who had discovered Salvador in Paris at his first show with the Pierre Colle Gallery in 1930 and had hung *The Persistence of Memory* (Dalí's famous melting watches) as the focal point of two blockbuster exhibitions at MoMA, readily gave his backing to the benefit.

By the beginning of August, invitations to "A Surrealistic Night in Del Monte in Honor of Senõr and Senõra Salvador Dalí" had been mailed out to film stars, socialites, and Monterey's most prominent citizens. The donation for dinner was $4; "just cocktails" was $2. Costumes were required. Partygoers could come either as one of their dreams, as a wild animal, or as an inhabitant of the forest.

Insisting that the party must be a work of art, Dalí and Gala planned it as a performance inside an installation. "The Dalís," Samuel Morse wrote in his memoirs, "were (and most of it came from Gala) founders of a new movement . . . I don't quite know what it means but he painted fantastical representations that were beautifully executed."

Morse's description is confused and confusing. Gala, who was known in Europe as the "Mother of Surrealism" was not the only founder of this literary and artistic movement that, championing the subconscious, took the Continent by storm in the late 1920s. She had, however been deeply involved in shaping the work and careers of two of its most famous proponents: her husband Paul Éluard, and the legendary visual artist Max Ernst. Gala had also inspired and coauthored

Dalí's *Paranoiac-Critical Method* (1931), which expands André Breton's *Surrealist Manifesto*, and was famous for stating that *illusion is real.*

What Morse, who was a natural-born promoter, did understand, and very clearly was the allure of fantasy for a country that was just coming out of a ten-year depression and going into World War II. "Let Dalí," he told Cerwin firmly, "do anything he wants . . . within reason."

Preparing for the party with the same painstaking care they applied to making a painting, the Dalís gave Cerwin a detailed list of everything they would need to create it. According to *Look* magazine, this included two thousand pine trees, four thousand gunnysacks, two tons of old newspaper, and twenty-four papier-mâché animal heads with twenty-four headless department-store mannequins to attach them to, as well as the largest bed in Hollywood, twelve hundred ladies' high-heeled evening slippers, two truckloads of squash and pumpkins, and one wrecked Buick sedan.[3] They also wanted ballet dancers and wild animals, like the giraffe that appears in Dalí's *Inventions of the Monsters*. This was going to make great newspaper copy, Morse and Cerwin agreed.

Herbert Fleishhacker, the financier who had underwritten the San Francisco Zoological Gardens, was a great friend of Herb Cerwin's. He agreed to take Salvador on a private two-hour tour of the zoo. Here the artist was spurned by a tigress when he tried to pet her ("So feminine," he concluded), and went on to enjoy a close encounter with a friendly giraffe. In the end, twenty animals were selected and nineteen were approved to be loaned for the party. (Fleishhacker, who thought the giraffe was too delicate to travel, wouldn't let him leave the zoo.)

ON AUGUST 25, a week before the big night, *Newsweek* published an article comparing the Dalís to Leonardo da Vinci, who had party planned for Lorenzo de' Medici in 1518. Four days later, the *Monterey Herald* ran a picture of Salvador discussing the upcoming festivities with Dorothy Spreckels, whose family had, in 1880, founded Hawaii's sugar industry. Later that day, the local magazine *Game and Gossip* was allowed backstage to take photos of Salvador wearing the round, mirrored glasses Gala had picked out for him while he painted Samuel Morse's daughter Mary's long blond hair blue and pinned Gala's low cut evening gown.

As the date for the party drew nearer, twenty men began work on the installation in the Del Monte's ballroom. Two thousand pine trees culled from the timberland were placed along the ballroom walls. The hemp sacks stuffed with newspaper were hung from floor to ceiling to conjure the effect of a cave. A huge bed that had been used in the 1925 silent film *The Merry Widow*, starring Mae Murray, arrived from Hollywood and was arranged as the end piece of the long table. This was where Gala would be dining "in bed," with her guests surrounded, as though in a dream, by the magical forest she and Salvador had created.

The bed was draped in red satin and velvet, its red velvet headboard flanked by two suits of armor suitable for a medieval-style joust. The wrecked car was placed where it could be viewed from the bed. Blue light bulbs were wound around poles and decorated with fir branches, transforming the grotto into a twilight zone. The animal heads, which had come from a production of *A Midsummer Night's Dream*, were fitted on top of the naked dummies. When the 1,200 stilettos arrived, the chef, who was coaxed into using them to serve the first course of crab and avocado salad in small paper bags, joked that the starter should have been "filet of 'sole.'"

The hotel was fully booked, and reservations for the party were still flooding in. Even though Pebble Beach was a five-and-a-half-hour drive from Hollywood, Millicent Rogers, Clark Gable, Jackie Coogan, Edward G. Robinson, Bob Hope, and Bing Crosby all wanted a role in the Dalí art performance and had promised to attend. Alfred and Alma Hitchcock and a posse of millionaires, among them seventeen-year-old Gloria Vanderbilt, were flying in from the East Coast. More than one thousand people had purchased tickets to the event.

Tables had to be placed in halls and adjacent rooms beyond the ballroom, which could accommodate only a few hundred guests. Dalí decided that those seated outside could come in, walk around, and enjoy the spectacle. They would be the denizens of the forest. By noon on September 2, the preparations were complete. The shop-window mannequins with their animal heads were strategically sited. The squash and pumpkins had been ingeniously arranged as table decorations. A tame performing bear and a caged tiger were carefully placed near the trees. A porcupine in a comfortable cage became one of the centerpieces of the bed where Gala would dine with her chosen guests. White-faced capuchin monkeys romped in the shadows.

By 5:30, Dagmar had finished sewing an anatomical chart onto Salvador's shirt for his costume. Half an hour later, a statuesque brunette model Dalí had selected to play the car wreck's casualty arrived. She took off her clothes and lay down in the vehicle, where she was given a mild sedative and covered with leaves. Partygoers would be encouraged to peer into the wreck and admire the pretty victim. At 6:45, the hotel's physician, Dr. Mast Wolfson, arrived to help Salvador dress the dancers in their bandage costumes. Dalí, who thought Americans were frequently in car accidents, had choreographed the "number," in which the bandaged ballroom-dance team Charlotte Maye and Burt Harger emerged from the car wreck to perform a preternatural pas de deux.

Just before 7:00 p.m., ice sculptures of animals were placed on the tables, and fresh white magnolias were pinned to the headboard of the bed, where a glowing Gala reclined with the five month old lion snuggled beside her. By 7:00, the newsreel cameramen from Paramount, Pathé Newsreel, and Universal were allowed in to shoot background footage before taking their places. *Life* magazine was planning a special feature called "*Life* Goes to a Party" and had sent its top reporter, Herbert De Roose. *Look* was permitted early entry as well, as was Robinson Jeffers, the famous Pacific Coast poet who planned to review Dalí's art event.

As soon as the rest of the guests, who arrived at 8:00, were settled at their assigned tables with their new animal-headed mannequin friends, they were greeted with Harger and Maye's spooky duet. The first course, of crab in satin slippers, was served by waiters dressed as nurses and followed with a double consommé, then a choice of Sardine à la Dalí or Beefsteak Forestière with wild mushrooms. Dessert was Coupe Surréaliste, but the pièce de résistance was a covered plate offered to the actor Bob Hope. When he lifted the lid, an army of live frogs jumped out. Everyone laughed. As the finale to the dinner, Salvador, who was acting as Gala's waiter, gallantly presented her with a jumbo Coke bottle with a very large nipple. It was filled with warm milk, and she was finally able to feed her ravenous baby lion.

There was dancing after dinner. Many of the guests wore horns or antlers. One came in a gorilla mask. Gloria Vanderbilt had little cat's-eye sunglasses. The festivities lasted all night, and the next morning *The Monterey Herald* reported that "by dawn most of the best people were subconscious." "I have attended a lot of parties, some of them quite fantastic," Morse wrote in his memoirs, "but this one topped them all. And," he added, Gala and Dalí "got as much publicity as we did."

Morse was right. Thanks to their party, the Dalís' spell had reached beyond the art world into the hearts and the minds of the American public. Within the week, millions of appreciative fans at movie theaters all over the world were entranced by the newsreel footage of Gala, whom they would remember as the captivating princess of her enchanted forest.

Naturally, many wondered who the ravishing, mysterious woman in the unicorn headdress really was.[4]

CHAPTER 1

FAIRY TALES AND SECRETS

Gala, who was so guarded that her friends called her "The Tower," was famous for being mysterious. "The secret of my secrets is that I don't tell them" was one of her favorite sayings. Even her birth date remains controversial. According to her teacher's certificate, she was born on August 26, 1894, but Michael Stout, who became Dalí's lawyer in the late 1970s, thinks there may be evidence that the year was really 1890.

She was born in Russia, an 8,800,000-square-mile, landlocked empire that stretched contiguously eastward from Sweden and the Baltic Sea to the Bering Strait in the Pacific Ocean, which separates Siberia from Alaska by approximately 50 miles. Three-fourths of the country was in Asia, and in the eyes of many Europeans, Russia had more in common with China than it did with them.

Ever since the first Romanov tsar, Mikhail Fyódorovich Romanov, made his father, Feodor Nikitich Romanov, head of the church in 1613, Russian Orthodoxy had been a force almost as if not more powerful than the emperor with whom it worked hand in glove. Thus, although the 350-year-old dynasty, conceived when a courtier named Roman (Yurievich Zakharyn) elevated himself by marrying his daughter Anastasia to Ivan the Terrible, was in decline, Nicholas Alexandrovich, the eighteenth consecutive Romanov to sit on the throne, believed he was God's representative in this world. All of

Russia was his personal domain. And although its people, the vast majority of whom were desperately poor manual laborers, were God's children in heaven, he was their tsar *batiushka*, their "little father" on Earth.

Since Catherine the Great's demise in 1796, the monarchy had become increasingly reactionary. It was at odds with the empire's creatives and thinkers, and much of its nobility, as well. Major suppressions of civil rights had been triggered by the 1881 Winter Palace assassination of Nicholas's grandfather Alexander II, who had survived six previous attacks on his life. By 1890; the political climate in Russia was palpably toxic.

Russia was the least developed of the great powers. Long after the end of Europe's industrial revolution, it was still an agrarian economy deeply dependent on the labor of its peasants, who made up more than 30 percent of the population. Many of these were slaves bonded to federally owned communes. The country's nonagricultural production was crude oil, sugar, and cloth. Most of the hardware, including rails, carriages, locomotives, and railroad switches for the magnificent Russian trains, world-famous through *Anna Karenina*, was of French manufacture. France was Russia's closest ally, and the Russian royals, nobility, and intelligentsia all spoke to one another in French, which was considered elegant, the language of culture.

Paradoxically, although the tsarist regime censored its artists and intellectuals so harshly that many, like Ivan Turgenev, immigrated to Paris and London in the mid-1800s, Russian culture remained the jewel in the empire's crown. Russian musicians, poets, playwrights, and novelists of the period—Tolstoy, Gogol, Dostoyevsky, Pushkin, Chekhov, and Lermontov, to name only a few—are among the greatest and most compelling creators the world has ever known.

Gala was born in Kazan, a Mongol stronghold founded in AD 1005 on the banks of the Volga River, approximately five hundred miles east of Moscow. It had flourished as a capital of the formidable Golden Horde khanate until 1552, when, after an arduous month-and-a-half-long siege, Ivan Vasilyevich IV of Moscow finally captured it and made it part of his empire, thus earning his sobriquet Ivan the Terrible ("fearsome").

By the time Gala came into the world, almost four centuries later, Kazan was best known for its august university, where Leon Tolstoy had famously studied and from which, in 1887, Lenin was notoriously expelled for revolutionary activities. A storied, beckoning hub of knowledge and self-fulfillment, this gleaming white Parthenon-like Greek revival temple of learning dominated the entire center of the city. Unhappily, since higher education was forbidden to Jews, females, and neo-Russians, it was also a Mecca Gala would never enter. Still, she could yearn.

Christened Elena Ivanovna Diakonova in the Russian Orthodox Church, Gala was the second of four children: three years younger than her older brother, Vadim (called Vadka) and two years older than Nicolai (Kola), who was the younger son. Her sister, Lidia, was seven years her junior.

Gala's mother, Antonine (née Deoulina), a warm and forward-thinking woman, was a trained midwife. She held a special license to teach children with disabilities and had published a series of children's stories. Antonine was born in Omsk, a lively frontier town in southwestern Siberia, where her family operated small gold mines and where, after being sentenced to four years' hard labor for allegedly conspiring against the tsar, that Dostoyevsky began work on *The House of the Dead*.[1]

Gala's father, Ivan, was a civil servant in Russia's Department of Agriculture who vanished in the snow fields of northern Siberia,[2] while prospecting for gold, when Gala was either nine or ten years old. I It had been an abusive alcoholic who beat his wife and neglected his children. Tellingly, there is no mention of him in the *Carnets Intimes*,[3] Gala's never-completed book of private memories.

Shortly after Ivan's disappearance, something equally frightening and decisive happened to Russia. On the morning of Sunday, January 5, 1905, a large group of workers marched, as for hundreds of years had been the custom of the Russian people, to the Winter Palace in Saint Petersburg to hand a petition for alms and protection to their tsar. They were led by their priest, Father Gaipon, who had promised them clearly and with quotations from the Bible that Nicholas, who was their *batiushka*, would answer their entreaty if they went to him humbly, because that was his obligation before God. The workers addressed their ruler as they approached the palace: "Sire . . ." they began respectfully, "we come to you to seek justice and safety." On orders from Nicholas, who was at his country palace, Tsarskoe Selo, playing dominoes, the imperial soldiers fired at the crowd to turn it back. Still, some sixty thousand protestors, intent on seeing the man they knew to be their true protector, managed to get through. The guards, who had been warned of insurgency, were alarmed. When the workers fell to their knees in the palace courtyard, took off their caps, and crossed themselves before their tsar, the firing began in earnest. It lasted for what seemed like eternity while one thousand kneeling, supplicant men were slaughtered. When the rifle shots were finally over and the survivors looked around at the dead and the wounded, they experienced a decisive moment of truth as their disbelief slowly changed to hatred and anger. In that moment of disillusion, the starting point to any revolution,[4] the people discovered that there was no Holy Emperor. The myth of the tsar *batiushka*, which for time out of memory had been the crux of Romanov power, was dead.

After her children's father disappeared, Antonine, who needed more work, moved the family to Moscow and enrolled Elena, who had previously been homeschooled, in the Potozkoi Lyceum, where the city's intelligentsia educated their daughters. There Elena made fast friends with the sisters and future poets Anastasia and Marina Tsvetaeva, whose father, Professor Ivan Tsvetaev, had founded the

Pushkin Museum. Anastasia renamed Elena "Gala," and Marina dedicated the poem "Mother in the Garden" ("Мама в саду") from her debut volume, *Evening Album* (Вечерний альбом), to her.[5]

IN HER FAMOUS *Memoirs*, published in 1971, Anastasia describes Gala as a little girl with an astonishing sense of humor and a laugh so huge it would overtake her entire body, until she was doubled up with her chin between her knees. But when something or someone displeased her, she would sneer suddenly and bolt, "turning on her heels without hesitation." Then Gala and "Stasia" would run away, "fast as arrows," holding hands. They shared, Anastasia remembered, everything: people, predilections, poetry, whims. She wrote of her friend, "The willfully determined curve of her lips and the devouring stare of her narrow eyes were more precious and more necessary to me than the gaze of all those others who looked at me with love."[6] Outside school, they enjoyed cozy Sunday afternoons curled up together on the little white sofa in Marina's bedroom, sucking caramels that stuck to the roofs of their mouths. The sisters liked to talk about the grand things they would accomplish when they were older—travel, adventures, and literary triumphs. Anastasia wrote that Gala took it all in as though it were "Water of Life." When they read *Les Petites Filles Modèles*, La Comtesse de Ségur's aspirational tale of French château living, Gala, who longed to live in a castle, braided her hair down her back, like the girls in the story.

"Gala had a simple, natural independence; a pride and a dignity," wrote Marina, "that made pity impossible. We never discussed her brilliant intelligence, which outshone her family's poverty, the blatant absence of her father, or her shabby clothes, which always reminded me of Cinderella."[7]

While she struggled to deal with the loss of her father and her new situation, Gala also drew closer to her older brother, Vadka, whom she admired and, during the years before she became a teenager, Gala and Vadka were virtually inseparable. For both siblings summer trips to visit their mother's brother Artemi were the highlight of their troubled childhood.

Artemi lived in Tomsk, a seventeenth-century university town on the Tom River in Western Siberia, more than two thousand miles from the capital. Gala describes her excitement when the train from Moscow stopped in small rural stations where "the villagers would arrive bringing roasted wild duck, freshly baked chicken pies, and delicious raspberries and strawberries picked in the woods," which her mother would buy for the children to eat. "Even after traveling the world," she wrote in her diary, "I consider this the best food I have ever tasted."[8]

Gala adored her uncle, whom she remembers as a colossus: "He popped one of us on each shoulder and a third on his head and went on walking and conversing with the other grown-ups as though nothing had happened."[9] Artemi, who owned a portfolio of country enterprises ranging from chalk pits to apiaries, cattle ranches, and dairies, lived near the university in a brightly painted, gingerbread-trimmed wooden town house that looked as though it belonged to the witch in *Hansel and Gretel*. Here he inspired Gala's lifelong love of gambling by teaching her how to win at card games, betting green beans instead of money, and thrilled the little girl with wild tales of her grandfather, who owned small gold mines four hundred miles to the south. This patriarch took such wonderful care of his laborers that he toiled underground by their side for months at a time, during which they all suffered great deprivations to get rich as fast as possible. At the end of each work period, the miners would burst into town to blow off steam by indulging in wild orgies, feeding their horses French champagne and terrifying the good burghers, who bolted their doors to keep the revelers out.[10]

While Artemi tended his businesses, Gala and Vadka roamed the dense neighboring forrests. There they discovered small glowworms, large snails with brown and ivory stripes on humped shells, and, peering out of the moss in bright clusters, brilliant red-and-white spotted toadstools. Their favorite game was searching for Karl Moor, the daredevil hero of Schiller's *The Robbers*, a Bavarian Robin Hood who gave up his rich lifestyle to live in the woodlands, protect the poor, and punish the powerful.[11, 12]

When Vadim set out to explore the Tom River, Gala, who went everywhere she could with her brother, insisted on going along. Soon they were caught in a summer squall. Their little dinghy was rapidly filling with water. Vadka rowed as hard as he could against rising waves that seemed gigantic to both panicked children. Gala kept them afloat by bailing desperately with a rusty old pail. In a stroke of pure luck: Just as the thunder and lightning began in earnest, brother and sister were saved by a group of fishermen astonished to see children out in such terrible weather.

Back home in Moscow, the duo gave themselves stomachaches from wolfing two pounds of strawberry jam left out by mistake on the dining-room table and made so much noise pretending to cross the Atlantic with Vadka as captain and Gala as sailor on an overturned table that angry neighbors complained to the janitor. They also played at being Native Americans. While Vadka and a tribe of classmates waged war in the park, Gala, as squaw, relunctantly stayed home. One day, Vadim came to her, as she describes it, "half dead, black and blue, and covered with blood." In his role as "chieftain," he had been taken prisoner by his enemies, who threw him into a gunnysack and beat him with sticks. When he stoically refused to cry out, his captors hit him as long and hard as they could. Not long after this incident, Vadka's health declined. Suffering from severe asthma attacks and chronic bronchitis, he became so weak that, by the end of the school year, he had to be carried to class for his final exams, which, Gala proudly records, "he passed brilliantly." Vadim was born,

Gala writes sadly, "with the will, wit, and courage of a leader. What he lacked was the strength."[13]

Tsarist Russia prohibited, and the all-powerful Orthodox Patriarchate refused to sanction, the remarriage of widows. Thus Antonine was flouting the law when, several years after Ivan's disappearance, she married Dimitri Ilyich Gomberg in a civil ceremony and became a "fallen woman" who was "living in sin."

Gomberg was a prominent, exceptionally well-connected Muscovite lawyer of Jewish descent. (In later life, Gala enjoyed explaining that she had acquired her business acumen and ability to negotiate from her Jewish-Armenian stepfather, who had somehow "managed to represent both the Tsar and the Bolsheviks at the same time.") So Antonine and her children abandoned their genteel poverty when they moved into Gomberg's spacious midtown apartment, complete with cooks, servants, and nannies: all luxuries that fourteen-year-old Gala, who was drawn to her mother's new husband, enjoyed.

After the move, Gala, who was slight and unathletic, distanced herself from Kola and Lidia, who laughed at her for being bad at the activities—riding lessons, ice skating, and tennis—that their new "father" arranged for the children. "[My sister] was so fragile and light," Lidia said later, "that when I was 10 and she was 17, I could carry her in my arms from the bath to the bed."[14]

Gala's brothers, who were sensitive to the social outrage their mother had committed by taking a second husband, loathed their stepfather despite his largesse, but Gala had a mind of her own. She showed her gratitude for the material advantages of their new situation by being affectionate and flirtatious with Gomberg and spending long winter evenings by the potbellied stove with her stepfather. She loved listening to him read—from Tolstoy and Pushkin, as well as Lermontov. Dimitri, who cherished his time with his stepdaughter and may in fact have been almost overly fond of her,[15] readily became Gala's adviser and mentor and, as Gala remembered, praised her so lavishly that she sometimes worried about living up to his high expectations.

When she turned fifteen, Gomberg paid for Gala to attend M.G. Brukhonenko Academy, an exclusive secondary school for girls, where she became an outstanding student with a special talent for languages. Here she excelled in French literature and expanded her knowledge of life by reading novels and poetry. It was an education that blurred the borders between fiction and fact.

Gala graduated at the top of her class with a diploma personally signed by Tsar Nicholas II. This document authorized her to work as a primary-school teacher or a private tutor. Because she was a woman, she was forbidden further formal education, but she audited literature classes at Moscow University anyway, where she discovered a strong affinity for Dostoyevsky, whose acute and poetic psychological insights fascinated her.

Lidia, who was jealous of the special attention Gomberg accorded her sister, described Gala insinuatingly as "the most practical of us all," and Gala's affection for Antonine's partner was viewed as treason by both Vadim and Lidia. But Nicolai, the younger son, who went on to direct a workers' theater in Moscow after the Revolution, saw things differently. Kola had acted out his anger at their mother's remarriage by bringing home horrible grades and wrecking Christmas dinners picking fights with his siblings. He interpreted Gala's behavior with Gomberg as a sign of her zest for life. "A petty, mean spirit was alien to Gala," he insisted. "Her vitality was a quality she inherited from Mother. Our mother always had a drive toward living a full life."[16]

In *Carnets Intimes*, Gala describes being the brunt of sibling anger and confusion. One evening, as a special treat, she and her brothers were allowed to read to each other from Lermontov's fairy tale "Démon," the story of an immortal fiend condemned to wander the earth in infinite isolation until he meets and falls in love with

Tamara, a beautiful princess whom he ruthlessly pursues. Pitying the demon's troubled soul, Tamara yields to his fatal embrace, but as she dies, she is wafted out of his reach to heaven, where he cannot follow. That night, after a special supper that included eggs "au diable" coddled over the gas flame of a lamp in the parlor, the children were all sent to bed much later than usual.

Very early the next morning, just before dawn, "the time when one doesn't know if it's night or day," Gala writes, she woke "abruptly. I knew there was somebody beyond my bed. Thinking it might be the demon; I opened my eyes and saw that indeed there was a shadowy shape breathing heavily. To calm whatever it was, I pretended to sleep deeply. Emboldened, it came close and began to run its freezing, trembling hands the length of my pale, thin little unformed body. I cried out. Frightened it hid itself in the shadows in the corner of my room.

"I decided to wait until the sun rose to discover who this intruder might be. Lermontov's story made me sure it was something sexual. And so the seemingly interminable fight continued. As soon as the trespasser advanced, I would make noise and it would hurry back to the darkness where it could hide. Finally, morning came and it ran away with its face in its hands. Then I saw the monster was my brother, Vadka. I was overwhelmed with dreadful shame, unqualified repulsion, an uneasy sense of superiority, and [like Tamara] agonizing compassion and concern [for my brother]. I lay rigid and sleepless until seven o'clock, when the chambermaid came to get me ready for classes. She found me ash-white and in such an awful state that she tried to keep me at home, but I protested so ferociously she finally gave in."

After this, Gala and her brother stopped speaking. He ignored her completely during the day. At night he visited her with "a passion which—as he remained subject to humiliation, regret, and naiveté"—he never acted on.[17]

Gala's description of Vadka's attention leads the reader to believe that he never actually assaulted her. And amazingly, throughout this ordeal, perhaps in imitation of the kindhearted Tamara, Gala managed to develop not only empathy but emotional resilience and an abiding faith in her own ability to survive. She did not, however, escape trauma. "These incidents," she wrote in her diary, "were emotionally excruciating, but I never told anyone. They were the first secret of my life." During this period, Gala, who had always been highly reactive, grew increasingly nervous and capricious. She acquired a dry, anxious cough and probably suffered from dysmenorrhea.[18]

In the spring of 1912, she was sent on a restorative vacation to the Côte d'Azur, where she was visited by Anastasia, who recorded tender memories of her little friend, sunburned and merry, wiggling her bushy eyebrows and squinting her brown "Chinese" eyes to make funny faces as she imitated Stasia posing as a lady, until they both exploded into fits of wild giggles and went shopping for extravagant hats.

Back in Moscow, Gala's cramps, mood swings, coughing, and retching got worse. On the advice of the family's doctors, who worried these symptoms might develop into tuberculosis, her mother and stepfather decided to send her to a new sanitarium intended chiefly for patients with lung disease. Clavadel, run by a Dr. Bodmer, was located in the German part of Switzerland, just above Davos, a resort town later described by Thomas Mann as the otherworldly setting of the Berghof sanitarium in his 1924 novel *The Magic Mountain*.

CHAPTER 2

PAUL

At the turn of the last century, 10 percent of all urban dwellers in Europe and America died of tuberculosis, a pandemic for which no one had yet discovered a vaccine. Like many of the famous clinics established to treat the disease, Clavadel was a combination of a glittering prison—designed to keep the ailing sequestered to prevent them from infecting friends and family while they hoped for recovery—and a luxurious retreat where rich patients who were overtaxed but not physically ill could retire quietly for a rest. It was as grand as a five-star hotel.

Gala was all alone when she made the 1,600-mile train trip through the ice plains of western Russia. Huddled in a corner of her gray upholstered compartment, she listened to the laboring engine pull her far from all that was dear and familiar. As she stared out her window at the frozen horizon, hugging her small bag crammed with religious icons, stuffed animals, tarot cards, and the books she loved, she was, as she wrote later, "on the verge of a nervous breakdown."

When she checked into Clavadel on January 12, 1913, the reason for her admission was listed as "nervous disorders." The forty-nine other convalescing inhabitants of the clinic's fifty balconied, south-facing rooms were by and large older, wealthy Europeans. These included prosperous Germans, Swiss-Germans, some Austrians, and one blond French teenager with a cumbersome name: Eugène Émile

Paul Grindel. At five feet ten, Eugène was exactly as tall as Vadka and just slightly more slender. He had a dreamy, faraway look in his blue-gray eyes and a sexy, asymmetrical smile. Gala was so struck when she saw him that she rushed upstairs to consult her tarot. And if she drew the Knight of Wands, (the tarot's symbol for Sagittarius, which was Eugène's astrological sun sign) that foretells travel, true love, creativity, and ambition, she accurately predicted what the boy destined to become France's most famous poet would bring to her life.

When pretty, round-eyed Jeanne Cousin married Clément Grindel on October 6, 1894, the groom's five brothers welcomed her with open arms. A close-knit band of left-leaning blue-collar workers, they had watched Jeanne grow up just across the street—rue Dezobry, in Saint Denis, the worst slum on the outskirts of Paris. They were sure that their new sister-in-law, who was pious and industrious, would be happy with Clément, who was a loving, generous man. Clément was also the best educated of the siblings. When their father, François Barnabé, a construction worker, was murdered at his site by a gang of thieves, Clément had decided that office work was safer. He became an accountant.

The newlyweds promptly moved to a small apartment opposite the Saint Denis primary school at 41 boulevard de Châteaudun, where, on December 14, 1895, at 11:45 in the morning, the longed-for son of their young love was born. But it wasn't until two years later, when the happy, outgoing toddler almost died from a sudden attack of bacterial meningitis, that, at Jeanne's frantic insistence, anticlerical Clément agreed to baptize his son. The ceremony took place in the church of Saint-Denis-de-l'Estrée on January 1, 1897.

The Grindels were enterprising. Jeanne, who was in charge of an *atelier de couture*, took "Gégène" to work every morning, where the little boy played on the cutting-room floor. Years later he described these happy hours to Coco Chanel:[1] *"Les aiguilles du midi / Cousent la traîne du matin / Je me vois moi ma jeunesse / Parmi les couleurs volatiles"* ("The needles of the afternoon / Sew the trains of the morning / I see my child-hood / In [their] ever-changing colors").

Meanwhile, Clément, who had observed that Saint Denis housing prices were on the upswing, cleverly began buying, selling, and developing neighborhood properties, and by age thirty he was well on his way to accumulating a fortune. Very soon Gégène, his "little white bunny," would be able to have anything he wanted. And dear Jeanne could be free to devote all her time to nurturing their only child, whose precarious health was a topic of great concern to the Grindel family and especially Eugène himself, who was traumatized by his early illness and grew up worrying he would always be weak and *inutile* ("useless and negligible").

The adorable invalid became an assiduous student. At six, he began bringing home prizes in literature, arithmetic, and vocabulary. His proud parents encouraged him to recite La Fontaine's fables "The Fox and the Crow" and "The Ant and the Grasshopper" for the amusement of uncles and cousins at large Sunday dinners. Although he later remembered these performances as "awful—I had no sense of drama, I mumbled and finished off the verses too quickly"—Gégène liked being the center of attention. He also enjoyed cultural outings: to the theater, to a M. Vlabel's dramatic poetry readings of Baudelaire and Marion, and to museums. He acquired an affinity for illustration, Aubrey Beardsley's in particular, and drew whimsical pictures of beautiful ladies in elaborate costumes and extravagant furs. When Eugène was sixteen, he won a school prize in English, which included a trip to Southampton to improve his fluency. There, blossoming in the freedom of British port life, he crafted the beginnings of a first poem. Jeanne and Clément were happy enough with these accomplishments. They were, however, also determined that when he had obtained his *brevet* (a certificate similar to a high school equivalency diploma), their brilliantly creative boy would become an apprentice in his father's flourishing business—a prospect that held no charm for Eugène.

That winter, Jeanne and Gégène vacationed in Glion, a small Swiss town near Montreux known for its pure, healthy air. There Eugène shared a sunlit room in the Victorian hotel with his mother, he enjoyed taking snapshots of Lake Geneva with his brand-new camera, and horrified both his parents by coughing up floods of blood one morning as he was brushing his teeth.

After panicked consultations with several doctors in Saint Moritz as well as Montreux and Lausanne, mother and son checked into Clavadel on December 19, 1912. Jeanne was instantly reassured by Dr. Bodmer's solicitous manner and the clinic's elegant atmosphere. Her husband concurred, "With the good care he will get, not to mention all the excellent food, our kid will be definitely on the mend by the end of winter," he wrote with relief to his exhausted wife, who for once was happy to leave her little boy in the care of his doctors while she boarded the train home to her beloved Paris and Clément's open arms.

At seventeen, Eugène was shy, spoiled, and overwhelmingly sheltered. He took all his vacations with a covey of aunts, uncles, and cousins at family houses in Nanterre at Easter and Bray-et-Lû in Val-d'Oise for summer break. At home he spent most of his time in the kitchen with his grandmother, an inspired cook whose famous *plats* were the delight of her family. And at school, the prestigious Lycée Colbert, to which he had been awarded a scholarship, he made only one friend, Fernand Fontaine, who was later killed in action during the First World War.

Through his first, lonely weeks in the sanitarium, Eugène felt like a misfit in the crowd of much older Germans, whose conversation he did not understand. When he met the fine-boned jolie laide from faraway Russia, he was immediately attracted to her gold-flecked eyes and masculine gait. At eighteen, she was only one year his senior and—even better—she could speak French.

Adding to his joy at this serendipitous encounter, Gala turned out to be wild, fierce, and outrageously opinionated, all of which he found utterly entrancing. When she explained to him that she preferred to spend her time with the gardener because she loathed "men with pretensions," adding that she refused "to countenance any kind of stupidity," Eugène found her severity charming. But when, after reading the new verses he had begun scribbling, she looked straight through him with her odd, piercing stare and declared he would become "a very great writer," he was over the moon.

An unintentionally candid snapshot of the young couple caught off guard offers an insight into their budding relationship. Eugène, clearly dandified for his portrait in an exquisitely cut tweed jacket and a large, floppy black velvet bow tie, with his hair parted down the middle à la Oscar Wilde, exudes impish pleasure as he shuts his eyes against the flash of the camera. Meanwhile Gala, looking earnest and a bit put out, has been captured midsentence with her mouth half-open, apparently giving him an order as she perches protectively over him on the arm of his wing chair. She is dressed down in a hand-knitted turtleneck. Her hands are perfectly manicured.

Gala and Eugène became constant companions. When they weren't being subjected to Clavadel's weekly routine of back-whacking checkups, thermometer readings, X-rays, and freezing showers, they held hands as they explored the crystalline edges of the snowy property, where, scrambling about the mist-wreathed rocks, they searched for crows' nests in the tall firs that rimmed the white-mountain lakes at the foot of Mount Günter.

Afternoons were spent lolling on adjacent lawn chairs in the glassed-in sun porch, sipping lemonade, getting winter suntans, and whispering to each other as time seemed to run both fast and slow. They developed a private vocabulary: When they were particularly excited and happy about something, they would say, "Hi-hi-hi." During "quiet hours," when all the patients were supposed to be resting their bronchial tracts in silence, Gala and Eugène passed surreptitious notes back and forth. In the evenings, there was Piper-Heidsieck, live piano music, and candlelight in the drawing room.

One day during rest period, Gala made a drawing that Eugène marked and returned to her for interpretation. It was a Cubist-style sketch in violet pencil of a young man in profile who looked like Eugène, attached to the enigmatic word "Triangulism."[2] Below this, a title printed in Gala's very neat hand read, "Portrait of a young man—the poet at seventeen." When Eugène asked her softly, "Who is the subject of the drawing?" she whispered back, "Today is the night you will dine with me." "I am your disciple" came the joyful reply.

In "Nuits Partagées" ("Shared Nights"), a prose poem written to Gala twenty years later, long after she had left him for Salvador Dalí, Éluard describes how much he wishes they were still enjoying that magical evening:

> *Que ne puis-je encore, comme au temps de ma jeunesse, me déclarer ton disciple, que ne puis-je encore convenir avec toi que le couteau et ce qu'il coupe sont bien accordés. Le piano et le silence, l'horizon, et l'étendue.*

("If only, as in the days of my youth, I could still be your pupil, if only you and I could still be agreeing together that the knife and its meat are attuned to each other: The piano and the silence, the horizon, and the wide-open spaces.")

Gala, who was Eugène's superior in both education and worldliness, was a warm and generous teacher. She shared her expansive knowledge of contemporary literature and her passion for the Russian Symbolists. She was particularly enamored with the critic and novelist Andrey Bely and his friend the poet Aleksandr Blok, two men who loved the same woman and whom she loved because they reminded her of her own country. She happily taught Eugène the nuances of French poetry by reading to him from the anthologies she had brought with her from home. When they discussed current events, Gala confided her worries that the outmoded belief systems of the world's ruling classes were paving the way to calamity. While Eastern Europe's tottering empires were filled with unrest Metternich's balance of power[3] had crumbled. There would surely be war. Eugène comforted her with mischievous verse: *"Ne pouvant pas entrer dans la voie inconnue / La vieille Humanité succombait toute nue."*

("Unable to walk down the undiscovered roadway / Old Humanity—stripped naked—lay down and expired.")

Gala was in love. "If I spent all my time with you," she wrote in one of the passionate letters the pair were still exchanging two years later, "it's that I was sure that with you, because I love you, all is pure, beautiful, and right." Being close to him was heaven: "I need your tenderness. . . . Never regret our caresses." Intoxicated with his love for Gala and his surging creativity, Eugène thought of changing his name. On his darling's advice, he dropped the hefty "Eugène Émile," picked up his grandmother's musical surname, and was reborn: Paul Éluard.

When Gala took him costume shopping in Davos for Clavadel's fancy-dress ball, they bought ruffs and white makeup. Paul transformed into Pierrot, a favorite character of the Symbolist poets, but instead of becoming Columbine in a tutu, Gala made herself into another Pierrot: Paul's identical twin.[4] She taught him to turn it all into poetry. Taking a leaf from Blok, whose explicitly erotic, Pierrot-centric verse had created a scandal in Moscow, Paul began writing about himself as an innocent romantic pining for sex. He also styled himself as Gala's puppet: a reference to *The Woman and the Puppet*, Symbolist Pierre Louÿs's novel about carnal obsession.

By November 1912, less than a year into their stay at Clavadel and under Gala's guidance, Paul had produced a collection of one hundred rondels, ballads, and sonnets, including "Pierrot," "The Ballad of Pierrot-White and Ugly," and a sonnet called "The Wet Pierrot." His mother was put in charge of working out the first printing with

Eymard & Co., a publisher Paul had contacted during a brief visit to Paris the previous summer. On December I, 1913, *First Poems*, by Paul Éluard Grindel, a 101-page volume with engravings by an illustrator named Ciolkowski and a single reproduction of a Beardsley drawing, made its debut to decent praise: *Revue des Oeuvres Nouvelles de la Littérature et du Théâtre* called Paul a "young poet bursting with ideas."

Jeanne was disgruntled. In her view, poetry, like acting, was a useless, vainglorious diversion. What she and her husband both wanted was a healthy son with his feet on the ground and solid, gainful employment. Worse, when she visited Clavadel the following summer, Eugène ignored her to spend all his time canoodling with Gala. The "little Russian," with her icons and tarot cards, was clearly a terrible influence.

Jeanne and Clément emphatically agreed that Gégène was much too young to be so deeply involved. They both wanted him to experience other women, and as Paul himself liked women in general, they enjoyed some victories in that regard. But these were short-lived. "At Clavadel," Gala wrote to Paul three years later, "when you seemed so happy with Miss . . . I prayed to God, perhaps for the first time, that the boy I adored would come back to me. And voilà! I have you. You know," she continued, solidifying the bond between them, "I understand these transgressions. I too have my *côté* putainesque [my whorish side]. When you saw me holding hands with 'H' and looking into his eyes, I was like you. It was only because he was pestering me. It meant nothing. You were my love always and always will be."

Disturbed by a flurry of worried letters from his parents demanding he break up with his sweetheart, Paul went to Gala for comfort, and she knew what to say: "Your mother is really in love with you," she observed curtly, "but when you turn 21, her consent won't matter. We can get married then." It was impossible for Paul to imagine his life without Gala. She was his soulmate. She was his partner. They quarreled. They made up. He pledged love eternal.

By the end of 1913, Gala and Paul had collaborated on another collection, *Dialogues des Inutiles* ("Conversations of the Useless"), which was published as a three-page insert in the literary magazine *Oeuvres Nouvelles* at the beginning of January 1914. *Dialogues* is a suite of fourteen breezily romantic mock-arguments between the poet and his beloved, in which Éluard takes both sides of the conversation. These are accompanied by Gala's introductory essay, signed *la Reine de Pauleùlgnn* ("The Queen of Paul-*eùlgnn*"), which reveals her to be the key to this work.

The importance of Gala's contribution to these early verses is strongly reinforced by the cache of drawings and poetry in the Sorbonne's Jacques Doucet Library titled, in Éluard's writing, "Manuscripts et copies par Gala et moi 1911–1918." It includes handwritten poems, some of which are now famous, in both Gala's and Paul's scripts. Those in his are visibly marked with her edits.

Later that January, the poet and playwright Émile Sicard, who complimented Paul on the originality of his talent, published another new poem, *"Le Fou Parle"* ("The Fool Speaks"), in his literary magazine, *Le Feu*: *"C'est ma mère monsieur, avec ma fiancée . . . Ma mère pleurait sur moi qui sanglotais / Pour l'autre refusant d'être à moi tout à fait."* ("Sir, it's about my mother, and my girlfriend . . . My mother sobbed at the thought of losing me while I was in tears / over the other one who refused to be mine completely.")

Jeanne was hurt and humiliated by Paul's little ditty, but there was nothing to be done. By February 1914, Paul and Gala, both pronounced "cured," had returned to their respective countries, officially engaged. They knew they had a wonderful future.

They just had to wait until Paul turned twenty-one.

WAR EVERYWHERE

Nineteen fourteen was a watershed year.

Defying opposition from both families, Gala and Paul had bravely announced their engagement, but they had gone home to different continents, and Gala wasn't sure when or even *if* she would see Paul again. After the sweetness and excitement of her adventures in Switzerland, Moscow seemed drab and forlorn. She developed a fever and chills. Refusing to go out, even to the ballet or the theater, she locked herself in her room, where, armed with pen and thermometer, she spent her days writing love letters to Paul.

Kola snickered. Antonine pursed tight lips anxiously but wouldn't say anything. Gomberg, startled at first, soon became furious at the thought of his brilliant twenty-year-old-daughter lovesick over an invalid Frenchman. At Kazan University, where he was preparing his doctorate, Vadim hid in his books.[1]

Then, on June 28, Franz Ferdinand, the heir to the Austro-Hungarian throne, was assassinated in Sarajevo by a Serbian student activist, and one by one, like a row of dominoes toppling against one another, the countries of Europe fell into war. Austria, backed by Italy and Germany, invaded Serbia. France, Russia, and England aligned themselves with the Serbs. On August I, when Germany declared war on the Russian Empire, France mobilized against Kaiser Wilhelm II. Suddenly, Europe was fire and blood.

Clément, who was forty-two, and Paul, who would turn nineteen in December, were drafted. Gala's fever grew worse. Now it was raging battles and mass burial grounds that lay between her and her intended. Paul spent all of 1915 and the beginning of the following year as a patient in one Parisian military hospital after another: first in Gentilly, with bronchitis, then in the Broca hospital with cerebral anemia and "chronic" appendicitis, and finally at the clinic in Cochin with debilitating migraines. Paradoxically, this miserable turn of events delighted Paul's aunts and especially his mother because it kept him safely away from the war. They could also visit his sickroom at will, where they spent hours knitting by his iron cot while he told them long stories that usually ended up being about Gala. Day after day, Paul praised and defended his fiancée so beautifully and stubbornly that, little by little, Jeanne, who prayed every night for her son's health and safety, felt her hostility toward "the little Russian" begin to evaporate.

He was equally tenacious with Clément. "Even joy is in tears," Paul, who never stopped repeating that he wanted Gala and he wanted her *now*, wrote to his father on October 17, 1915. When Clément refused point-blank to shelter the Russian, his only child threw him a curveball: If he couldn't have Gala, Paul would fight "like a man" in the trenches.

To the east, the remnants of Tsar Nicholas's troops were in tatters, starving and ill-equipped. Half-clad imperial infantry armed only with their bayonets, had been forced to charge against Germans brandishing machine guns. When the Austro-German army invaded Poland, Lithuania, and Serbia, more than three million Russian soldiers had been slaughtered. The imperial army was in panicked, chaotic retreat.

Gala's family remained in Moscow. Food was scarce in the capital, and the citizenship was disgruntled. In educated circles, everyone railed privately against the tsar who had pushed too far into Galatia, to support France instead of coming to a full stop while there was still time to save the day. No one thought Nicholas II capable of governing. Clearly, the worst was yet to come. Perhaps, Gomberg conceded, although there was scant hope for the success of this foreign marriage, Gala would be better off in France.

Then mid-June 1916, Gala received a telegram that arrived like a message from heaven. It was from Paul. It said: "Come."

In exchange for a hastily sworn promise to enroll in French classes at the Sorbonne (just like her friend the poet Marina Tsvetaeva, a parentally approved-of role model who had successfully traveled on her own to Paris just before the war). Gala finally wheedled permission from Gomberg to embark on the dangerous trip. Without yet setting a date, she alerted Paul of her arrival, prepared her trousseau, and plotted her itinerary to follow the mail route from Russia to France, her safest and only option, despite the fact that the Baltic was patrolled by German submarines. Gala would leave Moscow on September 1, travel by train to Saint Petersburg and from there to Helsinki, where she had an aunt with whom she could spend the night. From Helsinki, she would go on to Stockholm, and from Sweden she would sail to London and then on to Newhaven, where she would embark on the perilous crossing to Dieppe. By September 16, she planned to be in Paris, where it had finally been decided she would move into the Grindels' dark apartment at 3 rue Ordener in the 18th arrondissement.

Hoping to mend old grudges and begin her new life on the right footing, an exhilarated Gala wrote to her future mother-in-law, "Dear Madam, You may think me naïve because without knowing you very well it is *you* I will now turn to for comfort and advice in difficult moments. . . ." She signed her letter self-deprecatingly, "Gala, the little Russian."

At the end of June, Paul, whose migraines had abated, was sent to Hargicourt in the Somme, sixty miles northwest of Paris, to help complete the installation of a hospital for military evacuees just five miles from the front. On July 1, the French general Joseph Joffre, together with his ally and counterpart British general Douglas Haig, unleashed a four-month-long attack of such unprecedented ferocity that thousands perished, earning Haig his nickname: "The Butcher." The mutilated and traumatized survivors who had been rescued were treated at Hargicourt before being sent on to specialized hospitals. Appalled and demoralized, Paul wrote to his mother, "It's terrible to be so protected while so many are being massacred. . . ." It was his job to pen hundreds of condolence notes every day to the families of the dead and wounded. In his next letter home, he told Jeanne, "Being surrounded by all these 'real warriors' makes me ashamed to be living in such safety and peace." From then on, although he never stopped thinking about or writing to Gala, Paul spent most of his time trying to be sent into battle.

La petite chérie arrive à Paris / Paris fait du bruit. Paris fait du bruit ("The little darling is in Paris / Paris makes noise. Paris makes noise!"), Paul wrote triumphantly when, in the beginning of October, almost a week later than anticipated, Gala, to the great relief and joy of all concerned, finally arrived. She moved into Paul's old bedroom—just in time to learn that he had succeeded in getting himself sent to the front.

When Gala had transformed a lonely, sick teenager into a promising poet at Clavadel, she had, in true Pygmalion fashion, made him her reason for being. She felt so linked to him that in her mind they were almost one person, and she was determined to create their life as she dreamed it should be. But now she was alone in a foreign country with a woman she didn't really know and who hadn't wanted her there in the first place and Paul was going to war, where there was an excellent chance he would be killed.

"My most darling most adored most wonderful boy," she wrote to Paul in early November (as though she were his mother, even though she signed the majority of her letters, "I kiss you all over, your forever wife"), "I am by myself in the house, all alone in your bed. . . . I can't sleep. . . . I imagine crazy things. . . . I think that you've died." On November 17, she wrote similarly; then, on the nineteenth, she wrote for a third time, even more vehemently—as though holding up a cracked mirror to what she saw as his willfulness. "I came here to soothe your suffering [and make you happy]. If I have failed, I will go away and become a nurse. . . . That would be a totally clownish thing for me to do and very bad for me because I am so weak and so ill . . . but I don't have the courage to finish myself off all at once so I would let myself die slowly . . . *I don't want to be a little woman you love only when there is nothing grander or more serious for you to pay attention to.*"

They squabbled over sex. Paul found Gala's *côté putainesque* very intriguing. His teasingly pointed and wishful remarks about her sexual experience and their own intimacies nettled his intended, who answered him fervently. "You are thinking awful things! You must be in love with making love (because you don't write as though you are in love with me). I may have mentioned that I had a licentious side but I assure you that *I am not and do not* [or at least not in the way you are thinking about it]. Before I met you, I was never with *anyone* the way I was with you. If we did 'strange things,' it was because I *loved* you.

"I didn't kiss [or make love to] any other men. If I let one of them hold my hand it was only to get rid of him so he would leave me in peace. I disdained flatterers and they knew I despised them."

Gala deeply wanted to please. On November 20, she wrote confidingly, "My mother used to call me 'the princess and the pea' because I never did any work around the house. But I will do housework for you and I will do it very well (your mother thinks so too) and I will never look as though I've been doing a thing. I will be pretty and wear perfume and my hands will be beautifully manicured."

She did buy herself a bottle of Coty Blanc de Blancs, which she promised not to open until he got home—"You will see for yourself that the seal is not broken"—and she found attractive fabrics for dresses she designed to give pleasure to both of them, attaching swatches to her letters to Paul.

"When I imagine our wonderful life together," she explained to him, "I think of all the details—the carved chair I've found for our bedroom, the books for our library. . . ." Because they were so alike, she claimed, "we will live like kings with our books, our words, our thoughts and our *own way of love making that will be unique* to ourselves."

By the beginning of December, she had fully convinced him. Paul, who would write, "We will not go to the goal one by one but by twos," was eager to be married as soon as possible. He left it to Gala to work out all the technical details, which, since she apparently did not yet have a complete set of her own papers, she was nervous about finessing. Finally, she was able to confirm that the marriage license was being readied. "Today," she wrote triumphantly, on December 22, just six days after Paul's twenty-first birthday, "your mother and I went to the mayoralty."

A BABY FOR PEACETIME AND
A NEW BENEFACTOR

Looking to their future, the lovers had planned for some pitfalls. Gala, who vividly remembered the humiliation that dogged her mother's civil but not religious marriage, converted to Catholicism, which was France's official religion, so she could have a socially sanctioned wedding. While Éluard was on home leave, the couple also signed a prenuptial agreement that would supersede their marriage. To protect Gala if Paul died, the contract gave each of them one-half of any money they would make under Éluard, the new name Gala had helped Paul choose.

Their nuptials were formalized at the mayor's office of the 18th arrondissement and celebrated the same day, February 28, 1917, in one of the most storied churches in Paris, the elegant chantry Saint-Denys de la Chapelle, whose foundations had been established by Saint Guinevere in 475 and where Joan of Arc had once spent a full night in prayer. The wedding party included only Paul's immediate family. Gala's brothers, sister, mother, and stepfather, who had sent a small dowry, were one thousand miles away, in Moscow. The twenty-two-year-old bride looked shy, plump, and wide-eyed in a ruffled ankle-length afternoon dress of deep green taffeta (the color of luck, hope, and springtime), which she had probably designed herself and sewn with Jeanne. The groom wore a chic, oversize beret.

Paul had to report back for duty, so the newlyweds spent their honeymoon (their "little two days," as Gala bemoaned them) in a new, vast, and "exceptionally" soft bed that Jeanne had had made to her son's specifications and placed in the center of his old bedroom, from which the lovers emerged for just one hour each dawn for a short walk.

Ten days later, the February Revolution broke out in Russia. On March 15, Nicholas II abdicated. By the time the United States entered the war, in June, Paul and Gala were composing again. They wrote back and forth, working together on *Poèmes pour la Paix* (*Poems for Peace*). Once more, they were living on love. *J'ai eu longtemps un visage inutile / Mais maintenant / J'ai un visage pour être aimé / J'ai un visage pour être heureux* ("For a long time I had the face of someone who was useless / But now I have the face of someone who is loved / I have a face for being happy"), Paul wrote. And again in *"Un Seul Être"* ("One Lone Being"), a title that reflects Gala's vision of them as one person, "Our love is laughter in this Springtime / Like all your beauty / Like all your goodness / Our dream has come true."

That month, Paul had been sent back to Paris Plage hospital for severe bronchitis. He was reclassified as an auxiliary and relocated to Auvergne, where he was put in charge of grain storage at Montluc's famous trapezoidal fort. Ecstatic at having her husband away from the fighting, Gala rushed to be near him. When she wasn't trying to fatten him up with the best Lyonnaise cooking, she spent most of her time getting their new book ready for publication.

The Éluards began sharing their work with literary figures they admired, including Guillaume Apollinaire, who was generally supportive of young poets. Although they did not at first receive much of a response, they managed, on the recommendation of Ravel's muse, the poet Tristan Klingsor, to get "Un Seul Être" accepted for publication by the short-lived review *Les Trois Roses* ("The Three Roses"). It appeared next to writings by recognized authors Max Jacob and

Chanel's lover Pierre Reverdy. By September 14, the day the revolutionary Alexander Kerensky proclaimed the new Russian Republic, Gala knew she was pregnant.

Cécile Simone Andonyle Grindel, a sweet little girl who took after her father, was born prematurely at home on the evening of May 10, 1918, after an excruciating, prolonged, and life-threatening labor.[1] Jeanne, conscious of her daughter-in-law's postpartum fragility, swooped in to care for the infant. Thus Cécile, whose health was supervised closely, spent months at a time away from Gala in the salubrious air of the family house at Bray-et-Lû. There, forty-two miles outside of Paris, surrounded by the wild orchid trees for which the locality was famous, the infant was tended by Paul's solicitous aunts and Jeanne, who visited constantly. Mother and child did not bond.

It was Paul who chose the baby girl's musical name and celebrated her birth with a small gem of a poem, which Gala tenderly recorded in the little album of personal verses she and her husband kept together:[2]

Petit morceau de verre transparent
Petit enfant sur mes genoux
Ecoute le vent
Petit enfant
Lourd comme tout sur mes genoux
Ecoute:
je t'aime

("Small chunk of clear glass / Little child on my knee / Listen to the wind / Little child / Heavy as anything on my knee / Listen: / I love you").

Paul also arranged to be transferred yet again, this time to Mantes-Gassicourt, just twelve miles from Bray-et-Lû, so he could be close to his daughter and closer to his wife, who remained in Paris.

When Gala tried to reach her parents to tell them about their new grandchild, she discovered with a jolt that there was no way to get back to Moscow for even a visit. All communication had become impossible. Helpless in the face of circumstance, she made the difficult decision to turn her back on Russia and its political chaos. From now on (and this would become one of her trademarks), the past would not matter to her. Gala would live for the future.

Six months after the armistice signaled the end of World War I, on November 11, 1918, Paul was dismissed from the army. The newlyweds rented a studio apartment from Paul's parents on the top floor of the Grindels' narrow triplex, which Gala hoped would give them some privacy. Paul began his apprenticeship in Clément's office, where he collected rents, totted up numbers, and filed legal papers, all tasks he abhorred.

To compensate for this servitude, which tinged their yearned-for new life with an overall grayness, the couple amused themselves by discovering new restaurants, going to the theater, and spending as much time as they could at the movies, then a very new art form. They enjoyed French cinema by Pathé together with American films like Charlie Chaplin's *Sunnyside*, as well as *The Eyes of the Mummy*, starring Polish vamp Pola Negri, the first woman to lacquer her toenails. They also traveled as often as possible. While Jeanne looked after Cécile, who lived with her grandparents when she came to the city, the young couple vacationed in the south of France and Tunisia, where Paul gave a lecture on a new art movement called Dada, and Gala introduced herself and her husband to the glamour of the great palace casinos and the adrenaline rush of high-stakes gambling at cards.

In Paris, Gala did everything to make herself and their environment as attractive as possible. She continued to design and sew her own clothes. If she did happen to buy a ready-made dress, she would rip it up and remake it completely, adding her own accessories to individualize the look she was creating. She spent hours arranging and rearranging their one-room apartment, which contained the antique carved-rosewood Chinese throne chair she had found in the flea market, the broad, soft bed Paul had designed for their honeymoon, ample bookshelves for their exciting new library, and a long, wide, comfortable table where, sitting side by side, she and Paul could translate the Russian Symbolist Aleksander Blok, whose work they had discovered during their days at Clavadel.

For both Éluards, life without art was simply not living. Gala was more focused than ever on launching her husband's career as a poet and recognized member of France's intellectual elite. She began carefully planning their new role as creators, patrons, and collaborators who supported fellow artists by buying their work. In January 1919, when they were putting the finishing touches on their new apartment, their acquisitions began in earnest.

The couple started frequenting exhibition halls and the Galerie Druet, which represented Manet and Gauguin. They splurged on a Derain, and they met and befriended the Cubist painter André Lhote, who willingly provided five not particularly Cubist illustrations for Paul's new poetic anthology *Les Animaux et Leurs Hommes, Les Hommes et Leurs Animaux* (*Animals and Their Men, Men and Their Animals*).

Then in February, Paul received an enthusiastic letter from Jean Paulhan, who had succeeded André Gide as the director of France's most influential literary magazine *La Nouvelle Revue Française*. Suddenly it looked as though all their hard work had paid off. Paulhan, who would become Paul's friend and mentor, made a name for himself in 1913 by translating Madagascar's tribal folk rhymes into French verse. One year later, on Christmas Eve 1914, he was wounded while fighting with the 9th Zouave regiment. During his recovery he published a very personal and highly critically acclaimed novel: *Le Guerrier Appliqué* (*The Dedicated Warrior*, Paris, Sansot, 1917) about World War I as a tutorial in cruelty. It was a narrative both Éluards wholeheartedly embraced.

Paulhan, who began by praising Paul's linguistic experiments, ended his letter by wondering offhandedly if he might like to meet three promising young poets who had just started a new review called *Littérature*, dedicated to cutting-edge writing. They had included some of his own free verse in their second number, and Jean felt they would appreciate Paul's work enough to publish at least one of his poems in the third issue they were preparing for publication in May. It was a casually proposed introduction, but it provided the entrée to the cultural world to which Gala and Paul aspired. It would also irreversibly change both of their lives.

LITTÉRATURE

Almost the same age as the Éluards, the three editors of *Littérature*—André Breton, Louis Aragon, and Philippe Soupault—were well-educated, ambitious, and above all rebellious. At a time in France when poetry was so popular and widely appreciated that thanks to Arthur Rimbaud's lingering antihero charisma,[1] being a poet was like being a rock star today, these young men were bound by their common passion for verse. The periodical they had just founded was on the verge of becoming a crucial mouthpiece for avant-garde thought. In the scant five years it was in circulation, *Littérature* would publish the most important contemporary European artists and writers and become a key hub for cultural exchange.

The only child of an affable policeman, André Breton had a leonine head, intense gray eyes, and a reserved, commanding demeanor. Born in 1890 in Orne, Normandy, he was educated at the Lycée Chaptal in Pantin, a small city three kilometers north of the ring road that marks the outer boundary of Paris. At fourteen, he published his first poems in the school magazine, *Vers Idéal*, and by the time he turned sixteen, André had become a protégé of the world-famous poet Paul Valéry and a friend of Guillaume Apollinaire,[2] one of the most beloved cultural figures of the twentieth century. Apollinaire, who was famous for his masterpiece *Alcools* (1913), also invented the word "surreal," which he used to describe the heightened artistic reality of Serge

Diaghilev's 1917 ballet *Parade*, in which dancers dressed by Picasso to resemble skyscrapers and boulevards pranced insouciantly about on the stage. After a brilliant baccalaureate,[3] André had enrolled in the *faculté de médecine* just one month before France entered World War I. Now he was *Littérature*'s chief editor. Aragon and Soupault called him "the Pope."

Breton and Louis Aragon had bonded when they read their poetry to each other to drown out shrieks of the inmates in the hospital of Val-de-Grâce's fourth-floor psychiatric ward, where in 1917 they were both nurses in the medical auxiliary.

Dainty and deliberately charming, Louis was slim and elegant, with jet-black hair and translucent, almost colorless eyes, which he played up by dressing in black. The illegitimate son of Louis Andrieux, who was in charge of France's internal security, Aragon was born October 3, 1897, in Neuilly, Paris's poshest suburb, and passed his baccalaureate at the illustrious Lycée Carnot, where, like Breton, he had discovered his talent for writing at an early age. Now he was putting the finishing touches on his first book of poetry, *Feu de Joie* (*Fire of Joy*), which he would publish in 1920.

Littérature's patron was Philippe Soupault. He had been introduced to André Breton at the Café de Flore by Guillaume Apollinaire, who "ordered" the two aspiring poets to be friends. They bonded instantly over Picon-citrons (pale ales with lemon) and their mutual love of La Maison des Amis des Livres,[4] a bookstore on rue de l'Odéon dedicated to contemporary French literature.

Dark, angular, and gracefully catlike, with hazel eyes, high cheekbones, and a narrow cleft chin, Soupault, who described himself poetically as having come into the world "like a squirrel near trees" on August 2, 1897, at his grandparents' vast estate in Chaville on the outskirts of Paris, was the only artist in his industrial family. His maternal uncle owned the Renault car company. His father's father was a sugar baron.

Isidore Ducasse's dark, Gothic epic *Les Chants de Maldoror* was the major inspiration for his nearly finished collaboration with Breton, *Les Champs Magnétiques* (*Magnetic Fields*), the legendary first book of automatic writing (published by Au Sans Pareil in 1920). André and he dedicated this masterpiece to their scapegrace hero, Jacques Vaché.

Breton had become intrigued by the nonchalance of this eccentric but talented illustrator at the Nantes[5] hospital while bandaging a wound in Vaché's calf. An Anglophile fop who enjoyed dressing up as a woman, Vaché was a prominent member of a brotherhood of local pranksters called the Sâs, where he was idolized by his friends for his indifference and the monocle he affected. When he returned to the front, he and Breton wrote back and forth.

On January 6, 1919, Jacques Vaché was discovered lying naked in his room at the Hôtel de France in Nantes a few minutes before dying of opium ingestion. Next to him was the equally naked corpse of Pierre Bonnet, a fellow soldier who had expired earlier of the same cause. The police reported the sordid calamity as an accident, but the overt nihilism of the mysterious fatalities became a rallying cry for the cutting-edge art world, in whose eyes Vaché had become a martyr/poet, offering himself up as both object and subject. For Breton, Aragon, and Soupault, he was the mythical first "Dada Suicide." Thus Jacques Vaché, whose entire literary legacy consists of *Lettres de Guerre* (*War Letters*) sent to his friends and posthumously published by André Breton, who considered them "mail art," became one of the most influential forces of Surrealism.

For Breton and Soupault, the one and only possible cure for the painful aftershock of Vaché's suicide was the creation of a new venue for self-expression: the review for which Paul Valéry had suggested the name: *Littérature*.[6]

Gala was not invited to the March 19 meeting with the all-male editorial panel of the magazine, but she made sure Paul did not arrive empty-handed. When Éluard, dressed by his wife in his army uniform, knocked timorously on the door of Breton's cramped, dingy room in the splendidly misnamed Hôtel des Grands Hommes at 17 Place du Panthéon, he was equipped with a transcript of *Poèmes pour la Paix* handwritten by Gala on pink and green paper, and their notebook filled with verses from the just-finished anthology *Les Animaux et Leurs Hommes, Les Hommes et Leurs Animaux* (*Animals and Their Men, Men and Their Animals*).

In spite of his stage fright, Paul insisted on reading aloud. He blushed furiously, and his voice trembled, but the recital was a success. Interpreting Éluard's attire as a sign that he had suffered the same ordeals they had, the panel decided he was one of them. His poems, which they flatteringly described as simultaneously polished and innocent, captivated his judges. They selected "*Vache*" ("The Cow") for publication in *Littérature*'s third issue. It begins:

On ne mène pas la vache
A la verdure rase et sèche,
A la verdure sans caresses
L'herbe qui la reçoit
Doit être douce comme un fil de soie
Un fil de soie douce comme un fil de lait

("Don't take your cow / To dry prickly pastures / Fields without kisses / The grass your cow grazes / Should be as soft as silk is / A thread of silk soft as a thread of milk").
And it ends:

L'herbe devant la vache
L'enfant devant le lait

("The grass for the cow / Milk for the baby").
It was a defining moment. From now on, Éluard would be read by

the Parisian intellligentsia in conjunction with France's most highly regarded living authors, Jean Cocteau, André Gide, Paul Valéry, Guillaume Apollinaire, and Stéphane Mallarmé. Equally important, the Éluards had a new circle of dynamic friends. These lively twenty-somethings had done their duty as excellent students and good soldiers. Now they were making up for lost time. As their curmudgeonly idol, the Roman painter Giorgio de Chirico, remembered, they loved to party. "Despite their professed violent anti-bourgeois feelings," he wrote, "they always tried to live as comfortably as possible, dress very well, and eat excellent meals washed down with superlative wines."[7]

By the end of 1919, the hole left by Jacques Vaché's death had been filled by a raven-haired Romanian called Tristan Tzara, who had moved from Switzerland to Paris to become the fourth editor of *Littérature*. According to legend, Tzara, whose first language was Yiddish, had invented the term Dada, which means hobby horse in French, at six o'clock in the afternoon on February 6, 1916, on the terrace of the Café de la Terrasse in Zurich to describe the "electric imbecility" of his performances at the Cabaret Voltaire in Zurich.[8]

Dada, a wide-ranging cultural movement that flourished in Switzerland, Paris, and New York until around 1921, was born of Tristan Tzara and his friend the Alsatian sculptor Hans Arp's despair over World War I's massive mechanized killings. It was characterized by its rejection of logic, reason, salon art, and all the hypocrisy and aestheticism of modern capitalism. It enthusiastically embraced absurdities such as Marcel Duchamp's "improving" the Mona Lisa by adding a mustache.

While several other magazines, notably Francis Picabia's Barcelona-based *391*, were exclusively dedicated to Dada, *Littérature* whose tenets also espoused irrationality and political protest, was *not*.

The Dada Manifesto, completed by Tzara in 1918, was deliberate nonsense, and, effectively, the movement had no written philosophy or organized structure. It did have ambassadors who were called "presidents" and worked to spread its ideas. Tzara, who was one of the presidents of Dada, was best known for his well-attended theatrical performances.

Gala was invited to join in on more than one occasion. She enjoyed being onstage with Tristan. She was very pleased when he gave Paul exposure by publishing their poetry in his international magazine, *DaDa*, and when Francis Picabia, who was a transatlantic art star,[9] invited Paul to contribute to his paradigmatic journal *391*, Gala was throughly delighted. She loved going out and meeting interesting new people.

Gala went everywhere with Paul. Evenings often found them at the Certà, a blue-collar Basque café down the street from the Opéra, where they enjoyed cocktails and conversation with the gang from *Littérature*. Often they were joined by Marcel Duchamp, who had just arrived back in Paris from New York City. René Hilsum, a chum of Breton's from the *faculté de médecine* who had founded the Au Sans Pareil press, which was a combination bookstore and art gallery that sold work by Aragon, Breton, Soupault, and Éluard, was frequently in attendance as well.

Chatter at the café centered chiefly on the virtues and limitations of Dada (Éluard, Paulhan, and Gala believed too deeply in the importance of poetry to ever be totally pro-chaos). The men also critiqued one another's writing and amused themselves by grading fellow authors on a scale of −20 to +20. This was Breton's favorite game. Gala declined to participate, but Éluard generously gave a +20 to Jacques Vaché, a +19 to Dostoyevsky and Lautréamont, and a +18 to Breton and Tzara. When Breton asked him the name of his favorite novel, Paul's response was *The Eternal Husband*, a lesser-known novella by Dostoyevsky, about a man who is both delighted by and obsessed with his wife's lover.

Paul, who had never had a chance to enjoy the pleasures of male bonding, reveled in these games and the never-ending banter of his high-testosterone friends. Unfortunately for Gala, the group was really a men's club. The musketeers of *Littérature* who had welcomed her husband so openheartedly found the omnipresence of "Paul's wife" puzzling and inconvenient. None of them understood why, as a young mother, she wasn't spending more time with Cécile. At the group's get-togethers, where women, *if* they were tolerated, were expected to be silent, Gala's assertive personality and occasional fervently expressed observations were rapidly becoming irritating.

Soupault, who thought that Gala was provincial and pretentious called her a bed bug and nicknamed her "Gala *la galle*" ("Gala scabies") because she got under his skin. Breton found the elegant Mme Éluard in her sculpted suits, showy long gloves, and the "little furs" Paul tenderly wrapped about her shoulders to "keep away the chill" straight-out intimidating. When Gala snubbed his shy gallantries, he was humiliated. When she called him a flirt, he was enraged. For her part, Gala resented Aragon, who was always trying to get her husband to go out on the town "with the boys" for an evening of bars and bordellos, which meant she would be left alone with Cécile. So although she welcomed the advantages of being in the *Littérature* circle, Gala understood that its members weren't really her friends. She began shifting her attention to art collecting.

The Éluards both agreed that painting was poetic expression, so expanding their collection was a natural task for Gala to take on. She befriended Amédée Ozenfant, a post-Cubist painter who showed at Galerie Druet. Amédée, who liked Paul and Gala, was happy to introduce the eager young couple to the art world and its latest trends. With Ozenfant's guidance, they rapidly purchased paintings by Georges Braque, Juan Gris, and Giorgio de Chirico, known for his long shadows and eerie juxtapositions of everyday objects, from the German dealers Kahnweiler und Unde. Gala was beginning to develop her eye.

MAX

The most exciting artistic event in the spring of 1921 in Paris was the debut one-man show of a rising star from Cologne, Germany, whose name was Max Ernst.

Four years after Ferdinand Foch had signed the Armistice at Compiègne, memories of the First World War were still vivid and painful, and most Frenchmen referred to Germans as *"Boches"* (pejorative slang for "wood heads" or "monsters"). Accordingly, Tristan Tzara, who initiated the exhibition scheduled to open May 21 at the Sans Pareil gallery,[1] planned it to be an outrage, which he publicized vigourously to horrify all of Paris's "ordinary citizens."[2]

Ernst's scandalous reputation was already semi-established in Germany, where his fellow Dadaists admired the brazeness of his collaged compositions. In France, Braque or Picasso may have occasionally punctuated one of their paintings with a glued-on letter or a newspaper clipping, but in Ernst's oeuvre, the collages *were* the work. His best-known pieces, the so-called postcards, a name that underscored their literary character, consisted of startling collections of disparate, sexually charged, and often impudent cutout images, which, when assembled, took on a collective meaning of their own. As a result he was loudly if inaccurately disparaged by academicians for his supposed inability to paint. This criticism only added to his growing fame.

After organizing the Cologne branch of the Dadaist movement in 1919 with his lifelong friend Hans Arp and the son of a wealthy socialist baptized Alfred Gruenwald who had changed his name to Johannes Baargeld (German for "cash"), Ernst had further augmented his enviable infamy by publishing outrageously irrational French poetry in the radical magazine *Die Schammade* and getting himself jailed in his hometown for making pornography and inciting riots.

To top it off, Max was very good-looking. With his lean, athletic build, mocking blue eyes, and the shock of pale hair that fell over his right eyebrow, he exuded the sex appeal of a fallen angel. The third of nine children, Max Ernst was born on April 2, 1891, on the banks of the Rhine in the small township of Brühl, which is dominated by the graceful ruins of its rococo castle and bounded by thick, dark, and mysterious forests. By age ten, he had invented his own cosmology in which the birds of the forest were dragons and the death of his favorite pink cockatoo was caused by the birth of his youngest sister.

Max's father, Philipp, was an ardent Catholic and rigid disciplinarian who taught the hearing impaired during the week and spent his Sundays making religious pictures. He painted baby Max as the Christ Child and taught him to draw when he was only four, but when Philipp chopped down a tree because it disrupted the symmetry of a landscape he was painting, the little boy was so horrified that his love for his father was forever destroyed. He would spend the rest of his life in rebellion against what he viewed as Philipp's blinkered lifestyle and unimaginative thought process.

In the fall of 1909, Max entered the University of Bonn. He majored simultaneously in philosophy, psychology, and mathematics and spent most of his free time visiting psychiatric hospitals, where the inmates' artwork mesmerized him. He met Louise Straus, a brilliant art historian and the daughter of a prosperous Jewish hatmaker, in sketch class. The pair fell in love, and Max renamed her "Rosa Bonheur."[3]

Ernst was drafted on August 1, 1914, and married Louise, against the wishes of both sets of parents, on his first leave from the army. After the armistice, he briefly described his war experience as follows: "On the first of August 1914 Max Ernst died. He was resurrected on the eleventh of November 1918 as a young man inspired to find the myths of his time."[4]

Francis Picabia, who was the poster child for Dada, usually financed the shows at the Sans Pareil. But he was jealous of the German's notoriety and refused to put up any money for the Max Ernst exhibition. So Breton, who had abandoned his medical studies to become an art adviser, turned to his premier client, the great couturier Jacques Doucet, who gladly complied.

André, who had fallen in love with the "postcards" and who, in conjunction with Aragon, had paid for the publication of the catalog, not only wrote its polemical introduction but also personally hung each of the twenty-one canvases in the show. As he would explain in 1955 on French radio: "The suggestive power of Max Ernst's first collages came to us all as a revelation."

The vernissage, which ended up being more of a happening than an ordinary art opening, did not disappoint. Cultural celebrities such as André Gide and painter Kees van Dongen turned out to watch Aragon impersonating a kangaroo in the cellar and Soupault playing hide-and-seek by himself on the first floor. As soon as night fell, the lights were switched off, and Tzara, who was standing on a chair by the door, announced to the spectators that one of the "free" orangeades, which by that time everyone had ingested, was poisoned. This proclamation had the desired effect of inciting tumult and rage in the audience, and the newspapers went into shock for weeks over the incident, so although no art was actually sold, the event was considered an enormous success.

Because of his subversive practice and murky political affiliations, Max was not allowed out of Germany. Since no one in Paris had yet met the artist, his French friends decided to visit him in Tarrenz, a small town in the Austrian Tyrol where he had obtained permission from the German government to vacation. Tzara arrived at the beginning of August. Breton and his new wife, Simone Kahn, the daughter of a rich Alsatian banker, followed on September 15, as did Arp, who had traveled from Strasbourg.

The Éluards dallied. May 21 found them sunbathing on the Côte d'Azur, where they had gone, on the pretext of curing one of Gala's long colds, to gamble, relax, and write poetry. As a result, they had been conspicuously absent at the debut exhibition of Ernst's work in Paris and missed all the tumult of the now-famous opening. Gala and Paul were very intrigued by Ernst's art, his verses, and the poetic names like *A Week of Kindness* he gave to his "postcards." But they were waiting for a moment when they could have him to themselves. Paul pretended to be worried about the weather. "As you know," he wrote to Tzara, who was encouraging their visit to the Tyrol by extolling the exciting company and spectacular mountain scenery, "our vacations are mostly for my wife, whose health is precarious. Is it warm there in autumn?"

By the time Gala and Paul arrived in Tarrenz at the tail end of September, Aragon was back in Paris, Arp was ensconced in Strasbourg, and Ernst had gone home to Cologne. Meanwhile André and Simone were packing their bags for Vienna, where they hoped to meet "the Pope's" idol, Sigmund Freud. In Austria, Paul and Gala enjoyed themselves alone. For almost a fortnight they hiked in the luminous alpine sunshine and spent dreamy evenings stargazing from the carved balconies of the Bavarian hut they had rented. It wasn't until Breton was safely back in France and they decided the coast was clear for them to meet Max on their own. Early in the evening of November 4, the two radiant, suntanned Parisians knocked on the door of the Ernst residence at Kaiser-Wilhelm-Ring 14 in Cologne. They were welcomed by the artist, his baby boy Ulrich, who was sometimes called Jimmy but more frequently Minimax, and Louise, Max's plump, gemütlich wife.

Louise and Max were on the rocks. Their, in Louise's words, "not nice at all" civil wedding had isolated them from their families. They were living frugally on Louise's slim salary as a research assistant at the Wallraf-Richartz art museum in Cologne, irregularly supplemented by grudging handouts from her soon-to-be-widowed father. Louise, who had been brought up with servants, had no notion of housework or cooking. She was madly in love with Max, who required total devotion, expected his shoes polished, his studio swept, and his favorite meals served up warm when he wanted them. She also found him intimidating. As she wrote in her memoir, *A First Wife's Tale*, the war had changed the man she had married, who now "spoke little; was introverted and whose beautiful blue eyes had learned to stare coldly." To make matters worse, Max had many admirers but no buyers for the art he spent most of his time making, and Louise was not allowed to watch him paint or even ask him about an unfinished canvas. Since her wedding, Louise had broken off with those of her friends Max didn't like. She read only the books he loved and had even given up playing her violin. "I was supposed to live for him only and his interests and not follow my own," is the way she described her situation.

Because they entertained and went out constantly, the Ernsts were never alone, so in a sense they were already, in Louise's words, "separated." The wished-for birth of their son had only worsened the strain that already existed between them. The responsibilities that came with a child were too much for Max, and little Jimmy, who could sense the tension between his parents, was afraid of his father.

Max too lived in fear. Thanks to his left-wing political beliefs and status as a dangerous agitator, he was subjected to ongoing surveillance. Not only had Ernst been denied the visas he needed to leave Germany, he also worked under the constant threat that at any moment his precious art, now labeled "subversive," would be seized by the authorities and summarily destroyed. So he was very happy indeed to embrace the magnanimous Dada poet on his doorstep who, even though he was five years Max's junior, lived regally in Paris, that grand capital of art and of freedom to which Ernst was burning to escape.

For almost a week from the fourth to the tenth of November, the two couples and Minimax were inseparable. They spent their days in the amusement park and at the circus. Evenings were celebrated in all the dance halls they could discover. "We dance everywhere," a delighted Éluard wrote to Tristan Tzara. "We trail floating bits of ribbons and scare off the dogs." Back home they liked staying up all night chatting, debating, and gossiping until, finally worn out from the day's pleasures, Gala would curl up next to Paul and nod off on the sofa.

When Max showed the Éluards the new work in his studio, Gala and Paul, who only knew of his collages, were amazed. They could not believe he had never been formally trained as an artist, and Gala was thrilled to discover that she could easily parse Ernst's uncanny visual vocabulary. Paul immediately bought a just-finished painting of an enormous, dark gray, elephantine creature. The tank-like, lustful animal with a long, curvy trunk of a neck, a small bull's head, and big, bulging eyes is shyly ogling the beautiful naked body of a headless woman who floats in the lower right-hand corner of the composition. Ernst named the work *Éléphant Célèbes*. It was his first sale.

Bonded by similar war experiences (albeit on different sides of the conflict), the two men who quickly became allies called themselves "brothers." *"Le roi dansait sur marbre. Je ne suis plus fils unique."* ("The King danced on marble. I'm an only child no longer.") Paul wrote exultantly to Tristan Tzara.

In contrast, the two wives could not have been more different. Louise, who was blond, outgoing, and maternal, embraced the world openly, but self-effacingly kept her distance from her husband's inner thoughts and creative process. Reserved, complicated, and dark-complexioned Gala, without thinking twice, had left her daughter behind in Paris. She concentrated all her energies on Paul and was a respected, integral partner in his work.

Toward the end of the visit, Gala, Max, and Paul banded together to spend hours writing verse and picking out Ernst images for Éluard's new anthology *Répétitions*. Louise and Minimax were left on the sidelines. When Max presented Gala with his Croix de Guerre medal, the attraction between Louise's husband and Éluard's wife was palpable. For Louise, this was especially painful. She deeply resented Gala, who she remembered as "This floating, glowing creature with dark curls, crooked sparkling eyes and limbs like a panther. This nearly silent greedy woman who first tried to make her husband, who adored her, fall in love with me and when this did not work because of resistance by the two intended victims, just kept both men: hers and mine."

In Paul's poem "Max Ernst," which opens *Répétitions*, this situation is expressed more romantically and suggestively: *Dans un coin l'inceste agile / Tourne autour de la virginité d'une petite robe / Dans un coin le ciel délivré / aux épines de l'orage laisse des boules blanches:* In a corner agile incest / roams around the virginity of a little dress / In [another] corner the sky which has surrendered to / The prickles of the storm pelts white hail. While Paul wrote, Gala posed bare-breasted for Max. They named the finished gouache *Perturbation ma Sœur* (*Disruption My Sister*).

Just before the Éluards left to go home to Paris, Max gave Gala *Les Pléiades*, his portentous, eerily sexual collage of a naked female body floating in the night sky under the wings of an angel, which he dedicated to her. Also known as *Approaching Puberty*, the image underscores the beauty and purity of their new love, which, as its sensuality suggests, Ernst hopes will soon be consummated.

A postcard mailed right after the Éluards' departure further clarifies Max's understanding of the relationship. It's addressed to "big Paul," to whom Max "owes a great debt" and "dear Gala," to whom he hopes never to owe "so much as an apology"—and it concludes: "love stretched three ways is nevertheless love."[5]

When Sans Pareil published *Répétitions* in March 1922, Paul made a special trip to Cologne to give Max his own copies. Four weeks later, when the Ernsts and the Éluards, with their children in tow, got together again over spring vacation in Imst, a thirteenth-century Tyrolian Township that looked like a postcard of Christmas, the hurtful situation was reprised. Gala, dressed in a luxurious, long fur vest over a trendy midcalf skirt, went skiing with Paul and Max while Louise looked after the children. The coup de grâce came one rainy afternoon when they were all together in the same room. As Louise wrote, Max "was working with the Russian on the translation of one of his books and was very rude to her. I kidded her in a friendly manner. 'Why do you let him speak to you like that? I would never let him speak to me in that manner.' I admit it was clumsy but the answer [from Max] was the worst that could ever have happened. In a short moment he looked up and said, 'I also never loved you as passionately as I love her.' I realized then it was all over." "I wish," Max told Louise in one of their rare moments of solitude, "I could be happy just married to you, but it does not work."

There was a second reunion in Austria the following summer. The Éluards took a lake house in Tarrenz. Tristan Tzara, and the dancer Maja Chrusecz, together with the artist Hans Arp, and his fiancée Sophie Tauber were comfortably installed in the cozy, oak-beamed Gasthof Post Hotel. Matthew Josephson, a journalist from Brooklyn who was writing an article on Dada lifestyles for the American quarterly *Broom*, had a room near Maja and Tristan. And the Ernsts lived down the street in a rented apartment until Max very publicly abandoned his family to move in with Gala and Paul.

This open ménage à trois distressed almost everyone, except Max, who, in photographs of that period, looks quite pleased with himself. Gala, meanwhile, became increasingly melancholic and petulant, if not stormy. In an apparent attempt to telegraph that Russians had their own views on infidelity and that her newsworthy tryst was an effort to please her husband, she took to walking around everywhere with a copy of *The Eternal Husband*, Éluard's favorite novella about marital infidelity.

By the end of the vacation, Gala's performances were over the top to the point that Tauber and Arp began quarreling so fiercely over their meaning and relevance that they almost broke up, before deciding to get married. "Of course, we don't care what they do or who sleeps with whom," an irritated Tzara, who was on the verge of leaving his own lover, Maja, exclaimed to Josephson, "but why does Gala Éluard need to turn it into a drama à la Dostoevsky? It's intolerable."

Clearly embarrassed, Éluard did his best to take a larger, more civil view of the situation: "You don't know what it is to be married to a Russian woman," he told the American reporter. "I love Max more than I love Gala," he continued roguishly, underlining the fact that Max was a part of his intimate life and that Gala was in no way, or at least not yet, an issue between him and his new "brother." For his part, Josephson praised Paul's poetry in *Broom* and was quite taken with Mrs. Éluard, whom he described admiringly in his book *Life Among the Surrealists* as "lively," "dark eyed," and *very* Russian.[6]

While Josephson was writing his article, Paul, Max, and Gala continued their work on *Les Malheurs des Immortels*. It was published to good reviews in July 1923, under Philippe Soupault's imprint, Librarie Six. To make peace with Breton, who would have liked to have been a part of the collaboration, Paul and Max dedicated a special copy to him.

"You know," Max told Louise in August, "You do not need a man anymore. You are twenty-three years old. You have a son . . . what more do you want? You will be able to live quite happily with the child." "What are you thinking?" Louise answered angrily. "I am only twenty-three years old. I want to live." Max did go back to Cologne with Louise and baby Ulrich at the end of the month. But on September 2, he boarded the train to Paris. He could leave Germany now. He had Éluard's passport.

CHAPTER 7

THE DOLL'S HOUSE

Gala and Paul had abandoned Paris and their one room at the top of the Grindels' triplex for the clear air and privacy of Saint-Brice-sous-Forêt, a quick eighteen minutes north of Paris by train, where Clément had rented a small, rectangular bungalow with a flat roof, wide floor-to-ceiling windows, and the tiniest scrap of a wrap-around garden for the "children" so they could have their own home. When Max, Europe's most admired and notorious young painter, consented to become their houseguest, the Éluards considered themselves lucky.

Jean Paulhan, who was just as enchanted as Paul by Ernst's talent and charm, had helped out by procuring false papers for the German under the amusing sobriquet: Jean Paris. Max could now get a job without worrying about being extradited as a dangerous alien. Luckily, almost as soon as he began exploring the streets of Paris, he was "discovered" by a roving talent scout and enjoyed a brief film career as an extra in such pictures as Henri Diamant-Berger's *The Three Musketeers* and its sequel *Twenty Years After*. When Max was fired for disrupting an entire day of filming by refusing to wear his uncomfortable costume, Paulhan was able to quickly find him more stable employment as a polisher of fake gems in a Parisian souvenir factory, where his self-protective silence earned him the nickname "Le Taciturne."

Gala was much closer to Ernst's ideal of femininity than Louise had been. Keeping her prenuptial promise to Paul, she had become an exceptional cook and housekeeper. Unlike Louise, Gala (who had written to Tzara that Max would be as "great as Picasso") was unabashedly convinced of Ernst's genius. And despite her evident anxiety over the three-way affair her husband had encouraged, she was never someone to do things by halves. She treated Ernst as Éluard's equal in her affections. "I saw Paul and Max walking in Montmartre with *their* wife," Aragon wrote to André a week after Max had moved in. Every morning, Clément's chauffeur would drive the two "brothers" in one of the Grindel cars to Saint-Brice's station, where they would hop the commuter train to Paris and, because Éluard continued to work for his father, their boring day jobs.

Sometimes Gala would meet them in the city for a late-afternoon Picon-citron at the Certà or the Petit Grillon with their friends from *Littérature,* who continued to be slightly put off by her presence. Most nights, however, the two men would come home together to three-year-old Cécile and Gala's warm hearth, where, nurtured by the wife of his best friend and sole patron, Ernst's work was blossoming.

Even though he was only free to paint at night and on weekends, his first months in France marked the beginning of one of Max Ernst's most fecund periods. This included the completion of *Saint Cecilia (Invisible Piano),* a reference to Gala's daughter that channels a Raphael portrait by the same name, and *A l'intérieur de la vue (Inside the Vision),* an image of five crystal vases filled with flowers whose heads are in the water and stems in the air.

Ernst was also working on *Au Rendez-vous des Amis (The Meeting of Friends)* his famous portrait of *Littérature's* protagonists, in which he prophetically depicted Gala, the only woman in the painting, as an independent soul searching for new horizons. Gala, who is standing next to a bust of the group's idol, Giorgio de Chirico, has turned her back to the viewer as she points her right index finger to the left, away from the others. Ernst himself, prematurely white-haired and dressed all in green, sits snugly on the lap of a brown-suited Dostoyevsky, while at the center of the canvas Éluard, also in brown with his eyes half-shut, appears to gaze inward as he recites poetry. He faces a leaping André Breton, who looks as though he is about to make a proclamation. On the far right, their important new friend, the beautiful, bisexual novelist René Crevel, tickles the ivories of an imaginary piano as Hans Arp looks on protectively. Other players include the sixteenth-century painter Raphael, who evokes the birth of a new Renaissance, Soupault, Baargeld, Aragon, Jean Paulhan, and the mystical poet Robert Desnos. Breton had written recently to Doucet that he was about to denounce Dada in *Littérature*. In Ernst's painting a sign that "Dada" was waning is that both Picabia and Tzara are absent.

When the painting was finished in December 1922, and before it went on display at the Salon des Indépendants in Paris's Grand Palais the following February, the Éluards hosted a "soirée" to celebrate its completion. This was a festive evening that included all kinds of occult games. Breton's new friends, Robert Desnos and René Crevel, who had taken courses in hypnotism, led the séances while Gala read the tarot. The dinner itself, at which guests sat facing their own portraits to enjoy superb food and excellent wines, was a triumph. The only sour note was Éluard's blatant drunkenness.

Unfortunately, the months that proved so productive for Max Ernst were the opposite for Paul. In the latter half of 1922, the poet's entire output consisted of a single collaboration with Ernst, who provided its diagrammatic illustrations. This nadir of both of their creative efforts was a satirical exposé of the goings-on in their ménage à trois, which outlines puerile sex games two men can play with a woman. For example: "The lady is lying naked on a flat surface such as a table covered with a blanket folded over twice. Present an object to her, holding it above her head in such a way that it remains within her field of vision. . . . Always keep the object far enough away from the lady for her to be unable to grab it. Give it to her only when you wish to reward her for her efforts."

In reality, whatever initial titillation he may have experienced from seeing his wife in the arms of his friend had long worn off, leaving Éluard nostalgic for the heady, comforting intimacy he had enjoyed with Gala at Clavadel. Paul ached to retrieve his position with her but was reluctant to interfere with her relationship with Ernst, whose friendship he depended on now more than ever. This conflict left the poet visibly miserable with his current lifestyle. *"L'amour n'a pas d'ailes / le désespoir non plus"* ("Love has no wings. / Neither does despair"), he wrote movingly of his dilemma. Unwilling to face the situation at home, he did his best to obliterate his malaise in the company of Aragon and Crevel at the music halls, champagne bars, and brothels of Montmartre.

Despite evidence to the contrary, it was Gala who was blamed by their friends for her husband's depression. Breton, who was a bit of a prig and had never approved of the fashionable ménage ("imagine things like this actually go on in the suburbs," he exclaimed naively), concluded that Gala should never have permitted it. Aragon empathized with Éluard and felt pity for him, while Philippe Soupault, who had always detested Gala, openly accused her of using Paul's friendship with Max to torment her husband.

On a positive note: that April, Clément relinquished his Paris apartment for a grand estate in Montlignon on the edge of the ancient Montmorency forest that blankets the hills overlooking Paris. He bought his son a three-story pavilion nearby. At 4 rue Hennocque in Eaubonne, it was conveniently situated just three miles from the parental establishment and eleven miles outside of Paris.

Éluard was delighted with this pretty new home, which he described as a marriage of Louis XVI and modern.[1] It had a slate roof and a light, refined façade decorated with a band of white lotus flowers. Wrought-iron gates and a tall wall of pale bricks surrounded the property and sheltered the breathtaking gardens, which brimmed with chestnut trees, sequoias, and the plentiful multicolored rose-bushes Gala had ordered.

The public spaces—the kitchen, pantry, living and dining rooms—were on the ground floor. Private bedrooms and bathrooms were upstairs, while the third floor, which Jeanne and Clément had originally thought would be Cécile's nursery, was transformed by Éluard into a grand studio with a new wall of north-facing windows for his best friend Max Ernst. The Grindels could not have been more displeased and disappointed.

In February 1923, Tutankhamun's tomb in the Valley of the Kings just outside of Luxor, Egypt, was finally unsealed by British archeologist Harold Carter to a blaze of international publicity. All the Western World, including Gala, went mad for the paintings of spiritual and secular life in ancient Egypt's new kingdom that adorned the walls of Tut's famous burial chambers.

That May, Max Ernst, with Gala as his model and guide, began making his own ornamental murals on detachable panels for the new house in Eaubonne. These twentieth-century "Hieroglyphs" illustrated Gala's fantasy of "heaven on earth" and can be read as a first-hand account of life during the famous Eaubonne ménage.

Some found them disturbing. Cécile was four at the time, and although, as an adult, her dominant memory of Eaubonne was being ordered by Gala to "go play outside in the garden," she also vividly remembered that as a child she had feared and hated the paintings on the pavilion's ground floor. These were three highly stylized portraits of a naked, glowing, golden Gala with her arms outstretched as if greeting her guests. One is a perfect satirical image of a hostess who is literally but very abstractly and elegantly spilling her guts [turning herself inside out] for the benefit of her visitors, whom she greets with a warm, crimson-lipped smile. In all cases, Gala is in full motion.

She is either floating midair or dancing for joy with an unidentified androgyne, who is probably Paul.

A corner door adorned by Max with the narrow, long-fingered hands of a magician opened onto a cobalt staircase that led to the second floor. Here vibrant blue—the color of spirituality, femininity, dreams, and intimacy—was the dominant hue. The master bedroom was covered with murals of a Rousseau-like landscape filled with giant artichokes on exceptionally long stems. An enormous blue butterfly, the symbol of metamorphosis, adorned the door to the master bath. Opposite the fireplace in the middle of this dreamscape was a wide, passion-red velvet daybed where, according to Gala, who enjoyed enhancing her "bad girl" image, she, Éluard, and Ernst slept together every night.[2] Perhaps it was only most nights. Cécile had many happy memories of her beloved father lying on this couch for weeks at a time, too sick to get up but still well enough to hug his little girl and tell her long, funny stories.

Past the cosmic butterfly, the walls of the master bath described by Cécile as a joyful blue-green were filled with images of rare seashells and strange fishes, to give bathers in the vast claw-footed tub by the window the sensation of being submerged in an exotic underwater world. Cécile's little bedroom was decorated by Max with Egyptian-style friezes of quirky, imaginary games.

Between the panels, Gala displayed the Éluards' superlative library of first editions, and works by their friends Picasso, Derain, and Braque, along with the hand-carved kachina spirit dolls from Arizona Éluard had purchased through dealers in Europe. Gala loved the kachinas so much that, to please her, Paul named the villa "The Doll's House."

According to Gala's little sister, Lidia, who also visited during this period,[3] life in Eaubonne was filled with a mass of parties and séances that were famous in Paris's art world for becoming ever more psychological and insightful as they progressed:

BRETON: It's Ernst who is holding your hand. Do you know him?
DESNOS: Who?

BRETON: Ernst

BRETON: Will he live for a long time?
DESNOS: Fifty-one years – [This was in fact a prescient remark since Ernst, who was just thirty-four at the time, died fifty-one years later at age eighty-five.]

BRETON: What will he do?
DESNOS: He will play with crazy people.

BRETON: Is he happy with these crazies?
DESNOS: Ask that woman in blue.

BRETON: Who is the woman in blue?
DESNOS: There.

BRETON: What? There?
DESNOS: The Tour? Yes.[4]

No one was surprised when these table-turnings ended in tumult or when, one legendary, particularly drunken evening, Desnos chased Éluard into the garden waving a big kitchen knife. Incidents of this kind soon became so notorious in the neighborhood that rumors of orgies and witchcraft clung to the Doll's House long after Paul sold it in 1936.

There was also love. It was while he was working on the Eaubonne house panels that Ernst created his erotic masterpiece: *La Belle Jardinière* (*The Beautiful Gardener*), which is a luscious nude of Gala named after a painting of the Madonna by Raphael. As in the Doll's House murals,

Gala's luminous likeness is accompanied by a shadow: an ethereal androgyne composed of a wealth of fruits and vegetables—all the earth's bounty—who dances happily behind her. A large white dove placed provocatively over her pubic area suggests the Holy Spirit and gives her the appearance of being a hermaphrodite. The complex portrayal celebrates the seeming paradox of Gala's profound femininity and her epicene intelligence. She was at this time the woman Max had most loved in his life.

La Belle Jardinière became very popular. Braque, Gris, Cocteau, and Aragon all admired it. And Jacques Doucet was so taken with its beauty that he wanted to buy it for his collection until his jealous wife put her foot down and refused to let him hang the tantalizing image of Gala's naked body in their apartment.

That Christmas, Paul forsook his brothels and all-night binges to take Gala on a romantic long weekend to Rome. He planned to look at the new art in the Biennale and pose with his wife for their portrait by Giorgio de Chirico, who, at the top of his game, had eleven works on display in the exhibition. The holiday did not turn out to be what the poet had hoped for. Gala began composing the new painting with the Roman and became an instant favorite of Giorgio's, who pronounced her "the most fascinating and intelligent woman he had ever met."[5] Unfortunately, de Chirico so despised Éluard, who he described as having the "look of a mystical imbecile,"[6] that all three ended up being on edge. By the end of the sojourn it was apparent that the previous much-cherished bond between Gala and her husband was too frayed to be mended in a five-day vacation. Paul was shattered.

CHAPTER 8

ESCAPE FROM "THE DOLL'S HOUSE"

Back in Paris, on the evening of March 23, 1924, Éluard handed his editor Jean Paulhan the finished manuscript of his latest anthology, *Mourir de ne pas mourir* (*Dying of not Dying*), dedicated to Breton with a frontispiece by Max Ernst. The next day, without warning, he disappeared.

Clément was still fuming over his recent discovery of the true nature of Gala and Max Ernst's relationship and his son's new, very large gambling debts when he received a mail-o-gram from Éluard. It read: "I've had enough. I'm going travelling. You can take back the business you've set up for me but I'm taking the money I've got, namely 17,000 French francs.[1] If you send either the police or private detectives to find me, I'll see to the first one I spot. And that won't be good for your reputation. Here is what to say; and tell everyone the same thing: I had a hemorrhage when I got to Paris and I'm in the hospital. Later you can say I've gone to a clinic in Switzerland. Take best care of Gala and Cécile."[2]

It was as though Éluard had evaporated. No one knew where he was. André Breton, who ran into her in Paris, told all their friends that Gala was calm but she had to look for a job because Paul had left her with only four hundred francs to her name and her parents-in-law refused to give her or Cécile any money until Max moved out. But Max was all she had.

The next day, Simone Breton wrote to her cousin Denise Naville in Alsace, "André says we will never see Paul Éluard again."[3] Despite the fact that Desnos claimed to have had a vision of Paul sailing the Pacific, most of Éluard's friends believed he was dead. Their hope was that he had pulled what they called "a Rimbaud"—that is, abandoned everything as the Symbolist poet Arthur Rimbaud famously did when, in 1875, he abruptly left his lover Paul Verlaine and gave up his career as one of France's greatest writers for life as a solitary explorer.

Gala did not know what to believe. She trod water. Turning down the offer of a business partnership with de Chirico, she coped instead as best she could by having Ernst make salable objects, an idea she would reprise in America in the '40s, when the market for Surrealist artworks had temporarily turned cold. Under her direction, Max painted designs on scarves and ties, which she peddled door to door. To say she was miserable is an understatement: Max's sketches of Gala from this period show a frightening, wounded, witchlike creature with vicious, slanted eyes that radiate sorrow, rancor, and rage. According to Dorothea Tanning, Ernst's fourth and last wife, Max blamed himself for Paul's disappearance, and had guiltily begun to imagine Gala's famously smoldering eyes as live embers that were blazing straight through him.[4]

After slipping away south without anyone noticing, Éluard spent twenty-two days in Nice, where he checked into the five-star Hotel Beaulieu to nurse his misery alone. Then, on the rainy, gray afternoon of April 15, he boarded the French steamer SS *Antonius*, in Marseille, which was headed for New Caledonia, in the far west of the Pacific Ocean.

He arrived at Pointe-à-Pitre, Guadeloupe, on May 1. By May 6, he was in Fort-de-France, the capital of Martinique. When he reached Panama on May 12, he sent a letter to Gala. It read:

"My darling little girl, I hope you will pass this way some time soon. I'm bored. You know I always write. You should have made up envelopes for me but you will be consoled by the way I am going to love you. Wait till you get here to see the presents I have for you! You alone are precious; I have never loved anyone but you. I can love nothing else."[5]

Having emerged from the muddied coastal waters of Panama City, the SS *Antonius* nosed her way sluggishly through the Caribbean jungle to the clear blue waves of the Pacific, where, after two solid weeks of transoceanic sailing, on May 31, she put into Papeete, the capital of French Oceania, for five days.

The sugary smell of split coconuts, which were Tahiti's principal export, surrounded him as Paul, who owned some of the artist's work, entered the world of Gauguin. Here he began to enjoy himself. He dressed up in a pith helmet to climb one of the island's shark-tooth-shaped white mountains. And although he was fish-belly white and pitifully out of shape, he had his picture taken in a colorful native sarong.[6] He also sent Gala a written request to sell some of their paintings.

While Paul was skirting the Australian coast, Gala, without telling anyone except Max and her in-laws, reluctantly arranged for the Hôtel Drouot in Paris to auction sixty-one pieces from their collection, including six drawings by Picasso as well as oils by Odilon Redon, André Derain, Juan Gris, and naturally, Max Ernst, whose *Two Children Attacked by a Nightingale* had been recently reproduced in the Chinese publication *Art Wind*. Thanks in great part to Gala, Max was by now world-famous, but his work remained disappointingly uncommercial. Understandably, he was very worried about the psychological state of his only patron. To help raise funds for the trip, he managed to unload *La Belle Jardinière* to the gallery Mutter Ey in Hamburg, where it disappeared during the Second World War.

Gala used some of the money she collected to repay her father-in-law the seventeen thousand francs Paul had stolen from Clément's company, and with her usual meticulous attention to detail, she prepared to meet her husband in Saigon.

On July 17, the day the celebrated French explorer and novelist André Malraux was tried in Phnom Penh, where he was found guilty of theft for looting Angkor Wat's exquisite ruins, Gala and Max boarded the SS *Paul Lecat* in Marseilles. The French ocean liner dedicated to the busy Indochina run was not only grand; it was big enough to get lost in. Gala and Max were looking forward to a monthlong, sybaritically luxurious crossing, but the tropical weather refused to cooperate. By the time the ship reached its destination, several of the passengers were severely overheated.

"GALA HERE. LOOKING FORWARD TO COMING HOME AND TO PROPERTIES. YOU WERE NOT THE REASON. REPLY BY TELEGRAM. HAVE ALWAYS LOVED YOU. GRINDEL. HOTEL CASINO SAIGON," Paul, who had been tipped off by Gala that Clément was ready to forgive and forget, telegraphed his father on August 12 as a precursor to hitting him up for another ten thousand francs.[7]

Despite a mean temperature of eighty-six degrees Fahrenheit, Saigon in August 1924 was a dazzling Gallic colony filled with gracious villas surrounded by walled gardens of palms and mango saplings. The city that seemed to doze in the day came to life at sunset when its broad avenues, lined with a blaze of grenadine and scarlet trees in flower, were suddenly animated by a bustling mix of dressed-up locals and well-groomed tourists going out to fancy restaurants and into chic nightclubs.

It was in this torrid and glamorous setting at the Art Deco Hotel Casino that a resolute Max and a beseeching Gala managed to convince the still-wavering Paul of his duty to return home to his family. The ménage à trois was formally dissolved.

As if to commemorate their decision to disband the threesome, they had themselves photographed separately in the same location next to an elaborately carved stone likeness of a snarling Khmer lion. Here, an unsmiling, hollow-cheeked Gala, with very thin arms, crouches at the feet of the creature in a sleeveless lightweight dress with a wide cowl neck, and manages to look soignée and sad at the same time. Slightly behind her, a local guide in uniform with a narrow dark belt pets the lion, while Paul, almost completely obfuscated by the statue, gazes, as was his wont, into the yonder and appears to be sweltering. In a separate snapshot, Max, dressed head to toe in gleaming, impeccable white, with his arms crossed across his chest, stands proudly tall and alone in front of the lion, looking as though he has just tamed the beast.

Paul and Gala left Max in Indochina to wend his way home alone by way of Angkor Wat. Singapore, where they were scheduled to catch the Dutch liner SS *Goentoer*, bound for Marseilles, was their next stop.

By the time Gala disembarked in Marseilles on Sunday, September 28, she was glad to smell autumn in the breeze. Paul was still a little disoriented. He had been away for seven months and, according to Simone Breton, looked as though he had shriveled. "Travel has always taken me too far," he would write in 1930. "The reassuring knowledge that one's got a destination has always seemed like the hundredth ring of the bell on a door that never opens." And then, just like that, the Éluards walked back into Paris as though they had never been away.

On October 3, in a letter to her cousin Denise Naville, Simone Breton announced breathlessly: "Éluard is back—no comment, there's too much to say."[8]

"Great news," Aragon wrote to Denise's husband, the sociologist Pierre Naville, excitedly on October 5, "Éluard is back from Martinique, Tahiti; Java. André is depressed, happy to see Paul . . . and then the anger. As for me I can't tell you how much I missed Éluard."

A few days later the sculptor Alexandre Noll received what he thought was a sad letter from Breton:

"Would you believe it?
Éluard—it's a fact was happy in Tahiti
In Java and then in Saigon with Gala and Ernst
The latter will be back any day
But for Paul and Gala it's as though nothing happened—Eaubonne
I know you think that's fine
Well he drops me a line yesterday to let me know he'd be expecting me at the
Cyrano no more no less
It's him, no doubt about it
On holiday—that's all
He asked after you."

Predictably, most of the Bretons' anger was directed at Gala by Simone, who, since she was habitually ignored by her own husband, deeply envied Mrs. Éluard as a woman men appreciated "for her *intelligence*." When it turned out that Gala had actually known where Paul was for "weeks *without telling anyone*," Simone was beside herself with jealousy: "I don't accept that people play with my emotions, and especially not André's," she wrote indignantly to Denise.[9]

Paul himself was barely blamed: "So there was Éluard, like a comet back again as witty and cheerful as ever," wrote Naville, "and without wasting time, he got into the Surrealist Revolution."

On October 10, without Gala, Paul attended the inauguration of the Bureau des Recherches Surréalistes in the Duc de la Rochefoucauld's old town house at 15 rue de Grenelle. It had been set up to be used for experiments in the paranormal, and it was here that the first *Manifesto of Surrealism* was produced. At Breton's behest, Paul's signature had been hastily added to the document so he could appear at the opening as one of the presenters of the movement.

Meanwhile the recently released *Mourir de ne pas mourir* had become a succès de scandale when the columnist Jean Bernier commented on Paul's dedication, which describes the anthology as *"mon dernier livre"*:

(my most recent book, but "*dernier*" can also mean "last.") "'Dernier' takes on a *special* meaning," Bernier wrote, "when you know, as André Breton *himself* told me, that Paul Éluard disappeared mysteriously some months ago—and *no one* has heard from him since." This sensationalistic tidbit, published as Paul and Gala were sailing homeward, boosted Éluard's romantic mystique so successfully that the first edition of *Mourir* was a sellout.

The final Éluard, Ernst, Gala collaboration, an eighteen-poem homage to Gala titled: *Au défaut du silence* (*For Want of Silence*), came out in 1925. It was illustrated with the full range of Max Ernst's twenty sorceress-like ink drawings of Gala. The critics were stunned.

"Gala has vast powers of seduction that neither Éluard nor Ernst were strong enough to resist," Soupault, who was now convinced that Gala's allure was diabolical, wrote in his review of *For Want of Silence*. The anthology was, he said, a "miraculous" bouquet of some of the most beautiful poems written since Baudelaire's *Les Fleurs du Mal*" (*The Flowers of Evil*).

Gala's personal edition of *Au défaut* contains a note of apology from Max for his illustrations: "Gala my little Gala / I beg your forgiveness / I love you above all else and forever / I do not understand what is happening." But she didn't even bother to answer. The affair with Ernst was over and done.

Max, who was finally home from Saigon and Cambodia, rented an atelier in Montmartre, where he worked and lived by himself. He was so poor he didn't have enough money to eat every day. Then, in the spring of 1927, while making his rounds of the Parisian art galleries, he met Marie-Berthe Aurenche, a blue-eyed blonde who was just out of the Convent of the Faithful Companions of Jesus in Jersey and the daughter of a prominent Parisian judge. The attraction was strong, instant, and mutual. When Marie-Berthe's father called the police in an attempt to have Ernst arrested for corrupting a minor, the lovers, helped by Breton and Desnos, eloped to the island of

Noirmoutier, a seaside paradise off France's Atlantic coast, where they married in haste.

Éluard continued buying art from and supporting his friend. And for the rest of Ernst's life, his trip to Asia remained a major influence on his oeuvre, as can be seen in the lush tropical jungle in *Leonora in the Morning Light* and *Europe after the Rain*'s puzzling volcanic landscape.

That December, Gallimard brought out *Capitale de la Douleur* (*Capital of Pain*), a new collection of some older and more recent Éluard poetry. It contained *Répétitions*, the first of the trio's collaborations, and has been continuously in print since 1926. In 1965 it became even more famous for its influence on New Wave cinema: Jean-Luc Godard quotes from *Capital de la Douleur*'s love poetry throughout his AI cult classic *Alphaville*, in which *Douleur* is the "Bible" that saves men from turning into computers. The anthology also inspired contemporary music and Francis Poulenc composed melodies for several of its poems.

CHAPTER 9

ENTR'ACTE

Gala and Paul's life continued apace. More sought after than ever, they resumed the ritual of meeting their friends at the Cyrano a couple of steps from the Bretons' apartment at precisely five o'clock in the afternoon for a round of the new fetish drink: a Mandarin Curaçao. Paul commissioned their friend Man Ray to take an enticing nude photo of his wife, which he delighted in carrying around in his wallet to proudly pull out and show others and they did their best to settle back into the Doll's House. But Max Ernst's shadow haunted the villa. And Gala, who found herself at loose ends in the suburbs, would never fully trust her husband again.

Éluard, who was just turning thirty, had come to the dramatic realization that he was at a crossroads in his career. The publication he had been most associated with, *Littérature*'s, circulation had dwindled and the magazine had collapsed.

The war, which had been over for seven years, was a faded memory. Now was the time of "Les Années Folles": giddy prosperity and joyful experimentation. Paris was alive with artists, writers, and composers of myriad persuasions who had flocked to be together in the city of lights. Here, novelist Gertrude Stein, the self-acknowledged genius from San Francisco, held court in her salon surrounded by brilliant, rowdy Americans, including Ernest Hemingway, F. Scott and Zelda Fitzgerald, Gerald and Sara Murphy, and Ford Madox Ford, as well as James Joyce, an Irishman who was in the midst of transfiguring the novel as the world knew it. Although Paul and his friends did not mix with these authors and artists, they were certainly aware of them and what they were making, if only through Picasso, who belonged to both groups.

At night in Paris, American Jazz was the rage in every nightclub. Josephine Baker was the queen of the Théâtre des Champs-Elysées, and Éluard could not help but be affected by the extroverted American spirit. The political scene in France had become more expansive as well. The Radical Socialist Party was in power, and the newly elected Gaston Doumergue was the first Protestant to become President of the Republic. Although Paul was as antiestablishment as ever, Dada's nihilism no longer seemed pertinent.

The *Surrealist Manifesto*, whose philosophy and politics echoed his personal inclinations and promised a new criterion for his thirties, had captured Éluard's imagination, and since the adjective "surreal" is now part of the common vocabulary, he was clearly prescient. In 1924, however, what the *Surrealist Manifesto* expressed was a current of make-believe and illusion that had been a theme in European art for the previous twenty years. This could be seen in the architectural paintings of de Chirico and the musical canvases of Klee and Chagall,[1] which Breton and Éluard both admired.

Accordingly, Breton conceived of Surrealism as an encompassing cultural movement that included literature, philosophy, art, music, dance, and politics and legitimatized blurring the borders between disciplines. Unlike Impressionism or Cubism, which are recognized by their painterly technique, Surrealism did not endorse any one style. Alberto Giacometti, Pablo Picasso, and Joan Miró, whose works do not resemble one another, were all, at separate points in their careers, considered Surrealists.

What the *Surrealist Manifesto* advocated was fantasy and intuition. It denounced logic, capitalism, and Paul's bête noire, colonialism in conjunction with organized religion. Breton affirmed that: "Under the pretense of civilization and progress we have managed to banish from the mind anything that may rightly or wrongly be called superstition or fancy. Any form of search for the truth which does not conform to the traditions of our [own] civilization has been forbidden. *But now* creativity and inspiration are perhaps at the point of reasserting themselves."

Substituting personal dream imagery for religious iconography in art, Breton wrote that Surrealism was based on a belief in "the omnipotence of dream," and "the disinterested play of thought." By "play of thought," he meant automatic writing, which articulates the unconscious without editing its expression. André also praised Sigmund Freud, while continuing to decry bourgeois values. All of this was vastly attractive to Paul, especially because it was so different from his parents' belief system. He was in deep emotional agreement with Breton's call to *"Lâchez tout"* (leave everything) and follow the new order.[2]

Surrealism became Paul's cause, and during this fertile moment for the movement he spent many hours away from Gala with his fellow dissidents at "anti-conformist," "anti-bourgeois" protests. He participated in a demonstration against historian Robert Aron's conference eulogizing "The average Frenchman," which was being held at the Théâtre du Vieux Colombier. He then drafted an open letter to the distinguished playwright Paul Claudel, who, as France's ambassador to Japan, was doing his best to convert the Japanese to Catholicism, the religion of royalty and the right wing in France. This missive began, "We wish with all our might that revolutions, wars and colonial insurrections will come to destroy this civilization you promote and defend all the way to the Orient," and concluded rather immaturely, "We leave you to your ignoble catechism." When the letter to Claudel was read aloud to the guests at a banquet hosted by Breton in Montparnasse for the Symbolist poet Saint-Pol-Roux le Magnifique, it incited a riot, and Paul narrowly escaped being arrested by the Paris police. Although he and Gala were now reunited, Paul still clung to his concept of "free" marriage and continued to enjoy those long nights of dissipation that had consoled him during the years of the ménage and which he did not consider infidelities.

That April, an ambitious young artist from Catalonia named Salvador Dalí arrived in Paris. André Breton, who was introduced to Dalí by the art dealer Jacob Dalman, found the twenty-four-year-old's exotic Moorish bloodline, eccentric dress, and intense timidity delightful. He took the budding painter under his wing and became, in Dalí's words, his "second father."

Salvador met Paul Éluard in between floor shows at the fashionable nightclub Bal Tabarin, where the poet was drinking champagne with one of the establishment's dancers dressed in slinky black sequins by Érte. When it was explained to Dalí (sotto voce) that this "lady" was the poet's "friend," not his wife, who was currently traveling, the young Spaniard, who was exceptionally impressed by Éluard's fame and his way with women, decided that the wife of such a great Don Juan must be truly remarkable. He became very curious about Gala and invited Paul and his family to visit him in Cadaqués, a fishing village just south of the French border in Spain.

Eleven months later, in the spring of 1927, Clément Grindel, who was fifty-seven, died suddenly of medical complications during the aftermath of a gastrointestinal operation. The Grindel fortune was split between Paul and his mother. Jeanne kept the houses, the cars, and the real-estate investment properties. Éluard, who inherited the entirety of his father's stock portfolio and receivables, was now what he'd so often dreamed of being: independently wealthy and in charge of his life.

Gala, who had finally earned the esteem of Paul's colleagues, had come "into-her-own" as well. When André Breton met Léona Camille Ghislaine Delcourt, whose odd behavior, as his cousin in-law Pierre Naville noted, bore an astonishing resemblance to Gala's intuitive, mercurial persona, he renamed her Nadja, which is the beginning of the word "hope" in Russian. She became the subject of his most famous work, *Nadja*, whose heroine, rather than resembling Léona, was imbued with many of Gala's best-known characteristics. Like Gala, Nadja has mesmeric eyes with theatrically mascaraed lashes, and possesses "a certain power over men." Breton, who first sees her by chance on the street, is immediately infatuated with this exotic female, who, again like Gala, is both prophet and clairvoyant. Their reciprocal fascination takes them to the edge of madness, but when André discovers that, like Gala, Nadja is emotionally precarious, he ruefully withdraws. The relationship is over, but the *memory* of Nadja refuses to leave. Becoming a psychic omnipresence, the echo of Nadja haunts Breton's thoughts and his dreams. By the end of the book, it is clear that the Nadja/Gala persona, now more myth than living human, is the embodiment of Surrealism. Although Breton was never overtly fond of Gala, *Nadja* clearly indicates the breadth of her influence on Breton's thinking in particular, and by extension on the Surrealists in general. She was already famous for being adored and deferred to by two of the most revered artists of the decade. With the publication of *Nadja*, Gala became known in intellectual circles as "the mother of Surrealism."

Unfortunately, Paul's unstable health, strained by his journey to the Orient and weakened by his all-night excursions into the underbelly of Parisian nightlife, had deteriorated drastically. Gala could not find a way to change her husband or cure him. She felt entangled in circumstances she couldn't control, and although she struggled to hide her feelings, she was increasingly lonely and forlorn.

As Paul was settling his father's estate, Gala, hoping for comfort and Gomberg's advice on her marital dilemma, took her first trip to Moscow in eleven years. After the wreckage of the Russian Revolution, she found her parents impoverished and dispirited. They were still living in Gomberg's once-grand but now almost bare and drafty apartment, where the paper-patched windows had been smashed by the Bolsheviks. To make ends meet, they had taken in lodgers. They quarreled frequently and were no longer in love.

Tired and downhearted, Gala returned home to the delightful surprise of a chance meeting at the Certà with Anastasia Tsvetaeva, who had escaped Moscow in 1922 and was in Paris on her way to Berlin. The old friends enjoyed a warm, delectable dinner at Eaubonne, where Stasia, who found Éluard charming, describes being awestruck at how rail-thin the now worldly and elegant "little" Gala had become. This was the last time Gala would see her childhood friend.

In February 1928, Éditions Surréalistes published Éluard's *Défense de Savoir* (*Forbidden to Know*), a collection of verse about love and denial whose title poem begins, "I am not here / I am dressed in myself." *Défense* was edited and designed by Gala. It includes a frontispiece with a drawing de Chirico made for her, and the dedication reads: "for Gala who hides my life from me / and shows me all the love."

Now that Paul was rich, Gala and Paul decided to let Jeanne run the real estate business. They would become a pair of freewheeling art collectors, advisers, and dealers whose trusted and only partners were each other.

That March, Gala took the train to Berlin, where she planned to select and negotiate the purchase of a dozen Paul Klee watercolors to flip at a profit while Paul stayed in Paris, where he spent his time buying his wife turquoises and ordering dresses and furs made to her specifications by Parisian designers. So it wasn't until the end of April, after Éluard suffered a sudden tubercular relapse, that Gala met up with her husband in Switzerland. Paul had checked into the Parkensanatorium in Arosa, where, on doctor's orders, he was hospitalized for the better part of the year. There, in the lovely Schanfigg valley surrounded by snowcapped peaks and fragrant evergreens, Paul reread Baudelaire, watched the skaters on Lake Obersee, ate delicious fondue, and was sad and forlorn.

That June, to raise Paul's spirits, Gala invited René Crevel and his bisexual girlfriend, the Austrian set designer Mopsa Sternheim, to summer with them in Seelisberg, at the bucolic Hotel Bellevue, where she and Mopsa became fast friends. They were joined by Louis Aragon and his new love: British heiress and influencer Nancy Cunard. It rained almost every day. Drenched to the bone by the torrential thunderstorms, Crevel rapidly developed a high fever and chills. He took to his bed for the rest of the month while Gala escaped with Paul to Lucerne, where at the beginning of September they finally received reassuring news from René. He had chosen the name they'd suggested, *Êtes-Vous Fous?* (*Are You Crazy?*) for his new novel, which he dedicated to them.

January 1929 began raucously. Back in Paris, Paul and Max got into a serious fistfight over a nasty comment Marie-Berthe, who was uncontrollably jealous, made about Gala, and by February, the Éluards had decided it was time to move out of the Doll's House, crammed as it was with stale memories. Paul rented a spacious three-bedroom apartment in the 18th arrondissement on the butte (hillock) right next door to the gleaming, seven-domed Sacré Cœur. The flat had a panoramic view of the city, and Éluard determined that this time he would be responsible for the decoration. He hired the fashionable architect Jean-Charles Moreux, who had made a name for himself by combining art deco with elements from Egypt and Mesopotamia in his interior design, and wrote to his wife that the renovation would cost them "several primitive fetishes and a very large de Chirico." His vision for their new home, as he described it to Gala, was: "a peaceful, sumptuous and light-filled love nest" where she could luxuriate when she wasn't traveling.

A few weeks later, as Gala's tarot cards had apparently predicted, Éluard was introduced to Mopsa's friend, Mrs. Alice Apfel, a belle laide from Berlin "with a face like an Indian." Alice, who spoke English, gave Paul her address, and although he disingenuously insisted to Gala that it was Mopsa who was in love with her, the poet was smitten. He nicknamed his new acquaintance "La Pomme." A little bit later, he wrote offhandedly to his wife, "If there's nothing going on in Paris, I think I might pop over to Berlin for three days but naturally if that would bother you I won't." Then, just after the German jaunt, he continued, "We really shouldn't be apart for so long. I love having affairs but cannot be deprived of you, who are the perfection of Love. La Pomme is sweet and she adores me; she is very beautiful and makes love imaginatively, but I think that if I couldn't have you I would learn to hate her."

"Abuse your freedom, freedom should always be abused," was Éluard's advice to Gala as he "evened things out" by handpicking a new boyfriend for her. André Gaillard was the brilliant, disarmingly attractive editor of *Cahiers du Sud*,[3] who was publishing more and more of Paul's poetry along with important work by American writers such as Vachel Lindsay and making a name for himself in Paris and New York.[4] Alas, Paul's introduction was conditional.

In May, while she was with her new lover in Marseilles, Paul wrote to Gala that he had received a message from him: "André telegraphed me that he's given you drawings, photos and a manuscript for me." In the next breath he added dictatorially, "You are to understand and to make André understand that I am counting on him and me making love to you together as previously agreed." When she read Paul's letter demanding a threesome, Gala ended her flirtation immediately, causing Éluard to complain that Gaillard's attitude toward him had become "odious."

Gaillard was indeed so publicly shocked and hurt when Gala left him that his death the following December was rumored to be a suicide caused by Mme Éluard's abrupt termination of their brief affair. In fact, Gaillard, who had cerebral palsy, died of a fall caused by his disease.

In contrast to Gala, Éluard kept his affair with Alice Apfel going too long. Mid-June found the poet in Paris at the Hotel de la Terrasse with La Pomme and André Breton, who was sharing an adjacent room with the prostitute/photographer Suzanne Muzard. Simone, who was divorcing Breton for infidelity, had locked him out of their apartment, and André was retaliating by completely revising the *Surrealist Manifesto*'s position on sexuality. On June 15, Éluard wrote to Gala, who had asked to see him, "La Pomme has a long month to do as she pleases. I can't leave her now." He couldn't resist adding that he'd had a wonderful time traveling with Alice to Holland and Belgium, where he won eight thousand French francs at the gaming tables in Brussels. A couple of weeks later, at the beginning of July, he continued truculently: "You have B [perhaps a reference to a Herman Behr, who was also a patient at Arosa] and there will be other men who are attracted to you. La Pomme is beautiful, agreeable; submissive and a safeguard for me." He signed this missive: "I adore you, I kiss you all over" which was how Gala had signed her letters to him before they were married.

The dedication of Paul's latest book, *L'Amour la Poésie (Love Poetry)*, read, "Everything I have said, Gala, is so you can hear it. My mouth has never left your eyes." But while poetry may express love, love is more than poetry, and Gala clearly recognized the need to distance herself. The Éluards did not see each other again until the beginning of August, when Cécile, who had turned eleven in May, was out of school for vacation.

Driving up the cliff-hugging dirt lane through the highlands to Cadaqués was hazardous and very uncomfortable. Dust from the road swirled up in great blinding clouds, and once they climbed past the vineyards and olive trees rough sea winds began to slap hard at the car, rattling its windows. To make matters worse, Éluard, whose hands shook customarily, was a terrible driver, so Gala and Cécile were surely relieved when the large village church that jutted into the ocean like the prow of a boat appeared suddenly through a cleft in the hills and they knew they had nearly reached their destination.

The Éluards checked into Cadaqués's only hotel, a rudimentary white stucco building named La Miramar. It had a view of the Mediterranean and no electricity or running water. Then they went in search of their host, Salvador Dalí, whose family's whitewashed summer house sat at the far point of the bay beyond the village. There, shaded by eucalyptus trees and surrounded with geraniums, it stood alone on the Playa de Es Llaner, a sandy gold-and-tan crescent-shaped beach that was easily visible from the hotel. When they had gone as far as the muddy, potholed dirt track to the end of town would take them, they came upon their friends from Paris. René Magritte; his wife, Georgette; the poet and art dealer Camille Goemans with his mistress Yvonne Bernard; and Luis Buñuel, all in stylish bathing suits, were sitting by the water with Salvador Dalí.

According to Dalí's autobiography, *The Secret Life of Salvador Dalí*, he was totally out of control and laughing hysterically. "If you could see what I imagine," Dalí, who was doing his best to cover up his embarrassment at this involuntary hilarity, was telling his guests, "you would laugh even more than I do."[5] Gala, who was spattered with dirt from her difficult drive, took one look at the socially uncomfortable group and wished she had never come to this place. As for Dalí, who Paul kept telling her was so handsome, she was emphatically undecided.

CHAPTER 10

SALVADOR

Salvador Dalí, who for all of his life enjoyed pronouncing "Dalí" with a flourishing emphasis on the fancy final "í," loved his dramatic, unusual surname. He took great pleasure in repeating that it was proof of his descent from the Moors (fine-featured, dark-skinned Muslims originating from the ancient Roman province of Mauritania in North Africa) who had invaded Spain in 711, built the Alhambra, and established the city of Granada, which served as the lodestar of culture and science throughout the dark ages. Salvador claimed that it was from these origins that he derived his "love of anything that is gilded and excessive, my passion for luxury and my love of oriental clothes," not to mention his penchant for painting wide expanses of desert in some of his best-known canvases, including *Impressions of Africa*, and the readiness of his skin to turn the color of mahogany in the hot summer sun. In fact, the name "Dalí," which is almost nonexistent in Spain, is far more common in Africa. In Arabic, "Dalíl" means "omen" or "guide."[1]

By the sixteenth century, the Dalí tribe, who after the fall of the Alhambra in 1492 had chosen to convert to Christianity rather than be deported from Spain, had become agricultural laborers. They settled in Llers, a tiny municipality famous throughout Girona for its population of witches. It wasn't until almost three hundred years later, in the nineteenth century, that a Pere Dalí broke with family tradition when he became a forger, or more specifically a dagger smith. After the death of his first wife, this nonconformist journeyed on to Cadaqués, where in 1822 he married a local beauty, Maria Cruanyes, and where on July 1, 1849, their second child, Salvador's grandfather, Gal Josep Salvador, was born.

When Gal, who inherited his father's independent and eccentric personality, turned twenty, he moved in with Teresa Cusí Marco, a married woman from Rosas who was five years older than he. They had three boys, the second of whom was the future artist's father, Salvador Rafael Aniceto—otherwise known as Salvador Dalí y Cusí, who was born on October 25, 1872. After Teresa's estranged husband died, the couple married in March 1874. Nine years later they moved to Barcelona to escape the tramuntana, an almost mythic, high-pressure wind that howls down into Catalonia from the heights of the Pyrénées and is said to drive men insane. In the wake of the 1880 International Exposition, Barcelona had become a flourishing metropolis. Its newly opened stock market was all the rage. Gal invested heavily. Horribly, when the market crashed, he committed suicide by throwing himself off a third-floor balcony.

Luckily Teresa had been as prudent with her money as her husband was feckless with his. She was able to send her son to law school. He was a solid if not scintillating student, and, since there was apparently a plethora of lawyers in the north of Spain at that time, he decided to become a notary.

Notarios were public servants authorized to draw up wills, deeds, and contracts and witness signatures—all for a handsome fee. To become a *notario*, one had to pass a public examination that was administered by the Ministry of Justice only when a vacancy occurred. Once awarded a *notaria*, one was assured financial security and social respectability for life.

On the advice of his best friend from law school, Josep (Pepito) Pichot Geronés, who was the scion of a wealthy and artistic family in

Cadaqués, Salvador y Cusí applied and was accepted to the Notaria of Figueres, a modest municipality of eleven thousand citizens. Shortly thereafter he married his fiancée, a dimpled, brown eyed twenty-six-year-old named Felipa Domènech Ferrés.

Felipa, who was a talented and imaginative amateur artist, enjoyed drawing fantastical beasts to amuse and astonish her family and their friends. She had been born and bred in Barcelona, where her grandfather presided over a family-owned atelier known for its objets d'art and fine work with tortoiseshell. At the time of her marriage, the workshop was managed by her mother, Maria Anna, who was also artistically inclined and particularly talented at decoupage. Her younger brother Anselm would later own the most important bookstore in Barcelona, the Libraria Verdaguer.

On October 12, 1901, Felipa gave birth to their first child, a son the young couple named Salvador Galo Anselmo. Heartbreakingly, when their beautiful little boy was just twenty-two months old, he died of a gastric infection. On May 11, 1904, only ten days and nine months after this tragedy, a replacement child, conceived in the urgency of grief, was born in his family's apartment at 20 Carrer Narciso Monturiol in Figueres. He was baptized Felipe Jacinto *Salvador* nine days later in the parish church of St. Peter, and although this Salvador was not named after his older brother but instead in the Catalonian tradition of passing names down from one generation to another, he spent much of his life fighting hard to be recognized as his own person. As Salvador Dalí told Mike Wallace in a 1958 television interview, "What is most important to me is expressing Dalí."

It is evident from his memories of his father, his mother, and himself as a child that, from a very young age, Dalí had mixed emotions about his cloyingly attentive parents, who regularly indulged almost all of his whims. He wrote that, well into boyhood, he "deliberately" continued wetting his bed to humiliate his anxious and domineering father, who had promised him a tricycle if he would stop. And, contrary to all evidence, he vehemently insisted that his older brother had died of meningitis caused by a paternal blow to his skull. In contrast, Salvador adored his mother. Felipa was the only one who could soothe him when he was prey to one of his frequent tantrums and, as he liked to remember, would look lovingly into his eyes every morning and ask him: "Sweetheart, what do you want? What is it you desire?" But he also found her suffocating. She made constant comparisons between him and his late sibling. She gave him all his dead brother's toys and, whenever he went out, even in warm weather, she would caution: "Take a muffler, cover yourself up. If not, you will die like your brother." As an adult, Dalí claimed that his aversion to being touched stemmed from being too close to his mother when he was very young.

The one thing no one could fail to notice was Salvador's precocious talent for drawing. He began making images of small animals on the sides of his crib as soon as he could hold a pencil and before he could walk.[2] In 1910, when he was almost seven and Felipa's mother and youngest sister, Catalina, known as "Tieta," had just moved in with the family, Salvador scratched twenty tiny ducks and swans on an iron scrollwork balcony table. Beside herself with joy at her Salvador's obvious genius, his mother famously exclaimed: "When he says he'll draw a swan he draws a swan; when he says he'll do a duck, it's a duck!" That year Salvador also produced his first oils: a series of four miniature landscapes.

As soon as he began making art, Dalí's father enrolled him in a private school in Figueres, an offshoot of the prestigious French establishment Frères des Écoles Chrétiennes in Béziers, where he rapidly became a hopeless speller in three languages: Catalan, Spanish, and French. Despite this slight flaw, Salvador ended up his first year with three "excellents"—in geography, religion, and calligraphy.

Just after he turned eleven, he was invited to spend some time with his father's friend Pepito Pichot outside of Figueres at Pepito's sister

Maria's sprawling white house, which was skirted by pear orchards, surrounded with rosebushes, and filled with Impressionist and pointillist paintings by their brother Ramon Pichot. It was, Dalí wrote later, "one of the most marvelous places of my childhood."[3] There he was given oils, canvases, and a whitewashed storeroom that was sunny all morning to use as his own studio. Every day the boy happily set to work on a pile of drawings and oil paintings which he would tack up on the walls, and each afternoon Pichot would come to inspect the results. One day Pepito was impressed enough to say he would ask Dalí y Cusí to find him a drawing instructor. Looking up from his paper, small Salvador responded indignantly that he was already an artist and didn't need help.[4]

In a time when it was common to dress bourgeois children extravagantly, Salvador's haberdashery would have turned Little Lord Fauntleroy's head. When he was eight, he wore a long black cloak with a wide neck ruffle and carried a short walking stick. He was also photographed in an elaborate sailor suit with insignia embroidered in thick gold on the sleeves and stars on his cap. His shoes had silver buttons and were shined to a gleam, and he was the only one in his class to have an elegant silver thermos, which was filled with hot chocolate every morning. Salvador looked so different from the town's other offspring that he felt constantly on display. He had few friends his own age and developed a lifelong phobia of grasshoppers when some local bullies took to throwing half-dead ones at his head.[5] In his early teens, Dalí did manage to forge an important friendship with his wonderful art teacher at The Municipal School of Drawing in Figueres, Juan Núñez Fernández, and by the time of his graduation he had earned "excellents" in both Latin and French.

He supplemented his education with books plucked from his father's extensive library, where he discovered a special affinity for Voltaire, Nietzsche, who shocked him by writing "God is dead," and Kant, because he "couldn't understand a word he said." He got all the other books he wanted from his doting uncle Anselm, who owned the Libraria Verdaguer and introduced him to Barcelona's leading gallerist, Josep Dalman, a passionate Francophile. Around the dinner table at night, family discussions were invariably lively. Anna Maria remembered that while Dalí was preparing his baccalaureate, her father and brother quarreled constantly about anything, everything, and always ideology.

Disaster struck in 1921, when Felipa died at forty-seven from cancer of the uterus. Her sister Catalina, who had been living with the family as a second mother to both the children and possibly a mistress to Salvador Dalí y Cusí, was so upset that she suffered a complete nervous breakdown and had to be sent to recover in Barcelona, where she stayed for twelve months. To make matters worse, in July, at the age of fifty-two, Pepito Pichot expired unexpectedly of unknown causes.

Years later, when he was in America during World War II, Dalí would describe his mother's death as "the biggest blow" he had ever received. As an adolescent he countered his terrible losses by solemnly swearing to himself that he would become exceedingly famous. He grew his hair almost down to his shoulders and became a Communist, or at least subscribed to a Communist periodical: the French Marxist paper *L'Humanité*.

There were some small silver linings. In January 1922, Josep Dalman showed eight paintings by Dalí, along with forty of Juan Núñez's other students, in his gallery. The Barcelona daily, *La Tribuna*, commended Dalí's talent on its front page, while the Catalan picture paper, *Gràfica*, published a reproduction of one of his images: *Market*. Then, in July, when Dalí took part in the Exhibition of Empordanese Artists, an annual event in Figueres, he was awarded the coveted Barcelona University Rector's Prize. These successes clinched a gratified Salvador Dalí y Cusí's resolve to send his son to school in the capital, where Núñez had recommended Madrid's

Royal Academy Special School of Painting, Sculpting and Engraving for his brilliant student.

Dalí y Cusí found wonderful lodgings for his son in the newly completed Residencia de Estudiantes, which offered very comfortable if somewhat monastic rooms, grand Moorish-style public spaces, beautiful planted gardens, and informal interdisciplinary tutoring, as well as fascinating lectures by a wide range of intellectual celebrities. Over the years these would include H. G. Wells, Paul Valéry, and Albert Einstein.

Dalí deliberately caused a sensation among the other students when he arrived at his new home wearing a sweeping, floor-length black cape and carrying an ebony cane with a double-headed gold eagle handle. He then promptly repaid his father's solicitousness by refusing to comply with the rules of the Special School's entrance examination, which required a drawing from antiquity with the exact measurements of an Ingres sheet of paper. Instead of making work of the specified dimensions, Dalí intentionally threw his father into paroxysms of anxiety by submitting a beautiful picture that was much smaller than the school's stipulation and had the last laugh when he was accepted anyway.

Determined and almost sick with timidity, Dalí spent his first weeks in Madrid visiting the Prado, reading Amédée Ozenfant's periodical *L'Esprit Nouveau*, blushing frequently, and making paintings instead of friends. It wasn't until over a month into his university career that he finally bonded with Luis Buñuel, the son of a rich entrepreneur from Zaragoza who had amassed a fortune in Cuba and returned home to marry the prettiest girl in the locality, who was twenty years his junior. Buñuel, nicknamed Tarquin the Proud after the Roman emperor, was an independent, fiercely stubborn amateur boxer, a Francophile, and a budding poet whose fear of spiders matched Dalí's grasshopper phobia. He also enjoyed taking his remarkable new artist friend with him on long evening ambles through Madrid.

On October 9, 1922, just as Dalí was settling into his new life at the university, Maria Anna Ferrés, his maternal grandmother, died. Salvador Dalí y Cusí promptly asked both children for permission to marry Felipa's younger sister Catalina. When Salvador, who was heartsick at what he viewed as his father's betrayal of his vows to Felipa, responded that he didn't know why this marriage was necessary. Dalí y Cusí ignored his son's feelings, got a papal dispensation and married "Tieta" anyway.

Four months later, in early 1923, Dalí met Federico García Lorca, a dazzling young polymath from Andalusia who was just returning to the Residencia after a long absence. The son of a rich gentleman farmer, Lorca was born in Fuente Vaqueros, near Granada. He was a gifted musician and a fabled raconteur who was studying law and philosophy but spent most of his time writing ballads and staging his own plays. Six years Dalí's senior, Lorca was elegant where Dalí was flashy, temperate where Dalí was strident, and as attractive as he was charming. He was also an avowed homosexual at a time in Spain when, even at the ultraliberal Residencia, this orientation was totally taboo. Despite, or perhaps because of, their differences, the two young men, who shared a love of France and poetry, warmed to each other naturally. According to Dalí, this quickly developed passionate friendship, the most important of each of their lives, was defined by the contrast between Lorca's religious spirit and his own equally insubordinate animus.

Dalí got a chance to advertise his rebellious temperament on May 15, 1924, when King Alfonso of Spain paid a visit to Cadaqués. After lunch in Girona on the initial day of his stay, the king decided to inspect a large garrison in nearby Figueres. Alfonso XIII was an object of controversy in liberal, democratic, separatist Catalonia. So the authorities, fearful of demonstrations, decided to check their lists of potential troublemakers, some of whom they took into custody.

Since Dalí had participated in protests earlier that year concerning the election of a local art teacher, he was arrested in Figueres and jailed in Girona, where he cooled his heels from May 20 to June 11 before being released by a military judge. As he was the son of the city's public notary, the story circulated, and for a brief, heady moment, Salvador was able to revel in his notoriety as someone who had been imprisoned by General Primo de Rivera's detested dictatorship.

The following spring, Dalí invited Lorca to be his guest in Cadaqués for Holy Week, which was a big success. At his first lunch on their eucalyptus-shaded terrace, Lorca charmed the entire Dalí family, and especially Anna Maria, who fell in love with him almost immediately. By the end of the visit, he had begun his "Ode to Salvador Dalí," which he finished in twenty-eight stanzas, one of which reads:

But above all I sing a common thought
That joins us in the dark and golden hours.
The light that blinds our eyes is not art.
Rather it is love, friendship, crossed swords.

Once published, the poem was highly praised by Jean Cassou in the journal *Mercure de France* as a superlative example of Spain's new literary sensibility.

With love came jealousy. According to Dalí: "Sometimes we would be walking, the whole group, along El Paseo de la Castellana [in Madrid] on our way to the café where we held our literary meetings and where I knew Lorca would shine like a mad and fiery diamond. Suddenly I would set off at a run and no one would see me in three days."[6]

In April 1926, Dalí y Cusí granted one of his son's dearest wishes when he sent him, along with Tieta and Anna Maria, to Paris. Salvador was especially excited because he had an introduction to Picasso prearranged for him by Lorca. He wrote later in *The Secret Life* that meeting the famous Spaniard was "like being granted an audience with the pope." "I have come to see you before visiting the Louvre," Dalí told the great master. "That's right," Picasso shot back.

Back in Madrid, Salvador deliberately got himself expelled from the Special School for refusing to take his final exams. Passing them, which he could have done easily, would have entitled him to a comfortable, respectable career as a government-certified art instructor. When, on October 12, the expulsion was officially published in the *Bulletin of the Ministry of Education and Fine Arts*, Dalí y Cusí, who took his son's rebellion personally, felt shamed and disgraced.

As soon as he dropped out of school, Salvador began devoting more and more time to Lorca. He designed the sets for Lorca's play *Mariana Pineda*, about a political martyr who was executed for opposing the monarchy in Spain. Immediately popular, this tragedy is so famous today that it has become part of Spain's folklore. Dalí also began his celebrated correspondence with the poet in which he played the part of St. Lucy, who healed St. Sebastian after he had been nailed to a cross and shot full of arrows. Lorca, who was planning a series of lectures on the saint for the summer of 1926, would reply as St. Sebastian, the unofficial titular of homosexuals and also, as Dalí loved to remind him, the patron saint of Cadaqués.

By 1927, Dalí and Lorca were inseparable. As Buñuel wrote sourly to a mutual acquaintance, Lorca had completely "enslaved" Dalí. Or perhaps it was the other way around. Although for a variety of reasons, including Dalí's well-publicized dislike of physical contact, it's impossible to say if he and Federico García Lorca were ever physical lovers. That they loved and thought about making love to each other is incontestable.

Federico was consistently tender and supportive of Salvador's work, but his adoring attitude was not reciprocated. In 1928, when Dalí was finishing up his first clearly Surrealist painting, *Honey Is Sweeter than Blood*, he included an image of Lorca's head in the landscape. The poet flatteringly asked him to also "write my name on the canvas so that my name may amount to something in this world." Which request Dalí ignored completely. Then, that July, when Lorca's anthology *Gypsy Ballads* became a huge critical and popular success, Salvador was bitterly and openly censorious of his friend's achievement.

It was not the first time something like this had happened. Dalí had already hurt Lorca's feelings by telling him his verses were out of date: "Granada without trams. . . . an antique Granada far removed from today." "Our age has its own song," he wrote to Federico. "And you're not part of it" was the unmistakable implication. At the time, Lorca had forgiven the insult, but now he chose to withdraw. The name of the new film Dalí had begun working on with Buñuel: *Un Chien Andalou* (*An Andalusian Dog*) may also have had something to do with Andalusian Lorca's exiting the relationship.

Dalí and Lorca would see each other just once more before the poet's disappearance in 1936, yet fifty-nine years later, just three years before his own death, Dalí summoned Ian Gibson to meet him in Figueres. He urgently wanted his future biographer to understand that Lorca had "loved him sexually not merely platonically."[7] In 2004, on the French television talk show *Tout Le Monde en Parle*, Amanda Lear, a close friend of Dalí's in the 1970s, confided that according to Salvador he had once attempted to make love with Lorca—"But then it hurt—so he didn't want to [anymore]." Moreover, Salvador was famously loquacious and plain-spoken about sex, so it seems odd that he did not come right out and tell Gibson that he and Lorca had been lovers. This avoidance seems to signal that what Dalí really wanted his biographer to understand was that Lorca found him sexually attractive, which is easy to believe but does not solve any riddle. Was Salvador's request merely an old man's vanity? Or had the memory of Federico García Lorca never really left the artist's heart?

In the autumn of 1928, Buñuel was planning a film based on a series of short stories by Ramón Gómez de la Serna,[8] which he had talked his mother into funding. When de la Serna did not write the screenplay as he had promised, Buñuel sent the outline to Dalí, who decided it was "extremely mediocre" and returned his own short scenario. As soon as Buñuel read the pages, he set off for Figueres, where, after only a week's work with Dalí, the screenplay was nearly ready. As Buñuel claimed in his memoirs, he and Dalí were so attuned that there was no possibility of argument. They both intended to "create something which had never been seen before in the history of the cinema": to "make visible subconscious states which could only be expressed on film."[9]

The seventeen-minute-long *Un Chien Andalou*, which premiered on June 6, 1929, at the Studio des Ursulines in Paris in a double billing with Man Ray's *Les Mystères du Château du Dé*, was an instant hit. The all-star audience—including the Vicomte de Noailles, who was Man Ray's patron; a smattering of de Noailles's aristocratic camp followers; Jean Cocteau and Christian Bérard, who designed the sets of Cocteau's *Beauty and the Beast*; all the Surrealists (except the Éluards, who were otherwise occupied); as well as Fernand Léger, Constantin Brâncuşi, Hans Arp, and Le Corbusier—was electrified. Thanks in large part to the efforts of Charles de Noailles, who wanted to underwrite its sequel, *L'Age d'Or*, the news spread rapidly. When Dalí returned to Spain to prepare for his fall show in Paris at Camille Goemans,[10] with whom he had just signed a contract for the 1929–1930 season, he was on the brink of international success.

CHAPTER 11

GALA AND SALVADOR

B y the time Gala and Paul met up with Dalí's other French friends at the Miramar on the evening of August 10, 1929, the Éluards' arrival in Cadaqués had been trumpeted by the local newspaper *Sol Ixent*, which described Salvador's guests as "the well-known Parisian art dealer Camille Goemans, the highly distinguished painter René Magritte, and the *great* French poet Paul Éluard." The rest is art history. Salvador Dalí's dramatic courtship of Gala on the glorious Catalan coast was recorded in granular detail in *The Secret Life of Salvador Dalí*,[1] where it reads like the script for a silent film.

As the Surrealists gathered to drink Pernod under the plane trees by the Mediterranean, Salvador, who found Gala's "intelligent face" fascinating, made it his business to engage her in what he described as an "intellectual" discussion, during which he did everything he could to impress her with "the rigor" that he displayed in "the realm of ideas." For her part, Gala so obviously enjoyed and appreciated his conversation that when she told him his unbuttoned silk shirt and black vaselino[2] made him look like a tango instructor, the artist was more amused than insulted.

Dalí had recently begun experimenting with a new artistic alphabet that combined his own personally imagined imagery with Freudian tropes. Just before his second trip to Paris, he had completed a painting called *The Birth of Venus/Little Ashes*, which displayed the beautifully toned back, narrow waist, and full, feminine but-tocks of a naked woman he had seen in a dream. When he opened his bedroom window the next morning, Salvador had the impres-sion that he was looking down on the woman he'd painted. She had seemingly come to life and was joking and arguing right in front of him with Paul Éluard, Camille Goemans, and his other friends from Paris. It was Gala in her knitted bathing suit.

Suddenly, Dalí was seized with anxiety. He couldn't decide what to wear. He tried on several looks before he finally settled on turned-up shorts accessorized with his sister's fake-pearl necklace and a red carnation behind his ear. He tucked his latest, still unfinished and unnamed work under his arm and went down to meet everyone, looking as nonchalant as possible while being careful not to open his mouth for fear of dissolving into nervous giggles. Because he had already decided that at least in theory, he was in love with Gala, he did his best with many small attentions, like bringing her a cool drink and an extra pillow, to show her wordlessly how much he cared. This odd pantomime perplexed his guests, who found the scatological ref-erences in Salvador's still unfinished and unnamed new painting even more disturbing. Éluard sent his wife to question Dalí.

On the first of the romantic, seemingly endless seaside explora-tions that would frame their nascent passion, Gala got right to the point. She wanted to know about the lower-left-hand corner of the incomplete work, where a muscle-bound man was befouling his pants, and asked Salvador directly if he was "coprophagic" [sic], because if so "she would have nothing to do with him." As he was answering no—the image was intended to horrify his viewers—he succumbed to another attack of mad laughter. Instead of being put off, Gala, who could feel the panic behind this nervous hilarity, gripped Salvador's hand reassuringly and promised, "My little boy, we will never leave each other." Dalí was so shocked and deeply touched by Gala's intu-itive understanding of his fears and his yearnings that, as recorded in *The Secret Life*, this incident marked the beginning of a cure for his obsessive anxieties.

Over the course of many long hours and serious conversations on the high, windswept bluffs overlooking the ocean, Gala openly shared her own vulnerabilities with her new confidant. She revealed that she too had a similar long history of nervous dysfunction. When Dalí asked what he could do for her, she burst into tears. She wanted him to kill her. "When we have grown old together," she begged her newfound soulmate, "spare me a slow death." In a flash of intuition, Salvador recognized their psychic connection. He wrote, "Suddenly I understood that *like me* she had her own interior world of desires and tribulations . . . that *like me* she moved between . . . lucidity and madness."

He began to trust Gala, and the aggression that was the flip side of Salvador's shyness evaporated. He compared himself to the king in the Spanish fairy tale who ate beautiful maidens until one of them was clever enough to sugar her nose. As soon as the king discovered how sweet she tasted, he stopped wanting to bite her. Their relationship developed, and Salvador noticed his hysterical symptoms disappearing. As he mastered his laughter, his smile, and his gestures, Gala became more than a woman to him. She was, he was certain, his "Gradiva": the queen of intangibility who would lead him to his glorious fate.[3]

At the end of August, convinced that Gala and Salvador's friendship was just that, Paul Éluard boarded the train for Paris alone. Paul left his wife in Cadaqués with their daughter and strict instructions to come home with the now-decoded scatological artwork that he had named *Le Jeu Lugubre* (*The Lugubrious Game*) and Cécile. The Magrittes and Camille Goemans, with his girlfriend, took their leave at the beginning of September. Only Buñuel lingered behind.

The filmmaker, who found Gala intrusive and physically unattractive,[4] was apprehensive and exasperated. He complained in his

memoirs that Dalí had forgotten their friendship and the important movie de Noailles had commissioned from them for 220,000
francs—an unheard-of sum at that time. All Salvador wanted to do
was talk about Gala. One day while Gala, Salvador, and Cécile were
picnicking with the filmmaker in Cap de Creus, Buñuel praised the
glorious scenery, which he compared to the work of a second-rate
painter named Sorolla. When Gala sneered, "This is nature. What's
art got to do with it?" her condescension was the last straw. Losing all
self-control, Luis leapt to his feet and tried to strangle her. Dalí, on
his knees, sobbed and begged him to stop. Cécile was terrified.

Luis Buñuel was not the only one who felt threatened. As she
strolled along the rocky coast in the bespoke silk pajamas[5] Paul had
given her, eating sea urchins and combing olive oil through her hair,
Gala shocked the conservative locals, who had never seen a chic Parisienne and in whose eyes a liaison with any Frenchwoman was tan-
tamount to dating a prostitute. Tongues in the surrounding villages
started wagging, and Salvador's father became apoplectic when he
heard about his son's public involvement with a married woman who,
worse than French, turned out to be Russian. In retaliation, the notary disinherited his son.

Dalí y Cusí's estate had previously been divided equally between
his two children. Now, in a new will dated September 29, Salvador
would receive the measly fifteen thousand pesetas that was the sum
required by Spanish law at that time to prevent one sibling from suing
the other. His wife, Catalina, who had made the mistake of defending
her stepson in a family argument,[6] was bequeathed the use of only one
room in the Cadaqués house for her lifetime. Everything else went
to Anna Maria. Wounded, but defiant as ever, Salvador ignored this
deliberate humiliation.

Only vaguely aware of the turmoil she had caused in the Dalí
household, Gala was blossoming. Northern Spain suited her. She
loved the salty sea air, fresh food, and constant exercise. Her body

was perfectly toned, and under the Iberian sun her skin had become what Dalí described as the color of a golden mink. She had arrived in Cadaqués unhappy and anxious about her unraveling marriage. Her husband plainly loved her, but their relationship was a far cry from the union she had yearned for and described in her idealistic wartime letters to him. She had been unable to navigate comfortably between Max Ernst and Paul, and she had never given up wanting someone who was all hers.[7]

At first glance, Salvador was anything but an ideal partner. When Max's son Jimmy Ernst met Dalí in America in 1942, he couldn't understand how Gala could have replaced his gorgeous father with such a puny little person[8] but Gala, who had taken her time getting to know Dalí, had discovered a true connection. He understood her mood swings and quick intuitions. She could help him realize his talent, which in many ways expressed her own way of seeing. She was ten years older than Dalí, and she found the artist's youth and neediness very appealing. Here was someone she could take in hand, buck up, and lead. Importantly, it was unlikely that Salvador, who was twenty-five and still a virgin, would be unfaithful. By late September, when she returned to Paris with Cécile and the completed *Le Jeu Lugubre*, Gala had made her decision. She just hadn't made up her mind how to tell Paul.

Back in the beautiful Montmartre apartment her husband had prepared for her, Gala remained focused on Salvador, who had returned to his monastic existence. He finished a portrait of Paul he had begun work on in August[9] and began sketching out *The Great Masturbator* and *The Enigma of Desire*, both tiny 8x13 paintings, which would become two of his most famous works. He wrote longingly to his beloved, "All the pebbles on the beach remind me of you. They are calling our name. This is starting to get *real.*" Through the long autumn nights, alone in his bedroom, he hugged the little knit bathing suit she had left behind. Meanwhile, Gala was hard at work on his behalf, making notes on their discussions and organizing them into a coherent narrative. She sent him encouragement as well as critiques of the paintings he was planning to show at Goemans, and she helped him select what he would bring to the opening. As soon as the train from Perpignan pulled into the Gare de Lyon, Salvador rushed to the nearest florist, where he spent all his money on red roses for Gala.

The Goemans vernissage scheduled for November 20 was the talk of all Paris, but Gala had other plans for her suitor. Just before the opening, she and Dalí boarded the train for Barcelona, and by the twenty-fourth they were in Sitges, at the new and resplendent Hotel Terramar. Built at the very end of the pier, it had a private white sand beach, luxuriant gardens, and large, sun-filled rooms where Gala and Salvador enjoyed his sexual initiation. They might as well have taken out an advertisement in the newspaper. The pair's absence at Goemans was so flagrant that without being told, everyone now knew that Dalí was Gala's new lover. The Mother of Surrealism had spoken. Salvador Dalí was the next star of the art world.

The buzz was so loud that the show was a sellout. Charles de Noailles bought *Le Jeu Lugubre* from Paul, and Gala briefly went back to her husband, who was emotionally incapable of acknowledging what was happening in plain sight to his wife. Dalí and Luis Buñuel resumed work on their new film and traveled to Spain, where they stayed with Dalí y Cusí at the apartment in Figueres until familial tensions flared up again.

Salvador had used his art to publicize his anger over his father's quasi-incestuous relationship with Catalina, and one work he had just shown was particularly disturbing in this regard. It was an image of the Sacred Heart, a Christian symbol of love everlasting, on which Dalí had written, *"Parfois je crache par plaisir sur le portrait de ma mère"* ("Sometimes for fun I spit [ejaculate] on my mother's image"). The scene over this latest transgression was monolithic. As Buñuel remembered, "The father opened the door violently and pushed his son out into the street. . . . He told me he never wanted to see his pig of a son again in his house."

As Dalí y Cusí, who refused to believe that Salvador was on his way to becoming an admired, financially successful artist, wrote vindictively to Lorca:

> *I don't know if you are aware that I threw my son out of the house. . . . For dignity's sake it was essential to take such a tremendous decision. In one of the paintings he showed in Paris he committed the vile act of writing "I spit on my mother." . . . I asked him to explain himself but he would not do so and insulted all of us again. No comment. He is pathetic, ignorant and an incomparable pedant, as well as being totally shameless. He thinks he knows it all but he can't even read or write. Anyway you know him better than I do. He has even sunk to the level of accepting money and food from a married woman who with the consent of her husband is keeping him until she finds something better.[10]*

With Buñuel in tow, Dalí repaired to Cadaqués, where luckily, they finished the script for *L'Age d'Or* on December 6. This was also the day they received a message from Salvador's father sentencing him to permanent banishment. In a gesture of mourning for the part of his life that was now over, Salvador cut off all his long hair, which he buried in the sand of Es Llaner, where he had caught his first glimpse of Mme Éluard. Perhaps as a prequel to the famous William Tell paintings, he had Buñuel photograph him by the rocks with a sea urchin on top of his shaved head. Then he hopped a taxi to the station and caught the next train to France and Gala. It would be five years before he spoke to his father again.

CHAPTER 12

STARTING OVER

Salvador's return to Paris coincided with the publication of the twelfth and final issue of André Breton's latest journal, *La Révolution Surréaliste*, which was decorated with illustrations of the lips of the Surrealists' wives and girlfriends, including Gala, Alice Apfel, Suzanne Muzard, and Marie-Berthe Ernst.

It opened with the *Second Surrealist Manifesto* and included reproductions of Dalí's *The Accommodations of Desire* and *Illumined Pleasures*, as well as the screenplay for *Un Chien Andalou*. "Dalí," as Breton wrote in 1954, was "the incarnation of the Surrealist spirit. He made it shine with all its brilliance. . . ."[1]

This *Second Surrealist Manifesto* was Breton's personal response to an ongoing crisis in the movement over its sexual and political positions. André, who understood the necessity of anchoring Surrealist theory in concrete experience, now insisted that the movement was welded to Marxist thought in general and to Leon Trotsky in particular.

He wrote that although a "special function of Surrealism is to examine the notions of reality and unreality, reason and irrationality. . . . It is analogous. . . . with historical materialism"[2] In other words, nothing short of a total psychic revolution would satisfy the movement. Art, literature, and poetry were all secondary to the general aim of provoking a complete "crisis of consciousness."[3]

As for *sex*, as early as 1928, under Paul's influence, Breton had

STARTING OVER ▸ 103

found himself announcing that "everything that has to do with 'the field of perversity'" is "interesting."[4] Two years later he would finally agree that there was no such thing as "normal" sexuality.

Encouraged by Gala and awed by Breton's rhetoric, Dalí drew a fantastical frontispiece for the second *Manifesto*,[5] scheduled to be published in book form at the end of June. Then he and Gala went off to Carry-le-Rouet, a sparkling little port thirty miles west of Marseilles, where for two months they spent almost all of their time in their room. Gala read her tarot, which kept predicting a message from a dark-haired man about a new source of money, and responded sporadically to increasingly frantic missives from Paul, who after a brief visit with the lovers now found his wife's absence insupportable. Dalí, who later described this time as one of his happiest, worked on a new painting, *The Invisible Man*,[6] and wrote Buñuel a six-page letter describing the blisses of intercourse.

As usual, Gala's readings turned out to be accurate. Soon after Dalí's show closed, on December 20, Lou Coysin, Camille Goemans's rich wife, who was also his backer, left him. When Goemans closed his gallery, Dalí's income was gone, and Gala was proved right: Buñuel wrote to de Noailles to let him know what had happened, the viscount offered to make good on the monthly payments Dalí would now lose, and the dark-haired Buñuel was only too happy to give this excellent news to his friend.

With a check dated March 3 from de Noailles for twenty thousand francs, sent in exchange for the promise of a painting from Dalí's forthcoming 1930 output, Dalí bought a crumbling stone shack with a collapsed roof in the tiny cove of Portlligat, just around the corner from Cadaqués. This 220-square-foot hovel had originally belonged to Dalí's old friend, a local woman known as "Lidia la Bel Plantata." It was right on the beach, and had been used by Lidia's sons to store their fishing gear. De Noailles got the better part of the bargain. He received *The Old Age of William Tell*.[7]

Gala found the tiny dwelling, with its panoramic views of the vast ocean, incredibly romantic. The owners of the Miramar, who were afraid of Dalí y Cusí, had refused to let her and Salvador have a room at their inn, but she managed with Lidia's help to discover a dingy bed-and-breakfast that would take them. She had just begun renovations on their shack when she learned that Dalí y Cusí had sent the Civil Guard to harass his son. The situation became so difficult that when Gala and Dalí wanted to visit his friends, the Pichots, on the other side of the cape, they had to rent a small boat and sail to their hosts because it was too dangerous to use the road.

Gala and Salvador left Portlligat sooner than anticipated. The minute they were out of Spain, Dalí y Cusí wrote to Buñuel, "You must know where the 'Madame' [Gala] lives . . . tell her to inform [my son] that he need not try to return to Cadaqués, for the simple reason that he will not be allowed to remain in said village for even two or three hours. Then things will get so complicated for him that he will not be allowed to return to France."[8]

Safely settled in the Montmartre apartment with Salvador (Paul was presumably off with Alice), Gala used her significant influence to do everything she could to help her lover. Working as Dalí's critic and model, she also began to reach beyond these roles to create a real business plan around the work they were making together. She negotiated and organized Dalí's exhibition and sales contracts with Pierre Colle, the new gallerist Charles de Noailles had recommended. She also took charge of all matters relating to the presentation of Dalí's work.

Gala became her lover's "life coach." According to Salvador, she taught him "the principles of reality and proportion; how to dress; how to go downstairs (without falling six times); how to eat (without throwing chicken bones at the ceiling); how to recognize their enemies and how to stop losing *their* money."[9] From 1930, Dalí began signing paintings and drawings with their joint name: "Gala-Salvador

Dalí."[10] After all, as he would write later, "Gala, it is with your blood that I paint my pictures."

Gala worked so hard that she developed a nervous cough that threatened to turn into bronchitis. Both Paul, who claimed his hair was turning white from anxiety, and Dalí worried about her health. She looked, Salvador remembered, so fragile in her tea rose–colored nightgown that she reminded him of a little Art Nouveau fairy who "seemed on the point of dying from the mere effort of smelling [a decorative] gardenia whose blossom was larger than her head."[11] Her cramps had reappeared. So had her mood swings.

In April, at the invitation of his friend the poet José María Hinojosa, who was involved with *Litoral*, the most respected literary journal in Spain, Salvador took Gala to Málaga, Picasso's birthplace in Andalusia, where they stayed at the hotel el Castillo del Sol, a white turret on the cliff overlooking the dark cove of La Carihuela. Here Gala, costumed like a Cretan priestess, in a red skirt with her tanned breasts bare to the sun, made a lasting impression on the *Litoral* group, who could not help noticing how passionately involved she and Dalí were with each other. The gaudily dressed couple who loved kissing in public ended up attracting so much attention from passersby on the street that in self-protection, their tour guide started telling curious inquirers they were Egyptian.[12] A film clip from this visit shows Dalí standing behind a smiling Gala with an utterly dazed, slaphappy expression, as though he just can't believe his good luck.

In Paris, Paul, who was getting bored with La Pomme, began to pressure Gala to make up her mind about her living arrangements. The Montparnasse apartment was expensive to maintain, especially if he and Gala were never in it together. In another attempt to persuade his wife to come back to him, he wrote to Gala that his new friend René Char, a thirtysomething poet from the Luberon who would soon be counted among France's greatest living authors, had written his latest anthology, *Le Tombeau des Secrets* (*The Tomb of Secrets*), for her and dedicated it to both of them.[13, 14]

Meanwhile, Buñuel was putting the finishing touches on *L'Age d'Or*, and Breton had just published the first issue of his new journal, *Le Surréalisme au Service de la Révolution* (*Surrealism in the Service of the Revolution*); Éluard sent it to Gala in Portlligat, where she and Salvador had returned at the beginning of June. Happily, when he finally realized that trying to keep his son out of the neighborhood was impracticable, Dalí y Cusí's crusade against them had run out of steam and the renovations on their new home were progressing beautifully.

The cover of *Le Surréalisme au Service de la Révolution* was stamped with a mysterious astrological emblem that represented the conjunction of Uranus and Saturn, which had reigned over the collective births of Éluard, Aragon, and Breton. This icon can be interpreted as the marriage of creativity and pragmatism and was therefore the perfect image for Breton's artistic and political aspirations. The journal opened with a "Declaration" in which Breton's faithful swore allegiance to their guru. It was signed by Louis Aragon, Jacques Bousquet, Luis Buñuel, Salvador Dalí, René Char, René Crevel, Paul Éluard, Max Ernst, Camille Goemans, Yves Tanguy, and Tristan Tzara, among others. The issue also included *The Rotten Donkey*, a piece by Dalí that was edited by, and dedicated to Gala, and several film stills by Buñuel from *L'Age d'Or* showing the film's heroine orgasming.

For the next three months, Gala and Dalí lived by the indigo sea in their tiny beach hut. While Salvador continued to work at solving the technical problems inherent in his portrait of *The Invisible Man*, Gala gladly helped him with two new essays, a cursory reading of which reveals the continual use of her inimitable Russian-inflected sentence structure. She also completed the organization of her notes on their discussions about contemporary poetry and art.

That August they were visited by René Char, Paul, and Maria Benz—a leggy, dark-haired Alsatian artist and model who had an arrestingly beautiful, heart-shaped face. She had just arrived in Paris from Switzerland, without a cent to her name, when Paul, who was on his way to breakfast with René, picked her up on the boulevard Haussmann. He invited her along for coffee and croissants and discovered that her nickname was "Nusch." When Éluard checked into the Miramar, where he had been with Gala exactly one year before, he brought Nusch along as a signal of his willingness to accept his wife's involvement with Dalí and his own ability to handle the situation.

Buñuel, who had been recruited by talent scouts at Metro-Goldwyn-Mayer, was on his way back from Hollywood when *L'Age d'Or* finally opened in Paris, at Studio 28, in November 1930. Paintings by Dalí, Ernst, Tanguy, and Arp were on display in the studio's lobby. The exclusive premiere was attended by a knot of de Noailles's aristocratic friends and relatives as well as Brâncuși, Braque, Jean Cocteau, Gertrude Stein, Elsa Schiaparelli, and all the Surrealists. The film itself, which equated the Marquis de Sade's fictional hero, the Duc de Blangis, with Jesus Christ by depicting Blangis as "Our Savior," was an immediate and serious scandal aggravated by the fact that, on her mother's side, Marie-Laure de Noailles was the great-great-great-granddaughter of the Marquis de Sade.

A few weeks after the premiere, a large-scale demonstration was held to protest *L'Age d'Or*'s anticlerical imagery. Members of the Patriotic and Anti-Jewish Leagues marched into the theater screaming, "Death to the Jews" (Marie-Laure's father, Maurice Bischoffsheim, had been a rich Jewish banker). Then they began chanting, "We'll show you there are still Christians in France," while they slashed paintings and threw stink bombs at the spectators and ink at the screen. Art patron Étienne de Beaumont alerted the bishop of Paris. The right-wing newspaper *Le Figaro* launched a campaign to have *L'Age d'Or* censored. Charles de Noailles was accused of creating "a Bolshevik spectacle." He was asked to resign from the elite Jockey Club, which had always been his "second home;" and his mother, the princess de Poix, had to travel all the way to Rome over Christmas to personally apologize to Pope Pius XI, who was threatening her baby with excommunication. Finally, the film, renamed *L'Age d'Or-dure (The Age of Filth)* by its opponents, was confiscated by the police. Humiliated, the de Noailleses went into temporary seclusion at their sumptuous, all-white, Mallet-Stevens-designed Modernist villa over-looking the ancient Mediterranean port of Hyères. When news of the uproar reached England and America, Dalí and Buñuel became internationally famous.

That month, Gala put the finishing touches on Dalí's new manu-script, *La Femme Visible (The Visible Woman)*, and oversaw its publication in a limited, numbered edition by Éditions Surréalistes. The ravish-ing little volume is a gathering of the detailed notes she had been devotedly organizing and editing since meeting Dalí. It contains *The Rotten Donkey*, in which the artist's theory of "paranoiac criticism" is explained as instinctive understanding catalyzed by the juxtaposition of hallucinatory images; the lyric poem "The Great Masturbator,"[15] which is dedicated to Gala, and an essay on love that explores the relationship between dreams, sensuality, and the death wish. *La Femme Visible* served as both Dalí's artist's statement and his official letter of introduction to the Surrealists. Gala *was* the visible woman.[16] The book's first page is Max Ernst's 1925 portrait of Gala's penetrating gaze, drawn on Man Ray's most famous photograph of her. Éluard and Breton coauthored the introduction, which underscores the im-portance of Dalí's contribution to the Surrealist movement. And the frontispiece is illustrated with an elaborate etching by Dalí domi-nated by a nude hermaphrodite that signifies Gala and Salvador's eternal union.

By January 1930, Gala's abdominal pains were so much worse that Paul took her away for a rest from the uproar surrounding *L'Age d'Or*. They traveled south to Saint-Tropez with Georges Auric, who wrote the score for the operetta *Moulin Rouge*; Max and Marie-Berthe Ernst, now temporarily reconciled; and Valentine Hugo, who was separated from her husband, Victor Hugo's son Jean. Valentine's trip album includes a photograph of Gala and Paul snuggling like newlyweds, and three weeks later, Éluard sent his wife a poem written for her, which echoes the timbre of their early love letters. It's optimistically titled *"Par une nuit nouvelle"* ("On a New Night"):

> *Femme avec laquelle j'ai vécu*
> *Femme avec laquelle je vis*
> *Femme avec laquelle je vivrai*
> *Toujours la même*
> *Il te faut un manteau rouge*
> *Des gants rouges un masque rouge*
> *Et des bas noirs*
> *Des raisons des preuves*
> *De te voir toute nue*
> *Nudité pure ô parure parée*
> *Seins ô mon Coeur*

("Woman I lived with / Woman I live with / Woman I will live with / always the same / You should have a red coat and red gloves / A red mask / And black stockings / Reasons and proofs / To see you all naked / pure nudity o ready adornment / breasts—o my heart").

His charming, wistful verses turned out to be just that. Paul would never live with Gala again.

Later that month, Éditions Surréalistes published the limited edition of Dalí's poem *"L'Amour et la Mémoire"* ("Love and Memory"), for which Gala had hand-set all the type. Dalí's dedication reads, "To Gala for whom the speed of her life / annuls memory on her / body / with all the love of Salvador / Dalí." The illustration is Buñuel's photograph of Dalí with a sea urchin on his shaved head, taken when his father expelled him from Cadaqués.

The beginning of June marked a giant step forward for the Dalís when *The Persistence of Memory* (Dalí's famous melting watches) was exhibited for the first time at the Pierre Colle Gallery in Paris, where it caught the eye of Alfred Barr, the Museum of Modern Art's revered director, and an ambitious young American dealer named Julien Levy. Levy immediately purchased the work to take back to New York. "Once one has seen it, one can never forget it" was Gala's reaction when Salvador showed her the painting, which he had tenderly signed "Olive Salvador Dalí." "Olive" was his pet name for Gala, a loving reference to the oval shape of her face and the olive hue of her skin.

Later that month, Gala underwent a total hysterectomy for uterine tumors, performed in Paris by Dr. René Jacquemaire, whom she would never forgive for leaving her with hideous, irreparable scarring. On June 30, she returned to Portlligat with Dalí and René Crevel. While Crevel worked on his essay *"Dalí ou l'anti-obscurantisme"* ("Dalí or Anti-Obscurantism"), Gala swam in the sea, napped by the beach, and, encouraged by René, who was also urging her to write a novel, dreamed up her first known artwork, a Cornell box–like construction that was published in the third issue of *Le Surréalisme au Service de la Révolution* under the heading of "Objects Surréalistes" ("Surrealist Objects"), where it was grouped with similar fantasies by Giacometti, Salvador Dalí, and André Breton.

CHAPTER 15

PARIS WHEN IT SIZZLES

If the debut of *L'Age d'Or* humbled the de Noailleses, who would henceforth be regarded with suspicion by the *"particules"*[1] of Paris, it created a social bonanza for the now publicly indissoluble Dalís. Gala and Salvador were frequent dinner guests at Charles and Marie-Laure's much-photographed Place des États-Unis town house, where Jean-Michel Frank had wallpapered the grand salon with squares of shell-colored parchment and lit the rooms with Venetian and Baccarat chandeliers. Dalí, who was very conscious of being, in his own words, "a Catalan peasant," felt uneasy in the company of this incomparably social couple. Gala, who in contrast was naturally intrepid, remained unimpressed by their airs and graces. She clearly understood that the de Noailleses, who "played with ideas of revolution and sacrilege in approximately the same way that Marie Antoinette had played at being a shepherdess in the Trianon, lived to have the latest art world favorites at their table."[2] Correctly assessing her partner's value to these people, she concentrated all her efforts on guiding what Julien Levy would later refer to as the "missile" of Dalí's talent and personality in the right direction.

The Dalís were gratified to see *Le Jeu Lugubre* hanging next to a Lucas Cranach in the de Noailleses' dining room, where Gala's reassuring presence gave Salvador the confidence to be his normally rambunctious self. When he told his hostess he wasn't eating her dinner because of the wood-and-ice-cream dessert he had consumed before arriving (the ice cream was excellent, but the wood bothered his digestion), he was genuinely delighted to discover that his fellow guests found him incredibly amusing.[3] Soon the Dalís were being courted by Paris's top hosts. They were invited to the musical soirées of sewing-machine heiress Winaretta Singer, now the Princesse de Polignac, where they mingled with Erik Satie; Georges Auric; Arthur Rubinstein, and Gerald Hugh Tyrwhitt-Wilson, the 14th Baron Berners;. They were also included in Étienne de Beaumont's ultra-exclusive bal-masqués. At one of these, as Salvador wickedly recounted, he enjoyed "mistakenly" stepping on the Maharaja of Kapurthala's foot.[4]

Surrealism à la Dalí and especially his outrageous, conversational gambits became the rage of all Paris. Up-to-date socialites now enjoyed nothing more than talking "Dalí." At chic tables all over the capital, counts and duchesses could be found bursting into gales of knowing laughter as they whispered to each other, "For two days now I've misplaced my libido" or "I have this crazy urge to cretanize [sic] you, my dear."[5]

As a result of their newfound popularity, Gala and Salvador were spending the majority of their time with exceptionally rich people. Very different from Éluard's liberal, artistic bohemian clique, these new, worldly associates lived on ranches in South America, had inherited castles on the Continent, and spent Christmas in penthouses in New York. But the Dalís themselves had almost no money. Gala, who liked to say that "pity kills strength,"[6] kept their financial problems a secret while doing everything possible to find enough cash for Dalí to devote himself to his art. She scrimped on expenses. Weekly visits to the local cinema were her only indulgence. Nothing appears to have been spent on clothes during this period, although Chanel, to whom Éluard had sent a signed copy of Mourir de ne pas mourir, probably began lending Gala outfits as early as 1930.[7] The great designer, who became a lifelong friend of the Dalís, knew a winner when she saw one and certainly recognized the angular Mme Éluard's value as an informal ambassadress for Chanel haute couture.

Finally, Paul agreed to divorce. The process was completed on July 15, 1932. Gala took neither settlement nor alimony. She also agreed that because Dalí's finances were so uncertain, sixteen-year-old Cécile should remain in France, where she spoke the language and could live comfortably with Jeanne, who loved looking after her. The next day, Éluard published *La Vie Immédiate* (*Life Now*). He inscribed his ex-wife's copy, "For my Gala / For free Gala / whom I have loved since / 1912 / as much now as then." He visited Gala and Salvador in Spain two weeks later and stayed at the Miramar in Cadaqués with René Crevel, who brought the Argentine countess Maria "Tota" Cuevas de Vera with him as his guest.

The Dalís moved out of Paul's Montmartre apartment to an un-furnished flat in the blue-collar neighborhood of Montrouge. Here Gala made sure that the wide-open, loftlike space, whose best feature was its vast windows, would be alluring to potential customers com-ing to see her partner's work. With the exception of a multitude of mirrors, strategically placed to refract light, and long glass tables used for display purposes, the apartment had virtually no furniture.[8] But Dalí's most recent art, carefully spaced on the walls, enriched its ap-pearance, and everything sparkled. To celebrate their new home, the Dalís had themselves photographed near one of the mirrors. Brassaï, who took the shot, liked his subject so much that he included his own reflection in the composition.

Gala, who was becoming known for her inventive lunches and dinners, now entertained regularly. As Schiaparelli's publicist, a blond, blue-eyed American named Bettina Bergery, who was a friend of the Dalís', remembered:

"She would give you meals of mysterious little things you had never had before. At the time raw mushrooms in salad were a rarity. You would have a wonderful dinner, then she would proudly tell you how little it cost her. She was always thinking about two centimes and where she could buy the cheapest bread. I can still see the little scrunchy way she would wrinkle up her eyes when she was thinking about money."[9]

Prince Jean-Louis de Faucigny-Lucinge, an early Dalí aficionado and patron who had met Gala and Salvador through the de Noailleses, described Gala in the early 1930s as a fascinating personality, friendly yet reserved and so private that she sometimes almost seemed hard. When, many years later, Faucigny-Lucinge learned that Gala had a daughter, he was shocked that she had never mentioned Cécile to him. He and his wife, Baba, had proudly introduced Gala to all of their children. The prince couldn't imagine that what was a social occasion for him and the princess was real work for Gala, who worried daily about where the next commission was coming from and regarded him and his wife as clients, not friends. Still, he was admiring: "She was *someone* you know," he told Meryle Secrest, not beautiful but witchily attractive; "a creative, daring woman, with a great deal of common sense. And she kept Dalí painting. It was clear 'they' would be a success."

Gala needn't have worried, Faucigny-Lucinge turned out to be an excellent friend. That fall he, the American writer Anne Green, and Gala founded an exclusive society of twelve patrons, each of whom would support the Dalís for one month of the year in exchange for art. Gala laid out the conditions for inclusion: in return for their contribution, members could choose either one large canvas or a smaller work and two drawings. Because of the number of its fellows and the Surrealist affection for astrology, they named their new club The Zodiac.

Anne Green, who hailed from Savannah, immediately enlisted her younger brother Julien, who had recently met Dalí on a visit to the Pierre Colle Gallery. The Greens were heirs to a Georgia cotton fortune but had been raised in France, where Julien became the first American author to publish successfully in the French language and be accepted as a member of the Académie Française. Julien's life partner, the international journalist Robert de Saint-Jean, was Anne's second recruit. He joined because as he noted in his journal[10] he thought Dalí's tiny and provocative paintings glowed like the precious enamels of the sixteenth century. René Crevel enlisted his friend Tota Cuevas de Vera, whom he had already introduced to the Dalís, and Caresse Crosby, who had founded the Black Sun Press in 1927 with her late husband, J. P. Morgan's nephew Harry Crosby. Caresse was known as the "literary godmother of the Lost Generation" because she had published D. H. Lawrence and Ernest Hemingway and was currently printing paperback editions of work by Éluard, Max Ernst, and Aragon. Another very important new member, John D. Rockefeller's granddaughter, the just-wed Marchioness Margaret Strong de Cuevas, came through Faucigny-Lucinge, as did the Italian countess Anna Laetitia "Mimi" Pecci-Blunt, whose American millionaire husband Cecil Blumenthal was given his title by Pope Benedict XV as a wedding present. The decorator Emilio Terry; Marseilles soap heir André Hurst, who was also *Vogue Paris*'s premier photographer; award-winning journalist René Laporte; and the faithful Charles de Noailles rounded out the list.

They all met chez Gala on December 23 for a pre-Christmas dinner, where they drew straws to see who would get first pick of Salvador's upcoming work. Jean-Louis wrote that this clever and amusing financial arrangement flourished five or six years, during which time Dalí's art was seen and admired on the most envied and emulated walls of "the capital." It was only after the Englishman Edward James became Dalí's chief patron and Gala was able to get much higher prices for the work elsewhere that The Zodiac came undone. Although Faucigny-Lucinge wryly noted that he was not mentioned in *The Secret Life*, "great men are not always grateful"; he remained a lifelong advocate of the Dalís and was happy to second Serge Lifar, who had been Nijinsky's principal dancer until 1929,[11] in proposing Dalí for the important position of artistic director of the 1939 ballet *Bacchanale*.

While the Dalís were bolstering their finances and enhancing their artistic position in Paris, France was beginning to feel the vise of worldwide depression, intensified by angst from Germany, where Hitler had just been elected chancellor. At the same time, Spain and Russia went into tailspins of their own.

On April 11, 1931, Spain's thirty-five-year-old king, Alfonso XIII, fled his own country to avoid intensifying demonstrations and incipient war. When municipal elections held later that month clearly showed that the realm's biggest cities were overwhelmingly republican, Alfonso XIII was promptly dethroned. During the power vacuum created by the demise of his reign, Catalonia became the only autonomous government within the Spanish Republic. This balancing act began to unravel in 1936, when the Popular Front's electoral victory fell into chaos, followed by a gory military coup that began in July and grew rapidly into the Spanish Civil War, which lasted for three years of terror, death, and devastation. During this period, the Catalan state was demolished and the Catalan language was repressed. When Francisco Franco rose to power in 1939, the Spanish Republic was decisively squashed.

Russia, meanwhile, was in the fourth year of Stalin's first Five-Year Plan. The plan called for the reorganization of the country's agricultural workers. Accordingly, the government began converting individually owned, tillable acreage and livestock into state-owned farms. The peasants were no longer free to leave what had been their own properties. As in the reign of the Romanovs, they were serfs literally bound to the earth. This forced "collectivization" met vigorous resistance. Rather than hand their animals over to the Soviet officials, farmers slaughtered so many of their own cows and pigs that for years afterward Russia's livestock resources were lower than they had been in 1929. When Stalin retaliated by deporting resisters to Siberia, it turned out the rebels were such a large percentage of the workforce that starvation spread throughout the Soviet Union.

By 1933, Paul's brokerage account had dwindled to the point that, when his mother refused to give him any more money, Gala, if she could spare it, sometimes mailed him a check. In early February, after a sleepless night spent fretting over his investments, he sent Gala a letter from the Grand Hôtel du Mont Blanc wondering if the real estate she shared with Dalí might be in Dalí's name alone. This, Paul insisted, would be an unacceptable arrangement. "Excuse me," he wrote. "I have the right to say this because I am thinking of your best interests. . . . Imagine what might happen if Salvador died or [should it turn out he really is crazy] committed suicide. His father could take everything from you, everything in his son's house—and all YOUR paintings (and thus *mine*)," he added, invoking their prenuptial contract, "would strictly belong to him. It would seem that the father has disinherited the son but that the son cannot disinherit the father *or the sister . . .* that is the danger of not being married, consequently *you must get married.*" "Think," he concluded somewhat condescendingly, "you wouldn't even have the right to take your own dresses."

When he wasn't worrying about his personal finances, Paul, with André Breton and the other Surrealists, reacted to Europe's rapid and terrifying civil degeneration with an idiosyncratic mixture of radical rage and political mysticism. They published partisan articles. They consulted supernatural guides.

On May 11, 1931, six convents and a Jesuit building were burned to the ground by agitators in Madrid, and Éluard and Breton issued a tract called *"Au Feu"* ("To Fire"). In it they fiercely accused the Spanish Republic of having become a farce run by landowners and the Church. Two years later, as Hitler was turning Germany into a dictatorship, André switched course and decided to endorse the power of clairvoyance to solve governmental issues. He circulated a questionnaire titled "Recherches Expérimentales sur la Connaissance Irrationnelle de l'objet Boule de Cristal des Voyantes" ("Experimental Research on the Uncanny Knowledge Contained in a Fortuneteller's Crystal Ball") and asked Gala as the reigning Surrealist soothsayer to participate. In the resulting article that appeared in *Le Surréalisme au Service de la Révolution*, she described the crystal ball's infallible wisdom as feminine and aligned with the "air element." It was, she continued, favorable to love, occasionally menacing, and more ancient than pre-history.

Dalí began work on a similarly otherworldly series of paintings based on the French artist Jean-François Millet's 1859 *The Angelus*.[12] A pastoral masterpiece, Millet's chef d'oeuvre depicts a male and a female peasant with their heads bowed in prayer at dusk in a field where they have been gathering potatoes in a wheelbarrow beside them. It is famous for its subtle alignment of art with both the fruitfulness of the fields and (since the Angelus prayer invokes the Annunciation) man's connection to God.

In contrast, Dalí's *Gala and the Angelus of Millet Preceding the Imminent Arrival of the Conic Anamorphoses*[13] (1933) is a nightmare about Russia. Juxtaposing eerie images of governmental malfeasance, art, and spiritual transcendence, it portrays a tiny, terrified Gala dressed in the colorful garb of a rich Russian peasant in the back of a brightly lit chamber cowering under *The Angelus*, propped up on a shelf over her head. She is about to be assaulted by Stalin, who has been ushered into the room by a grimacing Maxim Gorky[14] with hands that are claws. In a second painting, *The Angelus of Gala* (1935), Gala (whose face now resembles that of Salvador's mother) and Dalí, wearing identical Russian peasant costumes, are painted as front and back of the same person. Behind them, a new version of Millet's composition provides a key to the work's meaning: Here the male and female farmer are next to each other *in* the wheelbarrow. *The peasants* have become the harvest that nourishes the viewer.

That year, Salvador also completed two profiles of Gala for his upcoming show at the Pierre Colle Gallery in June. The first is an exquisite Daphne-like Gala with shining dark locks that are olive shoots instead of laurel leaves. In the second, a chic Gala, whose nose is brushed by an airplane in flight, wears a lobster as her hat. These works were intended as "teasers" to be listed in the catalog as "not for sale." On July 12 from Portlligat, where she was sunbathing with Marcel Duchamp and his wife, Mary Reynolds, Gala wrote that one of the paintings she planned to exhibit in the upcoming Dalí show at Levy's New York gallery would be a portrait of her that was part of her personal collection. It would be shown *only* as an advertisement to give patrons an idea of "the kind of work they might be able to commission from Dalí."[15]

Meanwhile, in step with Breton's 1928 essay "Enquête sur la Sexualité" ("Research on Sexuality"), Gala began to conduct her own sex salons, which she held every Wednesday evening. Regulars included Éluard, Dalí, who was constantly trying to "intellectualize" the conversation, André Breton, and often Henri Pastoureau, a promising young author who recounted these "soirées" in his memoir, *Ma Vie Surréaliste*. Pastoureau, who clearly liked her, remembers Gala "with a great deal of nostalgia," describing her as "Russian to the tips of her fingernails and proud of it," with, he adds admiringly, "the keen insight of a natural soothsayer."[16]

Gala, who was invariably the only woman present, led all the conversations, in which the participants discussed their own sexual demons and preferences. She also contributed pertinently empathetic anecdotes from her own experiences with men, and sometimes—to tease Breton, who remained amusingly prim—she and Paul offered to demonstrate.

CHAPTER 14

AMERICA

To protect themselves from the insurrection in Catalonia, Gala and Salvador moved their belongings to Paris, where, to Paul's relief, they were married on January 30, 1934. The short civil ceremony at the Spanish consulate was witnessed by Yves Tanguy and their neighbor, still-life artist André Gaston.

Six days later, André Breton, alarmed by Salvador's political unorthodoxy, accused him of being "anti-revolutionary" and summoned both Dalís to a Surrealist meeting at which the painter's recent behavior and pronouncements would be judged. This "subpoena" arrived with an advance list of points to be raised during the "trial." Gala, who had coauthored Salvador's eight pages of answers, sat beside him through the entire interrogation. The critical affront was Dalí's 1933 painting *The Enigma of William Tell*, which unflatteringly depicts the Swiss father figure as a kneeling Stalin with one elongated buttock that's supported by a crutch. Breton, who was the proud owner of an earlier William Tell composition, found this current version disrespectful to Communism and was angry that Dalí was going to show it at the Grand Palais in an exhibition shunned by the other Surrealists. Dalí answered that the Stalin monster was really his own father, who wanted to eat him and kill Gala. Besides, since he always made work in order to disturb as many people as possible, the question of where he displayed it was irrelevant. Another primary concern was

Dalí's attitude toward Hitler, to which Dalí, who was famous for his phobia of alpha males, replied convincingly that if they were in Germany now, every copy of his artist's statement *The Visible Woman* would have already been burned by the Nazis.

Salvador, who had a cold, had arrived at the meeting carrying an oversize thermometer and wrapped in several layers of warm clothing, which, to everyone's hilarity, he kept taking off and putting on during the questioning and the event ended in laughter. When the Dalís were exonerated, Breton was so relieved that he inscribed a copy of his most recent book, *L'Air de L'eau* (*The Air of Water*), to the couple: "For Gala / and Salvador Dalí / the most beautiful weeds / in the stream. . . ." Just fourteen hours after Dalí's "trial" was adjourned, French Fascists provoked a violent riot in Paris, during which twelve people were killed. A general strike was called within the week, and Édouard Daladier, the radical Socialist who had been sworn in as prime minister just five days previously, was forced to resign.

Gala and Dalí visited Dalí's show at the Zwemmer Gallery that May in London, where they were regally entertained[1] by Edward James, an impeccably elegant poet and art patron. James had invited them to stay in his Paul Nash–designed town house on Wimpole Street, famous for its luxurious, modern bathrooms and richly tented study. Marie-Laure de Noailles,[2] who was James's lover and whose 1932 portrait by Salvador Dalí James had admired at Hyères, had introduced James and the Dalís a year earlier in Paris.

Edward James was the only son of the exquisite Scottish socialite Evelyn Forbes, one of the most admired hostesses of her era. King Edward VIII, who was Edward James's godfather and Evelyn's constant visitor, was rumored to be her lover and the real father of her little boy. James (who insisted that the king was really his *mother's* father) was also the sole heir to his American father's vast copper fortune, Phelps Dodge Corporation.

When he met Gala and Salvador, Edward had just turned

twenty-seven and was in the middle of a vicious, much-publicized divorce from prima ballerina Tilly Losch. Cecil Beaton, who was one of the many who commented on this debacle, described the beautiful Austrian as "that serpent of the old Danube," because after refusing to consummate their marriage, Tilly accused Edward of being homosexual. James was also making a name for himself in Parisian cultural circles as one of the underwriters of a short-lived but prestigious and beautifully printed new publication called *Minotaure*, produced by the famous Swiss luxury-book publisher Albert Skira, which Paul Éluard was helping to organize. More important, he was unstintingly generous and had a rich imagination, a keenly developed sense of humor, and an eye for talent that was almost the equal of Gala's. He rapidly became Salvador's patron and Gala's great admirer and friend.

After reading cultural critic Lewis Mumford's recently published *New Yorker* article "Frozen Nightmares,"[3] which praised his talent as "deeply revelatory," Dalí had decided American intellectuals were more objective and better informed than their European counterparts, who judged art through the lens of their own prejudices.[4] Now, further encouraged by the success of their English adventure, Salvador finally allowed Gala to persuade him to visit New York. Alfred Barr had just acquired *The Persistence of Memory* for the Museum of Modern Art, and Julien Levy's New York gallery was about to open a one-man show of Dalí's new work. On November 7, with exactly enough money from Picasso to buy two third-class passages, Gala and Salvador set out on their first transatlantic journey, aboard the SS *Champlain*. They were accompanied by Zodiac member Caresse Crosby, who was making the crossing for the thirty-fourth time.

As cofounder of the Black Sun Press, Caresse was revered for her varied and invariably talented friends and protégés. In addition to Hemingway and James Joyce, she had mentored, among others, Archibald MacLeish, Henri Cartier-Bresson, Kay Boyle, and Hart

Crane, and she had published Antoine de Saint Exupéry's 1931 novel *Vol de Nuit*. The Dalís who had enjoyed many visits to Le Moulin du Soleil, Caresse's country retreat, a honeysuckle-covered tower on the seventeenth-century de la Rochefoucauld estate, eighty kilometers northwest of Paris chose Caresse as their guide to America because they trusted her judgment and appreciated her taste. Still, Salvador, who was just thirty and spoke absolutely no English, was terrified by the prospect of the trip.

To distract him from his fears, once they were on board, Caresse, who had a first-class ticket, invited the Dalís to a formal dinner dance on the *Champlain*'s glamorous top deck. The evening was a flop. Remembering his mother's warnings about catching cold and dying like his brother, Salvador scandalized his fellow travelers by dressing for dinner in a heavy coat with a hat down over his ears and scarves twisted around his neck to ward off the lethal night air. In an effort to calm her husband, who was also convinced the ship would soon sink, Gala exacerbated the situation when she went above board the next day wrapped in a thick cork life jacket. She looked so much like the Michelin Man's twin sister that the only people who spoke to her were Salvador and Caresse.

As soon as the SS *Champlain* docked in New York, it was greeted by a group of jostling journalists hoping for royalty, film-star, or socialite snapshots for their party pages. Caresse, who knew most of them, pushed the Dalís forward, loudly announcing the arrival of a great Surrealist painter. Gala had tied a small portrait of herself with two lamb chops on her shoulder to one of the buttons of Salvador's coat. As Dalí tore the paper covering off *The Portrait of My Wife*, Caresse delivered a short speech on Surrealism. The cameras went wild.

Dalí, who communicated only through Caresse, somehow understood that the reporters wanted to know the reason behind the lamb chops on Gala's shoulder and was proud and pleased when they found his simple answer, "I like my wife and I like lamb chops," refreshingly funny. Newspapers the *San Antonio Light*, the *Decatur Daily News*, and the *Wisconsin State Journal (Madison)*, as well as the *New York Times* and the *New York Tribune*, shared Crosby's banter: under a headline that read, "Mrs. Caresse Crosby Sponsoring Salvador Dalí Sur-Realist [*sic*] Painter Discusses His Art.": "At first glance a piano fading off into a man's head out of which a tree is growing is a bit mad, and the painting of a watch lying on the edge of a table with part of it dripping off like butter on the floor will seem equally insane. But the minute they don't seem crazy I'll quit looking at them."

The *New York Times* called Dalí's practice "putting Freudian theories on canvas" and praised the delicacy of his brushwork. It further noted that Mrs. Stanley Resor had recently gifted *The Persistence of Memory* to MoMA, whose trustees were delighted to receive it for the museum's prestigious collection. The *Tribune* outdid itself. It printed a full page with photographs of Gala and Dalí and went out of its way to commend Salvador's showy outfit: "a dark suit with a yellow shirt and polka-dotted cravat," which Gala had picked out. Following the Dalís from the dock to their rooms at the hotel St. Hubert on West Fifty-Seventh Street, the *Tribune* further noted that their suite had been improved by Gala and Salvador with loaves of French bread exhibited on the fireplace mantel and a red Catalan *barretina* (nationalist hat) perched on a chair. Special mention was given to the portrait of Gala sprouting leaves from her head. All of the newspapers made sure to advertise Dalí's upcoming show, which was set to open on November 21 at Julien Levy's Madison Avenue gallery. Sales followed press, and in January, just before and Gala and Dalí planned to return to Portlligat to recover from the "tremendous excitement of their time in New York," he was able to proudly write his friend the journalist Josep Foix in Barcelona that twelve of the twenty-six paintings on view in the gallery had sold "at very high prices."[5]

Just before the Dalís' departure, Julien's wife, Joella Levy, and Caresse decided to cap the heady fortnight by throwing a goodbye party

New York would always remember. Once again, the newspapers were notified. The *Times* and the *Journal* hyped the event in advance, and invitations to a "Bal Onirique," or dreamscape dance, with music by Joe LaPorte and his Orchestra at Le Coq Rouge restaurant in Manhattan on January 18, were speedily sent out. Guests were asked to arrive dressed as their favorite nightmare. Caresse came as a virgin, in all white. Dalí wrapped his head up like a mummy's. Gala, whose outfit was the most controversial and self-revelatory, arrived braless in a very tight sweater and a semitransparent ankle-length skirt. A dead-looking baby doll covered in ants seemed to be growing out of her head. When the *Mirror*, which described the party as New York society trying to "out-Dalí the painter," asked her to explain the event, Gala answered that it was "an experiment to see how far New Yorkers would go to express their own dreams." "However," she felt, "only a dozen or so actually succeeded in this expression." The others were just "betraying themselves." A few hours later, still aglow from the triumph of their American journey, Gala and Salvador boarded the *Ile de France* and set sail for Le Havre.

CHAPTER 15

LOSS AND FAME

The talk of the town in February 1935 was the Museum of Modern Art's first Surrealist exhibition, with *The Persistence of Memory* as its centerpiece. Gala and Salvador were feeling so encouraged by their American sucesses that they decided to upgrade their Parisian living arrangements. The following month, the Dalís moved into an airy, recently constructed Modernist house designed by Gustave Perret in Villa Seurat, an artist's enclave on the shady Montparnasse cul-de-sac rue de la Tombe-Issoire. Gala, who enlisted the help of Zodiac member Emilio Therry, the Cuban sugarcane heir and celebrity designer, enjoyed turning the new residence into what Julien Levy, who was expecting a "neo-Baroque fantasy from Therry," described as an interior "surprising in its simplicity": all white and sparsely furnished with Spanish provincial pieces.[1] The entire top floor was a large, open studio.

On the evening of June 18, three weeks short of his thirty-fifth birthday, the Surrealist novelist René Crevel put his head in his oven and turned up the gas. Crevel, who wrote openly about how much he suffered from his conflicted sexuality, was widely and deservingly loved by the Parisian haute bohemia. He had a broad and dazzling variety of friends, including Gertrude Stein, Nancy Cunard, and the American artist Eugene McCown, with whom he enjoyed a stormy affair that he detailed in the lyrical cult novel *La Mort Difficile* (*Dif-*

ficult Death). And he had just discovered that his tuberculosis had progressed to his kidneys. A one-word suicide note was pinned to his lapel. It read, "Disgusted." Crevel had been a wonderful, devoted friend, confidant, and supporter of Gala in both of her marriages, and she was inconsolable. The British poet David Gascoyne, who was present when Gala heard the news, wrote that he had been genuinely startled to see a woman he had always thought hard and unfeeling dissolve into torrents of tears.[2]

Deciding to take a much-needed break from Paris, the Dalís accepted muralist Josep Maria Sert's invitation to stay at Mas Juney, his grand farmhouse in Girona, which was the most cosmopolitan spot on Spain's Costa Brava. Other guests included left-wing French politician Gaston Bergery; his American wife, Bettina; Countess Madina Visconti; flamboyant Mexican silver heir/art collector Carlos de Beistegui; and the peripatetic Edward James. Sert's wife, the exiled Georgian princess Roussy Mdivani, also invited her dashing brother Prince Alexis, recently divorced from his second wife, Barbara Hutton, who was the richest woman in the world.[3] Alexis arrived at the house party with his married mistress, Maud von Thyssen.

While the rest of the guests sunned, swam, and partied, James, who found Gala attractive and hoped to buy from her husband, spent most of his time with the Dalís, who gladly welcomed him to their studio. They were working on *Suburbs of a Paranoiac Critical Town*, a sophisticated composition, signed "Gala Salvador Dalí," that depicts Gala holding out a bunch of grapes to welcome the viewer to a place where the imagined is real.

Everyone's holiday was cut short on August 2, when, as was internationally reported, Alexis, who was driving his new Rolls-Royce eighty-five miles an hour on the blisteringly narrow road to Figueres with Maud beside him, crashed into a tree and died instantly.[4] The lovely Maud, who, as the newspapers assiduously recorded,[5] was wearing no underwear, was disfigured and became blind in one eye. Because he was a fellow houseguest and the son of the notary of Figueres, Dalí was called upon to identify the bodies. Both he and Gala were deeply affected by this wretched accident and its impact on Roussy, who was drowning in grief.[6] They left for Portlligat as soon as possible.

A few weeks later, Gala and Salvador welcomed Edward James in Barcelona. On September 28, they all had lunch with Federico García Lorca at the cozy eighteenth-century tavern Canari de Garriga, where Federico and Salvador had spent many wild evenings during their student days. It was a joyful reunion for the two artists, who hadn't seen each other in at least seven years. Gala and Lorca got along famously. According to Dalí, who was excitedly planning future collaborations with his old friend, Federico was "so impressed he couldn't stop talking about her for five solid days."[7] The poet did not, however, cotton to James's appearance. He described Edward as "a hummingbird dressed like a soldier" and, to Salvador's everlasting regret, declined the Englishman's invitation to travel with them to Italy.[8]

Disappointed, Gala, Dalí, and James set out by themselves for Turin and thence south to the Villa Cimbrone, a restored eleventh-century residence perched high on rocky cliffs overlooking the Bay of Naples that Edward had rented from Ernest William Beckett, 2nd Baron Grimthorpe. There, in the villa's sparkling, turquoise-tiled pool, Gala swam every morning to admire the unique beauty of the site, which Edward thought was "like a landscape by Poussin."[9] From Campania, the trio motored up to Rome, where they visited James's former colleague the composer and poet Gerald Hugh Tyrwhitt-Wilson, a former British attaché to Italy. They toured the eternal city in Berners's black Rolls-Royce Phantom, and enjoyed listening to his bright, dissonant compositions, which he played on the clavichord installed in the car when they stopped to admire the view. The Italian adventure ended back in Naples, where Gala got a letter from Éluard wondering if she had received a copy of Nuits Partagées illustrated with drawings by Salvador. "It's lovely," and, Paul added truthfully, "it's an especially beautiful text, one of the most serious, one of the deepest I've ever written, about our long life, yours and mine. Dalí's work fits perfectly."[10]

When Gala and Salvador returned to Paris that October, Pierre Colle was closing his gallery, so the Dalís decided that Gala, who was already the de facto commercial side of Dalí's practice, would assume the role of her husband's official impresario in Europe. Her first move was to develop their friendship with James, who had already bought several works straight off the easel.[11]

The Dalís visited Edward for a second time in November. This time they stayed at his three-thousand-acre estate in West Sussex. Here James, inspired by the model of a Surrealist dwelling that Gala was making, hoped to turn Monkton House, his Edwin Lutyens–designed hunting lodge, into a Surrealist fantasy. Dalí persuaded his new patron to paint the exterior of the lodge deep lavender and, for James's amusement, sketched *Man Finds Lobster in Place of a Phone* (in which a man grabbing for his ringing telephone discovers to his horror that it has turned into a bright-red cooked lobster[12]).

The following May, Gala, alongside her husband, Ernst, Duchamp, and Arp, exhibited in Galerie Charles Ratton's glowingly reviewed and exceptionally well-attended "Exposition Surréaliste d'Objets." The show was organized by André Breton as an introduction to the June 15, 1936, International Surrealist Exhibition in London, where key works from the MoMA overview would be displayed. Gala's contribution, *Ladder of Love and Psyche*, was a maquette for a Surrealist apartment with a winding stair to an enlarged print of a sculpture of Cupid and Psyche. The work was a precursor to Salvador's Monkton House project and intended as a fusion of art and interior design. It was the second of the only two noncollaborative artworks Gala is known to have made. A photo of the work that was scheduled to travel to England was included in Dalí's article

"Honneur à l'objet," and published in a special edition of *Cahiers d'Art*, produced in conjunction with the show.

Before setting out for the British Isles, Gala hosted an evening vernissage of Salvador's recent work in the Villa Seurat. Her invitations, engraved with Dalí's new crest—a splash of milk stopped midmotion to form a pearly coronet—were sent out to everyone she knew or wanted to meet. According to Julien Levy, who attended the opening of this "one-day only" exhibition with Leonor Fini, "*le Tout Paris*" turned out.

As he entered the room crammed with beautiful people, Levy immediately noticed a sea change in Salvador. The "half timid, half malicious" outsider in a threadbare overcoat he had first glimpsed on the streets of Paris had disappeared. The new Salvador was "elegant, expansive, and . . . formidable." Because of what had happened with Pierre Colle, Levy was unsure of his ongoing status as Dalí's American dealer and spent some uncomfortable minutes watching the artist tour his party with Gala, clad in haute couture, by his side, playing interpreter. His discomfort turned to despair when Marie-Laure de Noailles explained that none of the stunning paintings on the walls were for sale: "The English"—Edward James—had all already bought everything.

Marie-Laure was telling the truth. On June 30, just before the vernissage, Gala had negotiated a statement of intent stipulating that all the work Dalí produced between July 1936 and July 1938 was to be the sole property of Edward James, who agreed to pay Dalí every six months. In the end, though, the evening was a success for the dealer. The Dalís wanted a show in New York and introduced James to Levy, who was thrilled to learn that although "the English" did own every piece of art in the room, all the work could be resold with Dalí's consent.

There is no question that James's calculated investment in Dalí had everything to do with his opinion of Gala. In private notes,[13] he wrote that the stylish Mme Dalí was outstanding in education, intelligence, and character. Emphasizing that she avoided idle chitchat, he added that though she never gave herself airs or pretended to know more than she did, Gala's knowledge and understanding of art was impressively encompassing. James, who could not imagine ever tiring of her company or conversation, wrote, "What a wonderful thing for an artist to find exactly the right wife for him." Gala, he felt, would make all the difference in Dalí's career: the difference between being an "interesting phenomena [sic]" or "a leading figure for the coming age."[14] That October, James commissioned the eight-by-twelve-inch portrait *Geodesic Gala*, in which Gala, viewed from behind, sparkles like a crystal in an encrusted jacket.

Gala and Salvador landed in England on June 22. Guests of a guest, they headed (with James, who had secured their invitation) straight to Wiltshire and the party Cecil Beaton was hosting at his Georgian manor house, Ashcombe. To celebrate this visit, Cecil photographed the Dalís posed beneath a pair of gilded putti fluttering over the fireplace. By the end of the week, they were back on Wimpole Street for Salvador's July 1 lecture at the New Burlington Gardens titled "Authentic Paranoiac Fantasies" and subtitled "Immersion in the Subconscious."

It was a sunny, warm day when Dalí arrived for his presentation. He was wearing a locked, old-fashioned metal-and-glass diving suit decorated like a Christmas tree.[15] Speaking in French through loudspeakers, Salvador began to address the expectant crowd of three hundred about the depths of Gala's intuitive powers. Unfortunately, the globe-shaped helmet was so airtight that the artist, who was beginning to feel hot, started to pant, and the audience had difficulty understanding his speech. He gestured for help. They applauded. He became frantic. They roared with laughter. He rolled on the ground. The spectators cheered him. Finally, Roland Penrose sent for assistance, and Gala, who always selected her husband's outfits, appeared with the key.[16] Dalí, who later claimed he had been at the point of asphyxiation when help arrived, told the excited journalists he had worn the suit "to show I was plunging down deeply into the human mind."[17] Whatever the reasoning, this widely reported near calamity, which marked the beginning of Dalí's career as a performance artist, captured the public's imagination on both sides of the Atlantic. The publicity kindled attendance at Dalí's one-man exhibition at the Alex Reid & Lefevre gallery, which had opened at the same time as the Surrealist exhibition and contained several portraits of Gala, including *Suburbs of the Paranoiac Critical Town.* By lunchtime the first day of the show, ten paintings had already been sold.[18]

The Dalís, who were pro-Republican,[19] were still enjoying London when, on July 18, they learned of Franco's right-wing uprising in Morocco, which would ignite the Spanish Civil War. Instead of going to Catalonia as usual in August, they accepted Berners's invitation to stay at his family estate, Farringdon, a "grand but not intimidating"[20] Palladian villa with a graceful, pillared porch. This beautiful old house, by all accounts an aesthete's nirvana, was located in Berkshire, just west of Oxford. It had extensive, classically landscaped gardens planted with real and paper flowers and grand, sweeping lawns dotted with joke notices like "Mangling done here" or "Defacers of this sign will be prosecuted." The dovecote housed a homing of magnificent pigeons powdered every color of the rainbow. The chandeliered orangery was filled with Aubusson rugs and large portraits of Gerald's ancestors. And the Farringdon "folly," a looming brick tower, afforded an astonishing 360-degree view of the countryside.

Gerald had built the folly in honor of the twenty-first birthday of his partner, Robert Heber-Percy, aka "Mad Boy." But Robert, who would rather have been gifted a stallion, was no fan of the turret. He did, however, appreciate Gala—so much so that, years later, when he (briefly) married Jennifer Fry, he named their only child Victoria Gala. At Farringdon, the Dalís dined with the writer Penelope Betjeman. Penelope was the wife of the soon-to-become-poet-laureate John Betjeman and the object of Evelyn Waugh's unrequited adoration. She was also Gerald's neighbor, and with her permission her horse Moti, had famously taken tea in Farringdon's dining room as a guest of Lord Berners, who invited the filly sans owner to tea. After her evening with the Dalís, Penelope, whose defining characteristic was her preference of animals to people, surprised everyone by going out of her way to report that, while Salvador's continuous conversation was endlessly irritating,[21] she found Gala both original and elegant.

On August 16, Federico García Lorca, who had been working in Granada, disappeared, almost certainly felled by a nationalist firing squad. Sensing that his friend's death was the result of his "nonconformist" sexuality, Dalí wrote, ". . . in that Civil War people killed one another not even for ideas but for personal reasons; for reasons of personality; and like myself Lorca had personality and to spare."[22] Salvador was profoundly disturbed by the murder, not just because he had lost someone he loved deeply but because he felt it could easily have happened to him. Ever protective, Gala agreed. The Dalís would not see their beloved Catalonia again for eleven years. They traveled instead.

In September Gala and Salvador visited Cortina d'Ampezzo, a small town in the Italian Alps with their new acquaintance, Peter Watson, who was Cecil Beaton's close friend. The first-generation heir to a margarine fortune, Watson was one of the richest men in England and an eager collector of Dalí's work.[23] Following their visit to the Dolomites, the trio accepted Zodiac member Mimi Pecci-Blunt's invitation to her monumental late-Renaissance palazzo in Tuscany, the Villa Reale di Marlia, which was famous throughout Italy for its potted lemon tree gardens and ornamental pools. Their fellow guest in this sun-drenched corner of paradise was the brilliant jeweler Duke Fulco di Verdura.

On December 7, 1936, Gala and Salvador arrived in New York to attend the opening of Alfred Barr's MoMA blockbuster *Fantastic Art Dada and Surrealism*, that was the second in a series of surveys "planned to present in a historical and objective manner the principal innovations of modern art."[24] The show starred *The Persistence of Memory* along with three other recently acquired Dalí paintings—*Illuminated Pleasures* (1929), *The Font* (1930), and *Puzzle of Autumn* (1935)—as well as a work lent by James from his personal collection, called *Paranoiac Face* (1936). It established Salvador as a critical player in art history.

The man on the street's response to the Dalínean imagination was enthusiastic. A window Bonwit Teller had commissioned from four artists, including Salvador (whose display, inspired by Gala, was called "She Was a Surrealist Woman"), drew a crowd standing six deep to gape at a dummy in a slinky black evening gown with a head of red roses.[25] By December, when the cover of *Time* magazine was a portrait of Dalí by Man Ray, the word "Surrealist" had become so popular in New York that people were now applying the adjective to everything from films to paint colors.[26] Gala could no longer walk down Fifth Avenue with her husband without being stared at and sometimes even stopped. Dalí was euphoric. Gala was his rock.

Gala and Levy had planned the debut of Dalí's second one-man exhibition in America to coincide with MoMA's opening, and James, who sailed in for both events, kept his word and lent Levy several works from his personal collection. Needless to say, the gallery show, which contained one of Dalí's most-praised compositions—the 1936 *Soft Construction with Boiled Beans (Premonition of Civil War)*—was a great success. By December 21, Gala had finalized another new, revised Dalí/James contract. It specified that for £2,400 (approximately $400,000 today), to be paid in monthly installments, James would purchase all of Salvador's work completed between June 1937 and June 1938. James further agreed to provide Gala with an haute couture wardrobe by Elsa Schiaparelli. It was more money than the Dalís had ever seen.

Abandoning what Salvador described in a letter to Breton as "the uninterrupted agitation"[27] of Manhattan, the Dalís were on the move. After Christmas in Quebec to enjoy the snowfall, they journeyed south with Peter Watson to Arizona, where they visited the sunny Mission San Xavier del Bac in Tucson. They sent a postcard signed by both of them to Mimi Pecci-Blunt, inviting her to visit the American desert, where Salvador was working on a film script called *Giraffes on Horseback Salad* with his friend and patron Harpo Marx, for whom he had made a real harp with barbed-wire strings as a Christmas present.[28]

Spring found them back in Europe, touring Austria with Edward James just a few months before the "Anschluss," the political merging of Austria and Germany. Here Dalí painted a dark, fiend-littered landscape called *Inventions of the Monsters*, where a double-skulled Death holding an hourglass cradles a butterfly, the Surrealist symbol of transformation and rebirth.[29] Shortly thereafter, in *Metamorphosis of Narcissus*, Dalí revisited the triangulated themes of double imagery, death, and rebirth. *Metamorphosis* is the second painting begun on the Austrian trip. It seizes the instant that Narcissus, fossilized by the view of his own reflected likeness, turns into a hand that, seeming to rise from his own watery image, holds the cracked seed that was the hunter's head. Beside him, his doppelgänger, a stone hand growing out of the earth, holds an egg from which a new narcissus flower blooms.

The painting was accompanied by an eponymous book published in 1937 by Éditions Surréalistes. Its cover image is the 1935 Cecil Beaton photograph of Gala carefully made-up, and dressed by Schiaparelli, in front of *A Couple with Their Heads Full of Clouds*.[30]

CHAPTER 16

EVERYDAY MARVELS

Gala's maquette of a Surrealist apartment, *The Ladder of Love*, paved the way for the latest James/Dalí experiment: the "Surrealization" of design and decor. In May 1936, Edward hired the architect Sir Hugh Casson to help Salvador with Monkton House's transformation. The Dalínean "improvements," which had begun in 1935, when he had the lodge painted aubergine, included sculptured blankets thrown over chimney tops, a big stained-glass clock that showed days instead of hours in the middle of the smokestack, plaster bedsheets thrown out from the windows, and bamboo columns for drain spouts, all of which Casson completed. A plan to make the drawing room feel like an out-of-breath dog's insides, replete with piped-in sound effects that mimicked panting, was, mercifully, never executed.

Casson, who was initially impressed by the sophistication of James's linen shirts and Parisian ties, disliked Salvador's flamboyance. Describing Dalí as someone who enjoyed complaining about how hard it was "to shock the world every twenty-four hours," the architect confided to Meryle Secrest that "the whole endeavor [*sic*]" was dotty and decadent.[1] Nevertheless the Monkton adventure sparked a series of delightful furniture inventions, including the scarlet "lip sofa" based on the contours of Mae West's mouth and an "arm chair" for which two long, skinny arms with yearning hands stretch to the heavens and substitute for a backrest. The lobster that made its debut on Gala's head in Dalí's 1934 portrait became a telephone with a lobster receiver. Edward James commissioned ten lobster phones, five in red and five in white. And despite Casson's misgivings, the overall results of the collaboration were more charming than they were weird. The ex–hunting lodge is now admired as one of the world's notable examples of environmental Surrealism.

In 1922, Elsa Schiaparelli, "that artist who makes clothes," as her archrival Chanel invidiously described her, landed in Paris with a sick two-year-old daughter, no money, an abundance of verve, and a wealth of ideas.[2] When Francis Picabia's wife, Gabrielle, introduced her to the great couturier Paul Poiret, Schiap, as she liked to refer to herself in the third person, immediately became his protégée. By January 1927, with Poiret's encouragement, she had launched an ingenious collection of trompe l'oeil knitwear that was featured in *Vogue*. Seven years later, she was rich enough to buy an elegant ninety-eight-room, five-story town house at 21 Place Vendôme, where she set up workrooms for her couture collection and opened a head-turning, all-black boutique, decorated by Jean-Michel Frank, on the ground floor.

Elsa's publicist, Bettina Bergery, wrote that when she first saw Gala in 1935, Gala was wearing a Schiaparelli newspaper-print blouse,[3] which was probably a gift of the designer,[4] and it is clear from photographs of the period that Gala's favorite designer in the 1930s was Elsa Schiaparelli. There is no record of the Dalís' introduction to Elsa, but Schiaparelli expert Dilys Blum believes they probably met randomly in the "everyone knows everyone" fluid high society of the interwar period.[5]

1935 is also the year Schiaparelli archivist Francesco Pastore[6] gives for the first actual Dalí/Schiaparelli collaboration: an amusing round powder compact with a black-and-white enamel telephone dial for its cover. The case became so popular that Schiap re-created it in a variety of materials, including all-white enamel and tortoiseshell. Less than a year later, when a group of coats and suits with pockets mimicking miniature drawers with dangling wood handles, specified by Dalí[7] and directly referencing his 1936 painting *Anthropomorphic Cabinet*,[8] appeared in Schiaparelli's August collection, the translation of Dalí's art to haute couture was in full swing.

Twelve months later, Gala and Salvador, who had spent July with the Faucigny-Lucinges at their bastide in Menton, hopped the train to Paris, where they would watch Gala's red lobster in Schiap's 1937–1938 fall/winter fashion show. The phallic crustacean had pride of place on the runway, where it crawled down the front of a demure white organza evening gown. Wallis Simpson, who fell in love with it, commissioned Cecil Beaton to take her picture wearing the Lobster Dress just before she became the Duchess of Windsor.

Schiaparelli's principal accessory that season was the "Shoe Hat,"[9] a large upside-down felt stiletto taken from a playful 1933 photo Gala had snapped of Dalí with a shoe on his shoulder and another on his head. Anointing the triangulation of herself, Dalí, and Schiaparelli, Gala posed for her photograph wearing the headgear she'd inspired. She is seated next to her husband's sculpture *Retrospective Bust of a Woman*. The black wool suit she is wearing, which was made to be part of her outfit,[10] is decorated by Lesage with vermilion embroideries of Dalí's Mae West lips.

In October, the Dalís moved to 88 rue de l'Université, a grand eighteenth-century limestone apartment building in Saint-Germain-des-Prés and Gala placed Edward James's gift of a polar bear dyed pink by Dalí in the flat's foyer, where it greeted their visitors like a majordomo.[11] Bergery thought this bear was so funny that she dressed it up in an orchid satin opera coat with lots of sparkly fake jewels and put it in the window of Schiaparelli's boutique, where Edward, who was on his way to a Schiap fashion show, saw it and burst into tears. That day passersby in the Place Vendôme were charmed and surprised by the sight of the tiny, elegant British gentleman in Elsa's shop window crying and hugging his old, eight-foot-tall stuffed bear.[12]

On January 17, 1938, the day Hitler declared his decision to destroy Czechoslovakia by military force, the presentation of Schiaparelli's notorious "Circus" collection coincided with the black-tie opening of the Exposition International du Surréalisme.

Elsa Schiaparelli's last prewar show featured the alchemical Tears Dress. It's a reference to Dalí's elaborately titled split canvas *Dreams Puts Her Hand on a Man's Shoulder* that was part of Schiap's personal collection. The painting contrasts the frayed flesh of a naked, wounded woman with the image of a fleeing girl dressed in tatters and poses a question about the relationship of our skin to our clothes. The gown, in which Dalí's painted wounds have become an exquisite silk print, is simultaneously a trompe l'oeil trick, an icon of transformation, and a comment on the atrocities of war. Last out on the runway was the Skeleton Gown: a long black formfitting knit adorned with quilted skeleton ribs. Like a specter of Death at the circus, it foretold frivolity's demise.

These pieces, made when the world seemed to be ending, transformed the commonplace into the strangely beautiful and changed fashion forever.[13] Thanks to the creative synergy of the Dalís and Schiaparelli, a dress was no longer merely a dress. It was an expression of vision and interiority. Fashion became art.

CHAPTER 17

END OF THE ERA

Surrealism's "last hurrah,"[1] the January 1938 Exposition Internationale du Surréalisme, was held in George Wildenstein's[2] magnifient Belle Époque Galerie des Beaux-Arts at 140 rue du Faubourg Saint-Honoré in Paris. It was supposed to be curated by Paul Éluard and André Breton. But Breton, who was always more attached to his ideology than his friendships, quarreled so fiercely with Éluard while they were organizing the exhibition that, as Paul wrote to Gala, their friendship had been shattered.[3] Dalí and Ernst were technical advisers. Man Ray masterminded the lighting, and Marcel Duchamp did his best to keep it all together.

The holistic presentation opened with Dalí's water-drenched *Taxi Pluvieux* (rain cab). It included paintings, objects, and unusually decorated rooms as well as reconfigured mannequins. The Exposition showed 229 works by 60 artists from 14 countries. By the sheer mass of its volume and inclusivity, it became so wildly popular that it rewrote exhibition history, attracting more than thirty thousand visitors in the twenty-seven days it was open.

The seventy-six-page *Dictionnaire Abrégé du Surréalisme*, with cover art by Yves Tanguy, was published by Breton and Éluard to complement the show. It contains photographs of the Surrealists and their work. A reproduction of Gala's 1931 *Surrealist Object Functioning Symbolically* appears on page forty-six with objects by Joan Miró, Méret Oppenheim, and André Breton. The dictionary part of the *Dictionnaire* is a long list of fanciful sound plays and tongue-in-cheek definitions. Under "E," for example, Éluard defines the "adjective" "Elephants," which sounds like sneezing, as "contagious," while under "G," Dalí's gag definition of the "noun" "Gala" is "a violent and sterilized woman."[4] Like all good jokes, it holds a sad kernel of truth.

Breaking free from the Surrealists' squabbling, the Dalís borrowed Lord Berner's terra-cotta town house in Rome for eight weeks starting in March. The studio, where Gala and Salvador spent most of their time, had elegant, wide Palladian windows and an astonishing view of the Forum in ruins. There they enjoyed the warbling of Tito the cook's beloved canaries as they completed *Impressions of Africa*. A complicated collection of images, the painting invokes the past to shed light on Dalí's fear of the future. Gala appears as the phantom of memory. The eternal yet ever-shifting Mauritanian Sahara provides a poetic framework for the composition and reminds the viewer of Salvador's Moorish roots.[5]

When Hitler invaded Austria, on March 11, Sigmund Freud, who had spent the past seventy years of his life in Vienna, where he was now dying of cancer, was immediately put under "close observation" by the Nazis. Six weeks later, the father of psychoanalysis, his wife, Martha, and their youngest daughter, Anna, who just that morning had been arrested and released by the Gestapo, fled Vienna. They traveled rapidly through Paris to London, where with the help of their friend the Jewish journalist Arthur Zweig they were able to rent a house at 39 Elsworthy Road in Primrose Hill.

As soon as they heard Freud was in England, the Dalís wrote to James requesting an introduction. It turned out that Zweig was also a great admirer of the Dalís, and a meeting was arranged for July 19. Salvador, as he had promised Edward, brought his most recently finished, best painting to Freud's home for inspection. To everyone's amazement, Freud, who had absolutely no interest in Surrealism, not only looked carefully at *Metamorphosis of Narcissus* but in his thank-you note to Arthur commented appreciatively: "Until now I was inclined to regard the Surrealists who seem to have adopted me as their patron saint as 100% fools (or let's rather say with alcohol, 90%). This young Spaniard with his ingenious fanatical eyes and his indubitably technically perfect mastership has suggested to me a different estimate. In fact it would be very interesting to explore analytically the growth of a picture like this. . . ."

The following day, Edward James gushed to his friend the novelist Christopher Sykes that Dr. Sigmund Freud, who at age eighty-two was adorable, had whispered to him in German, "That boy looks like a fanatic. Small wonder they are having a Civil War in Spain if they're all like that." For his part, Salvador, who had spent almost all of the audience with Freud sketching his hero, was overjoyed with the meeting.

André Breton, who was just back from hunting butterflies with Leon Trotsky in Mexico—where, with the Marxist's input, he had been rewriting the *Surrealist Manifesto* for a third time—received a letter from Salvador that week. It reported excitedly that Freud, who habitually shrugged off the superficiality of contemporary art, had compared *Metamorphosis* to the paintings of the old masters and found that *just like them*, it was worthy of analysis. This insight, Dalí wrote, had revolutionized his thinking about art.

After London, the Dalís returned to Italy, where Gala, who had just sent Cécile a check for approximately $20,000 in today's money, received a flood of letters from Paul begging her to get out of Tuscany, where the political situation was too dangerous. The poet wanted her and Dalí to join him, Nusch (now Mrs. Éluard), Picasso, and Dora Maar in Cap d'Antibes as soon as possible.[6] The decision to leave Florence was clinched by a telegram inviting them to visit Coco Chanel on the Rivera. By September they were settled into Chanel's mansion on the doorstep of Monaco, where they decamped for four months.

Bettina Ballard, *Vogue*'s fashion editor in the 1940s and 1950s, vividly remembered La Pausa as the most relaxing place she had ever experienced.[7] Indeed, Chanel was famous for spoiling her guests. The villa, which was known for its enchanting views of the Mediterranean, was perched on a hilltop in Roquebrune-Cap-Martin, encircled by 350 ancient olive trees, fragrant orange groves, and gardens bursting with roses, lavender, iris, and daisies. La Pausa was as graceful, pared down, and mysterious as the woman who built it. The grandeur of its proportions and high, elegant arches was inspired by the twelfth-century Abbaye d'Aubazine, in whose orphanage the designer had spent part of her childhood. Its capacious beige- and cream-colored great rooms and the all-white guest rooms, each with its own private entrance, were sparsely but very carefully and comfortably furnished with handsome Spanish antiques. Curtains of ivory taffeta matched the walls of the dining room, where days began at noon with an abundant buffet displayed on massive silver salvers. After lunch there was tennis, swimming, or reading. Small cars were available to take guests to town or up winding paths into the hills, which they could also explore on their own.

The dress code was elegant but very relaxed. Chanel favored her signature chic, tight sweaters over flared navy trousers and red rubber–soled espadrilles. Ever provocative, Gala dressed in Schiaparelli clothing she had either inspired or helped design.

Salvador had been given a little pink house at the bottom of the garden to use as his own private studio.[8] Here, working from the many photos of Gala taken at La Pausa, he completed *The Endless Enigma*, which is made up of the layering of six different images, including one of Gala's face, and the portrait *Gala*, where, as a tribute to her hostess, Mrs. Dalí is wearing a turban by Chanel.

Gala's tarot predicted war, although "not yet," so she lived with her ear glued to the telephone, while Salvador, inspired by the Munich Agreement,[9] chronicled the nightmares behind the headlines by painting *The Enigma of Hitler*, which juxtaposes Neville Chamberlain's impotent, furled, colorless umbrella, a sinister, equally pallid bat, and a giant, black, broken cordless telephone receiver that's oozing pus.[10] In the evenings at news hour, Coco, Gala, Salvador, and fellow guests, who, to Salvador's delight, included the great poet Pierre Reverdy, Coco's lover, Diaghilev's right hand Boris Kochno, and Jean Cocteau,[11] hovered anxiously around the radio to hear the latest news flash on Germany's progress in Eastern Europe.

Encouraged by Boris and their proximity to Monte Carlo, Salvador also resumed work on *Bacchanale* with Léonide Massine. This was the work based on Wagner's *Tannhäuser*, for which Serge Lifar and Jean-Louis de Faucigny-Lucinge had recommended Dalí as artistic director. Edward James was planning to stage it in London the following year.

Salvador had repopulated the ballet's original libretto with all manner of new characters, including Mad King Ludwig of Bavaria, Leda and the Swan, and Leopold von Sacher-Masoch. The score was to be Wagner's *Tannhäuser* overture, and Chanel, who loved Symbolism and came alive when she collaborated with artists, agreed to design the costumes.[12]

Meanwhile, Gala, who had begun planning the forthcoming exhibition in New York with Julien Levy, wrote to ask Julien's wife, Joella, to see about getting a discount at the Hotel St. Moritz on Central Park South and fretted over choosing a date for the opening. She thought a time when the well-to-do New Yorkers who could afford Salvador's paintings would be back in town from their winter vacations in Palm Beach would be best.[13] When Levy wrote back suggesting a simultaneous participation in the Surrealist pavilion at the upcoming world's fair, scheduled to open in Queens on April 30, Gala was intrigued.

Back in France after his intoxicating Mexican adventure, André Breton perused Dalí's March letter from England and found it unpleasant. Salvador's description of the afternoon with Freud made Breton jealous.[14] When, to his growing displeasure, André read that Salvador, who disagreed with Trotsky's theory of class conflict, "distrusted" what he called Breton's "compulsive organization" of the new *Manifesto*, he decided it was time for a chat. Just before he and Gala were scheduled to set sail for New York, Salvador, at Breton's invitation obediently, traveled to Paris. The meeting was an explosion.

In a vindictive, purposely damning article on the recent developments of Surrealist painting, published in the *Minotaure*'s final edition,[15] André Breton, who after Éluard's resignation had taken charge of the magazine,[16] proclaimed: "Salvador Dalí's influence is in *rapid decline*."

"It could not," he went on to explain, "have been otherwise": Dalí was "a crowd pleaser" trapped by his "never-ending need to perfect his own paradoxes."

Breton had been particularly affronted the previous February, when Salvador, who was very proud of his dark-skinned Moorish origins and may very well have also accused André of being an intellectual Simon Legree,[17] had apparently alleged that *"racial tension"* instead of *"class conflict"* was the root cause of misery in this world. According to Dalí, the "white races were by tacit agreement subjugating people of color." A scornful Breton had *"no idea"* what doors Dalí, who now "oscillated between Italy and America," thought his current assertions would open for him in those countries, but he was very clear "which doors they *will close*." After such a statement, it was impossible to imagine how independent thinkers could take Dalí seriously. Factually, Breton concluded, Dalí's art was already "profoundly" banal, and, by dint of being constantly refined and edited, his Paranoiac Critical theory had dwindled to a "crossword puzzle"–level "diversion."

In other words: Salvador Dalí was publicly expelled from the Surrealist circle.

To generate excitement for the show in his Madison Avenue gallery, Julien Levy had once again persuaded Bonwit Teller to commission two signed window displays, named respectively "Day" and "Night," as a preview to the Dalí opening. Gala and Salvador spent all night perfecting their presentation. In the "Night" window, an unkempt mannequin sprawled on a black satin bed with a taxidermied water buffalo for a headboard and a mattress made of what looked like glowing coals. The central figure of the "Day" window was a naked vintage mannequin with a red wig. Gala had unearthed the doll in a secondhand store, decorated her with pasted-on green feathers, and placed her next to an old claw-footed bathtub lined with black Persian lamb and half-filled with water.[18]

After a few hours' sleep at the St. Regis, where Edward James had arranged with the manager, Serge Obolensky, for free rooms for the Dalís—an understanding that subsequently became permanent—Gala returned to Fifth Avenue to review their creation with Levy. When she discovered to her horror that Bonwit Teller's management had replaced the old feathered doll with a new mannequin in a modern, sellable suit, she promptly sent Salvador to solve the problem. After arguing fruitlessly with the store's guard in French and Spanish, Dalí pushed his way into the display, where he somehow managed to crash the bathtub through the store's plate-glass window, narrowly missing decapitation by a falling glass shard. Gala, who according to Levy looked as though she wanted to claw someone's eyes out, shouted desperately to the dealer that they needed an *avocat* (lawyer) immediately, and to telephone Edward James.

Salvador was arrested and briefly jailed for "malicious mischief" before being released in night court by a magistrate named Louis B. Brodsky, who believed there were some "privileges that an artist with temperament [is allowed] to enjoy."[19] The incident, which generated a barrage of amusing headlines like "Store Window Fails to Stop Raging Artist,"[20] was noticed by Éluard, who read all about it in the

Paris newspapers and immediately wrote to Gala congratulating her on this magnificent publicity. It would certainly yield "wonderful results." The poet was accurate. Gala needn't have worried about Levy's attendance. There were lines around the block to get into the gallery. In fact, *Life* reported, no show had been so popular since *Whistler's Mother* had gone on display five years previously.[21] In less than fourteen days, almost all of the paintings, except *The Enigma of Hitler*, had been bought.

That April, *Harper's Bazaar* published a double-page spread devoted to Salvador and Gala by George Hoyningen-Huene, who photographed them in the tall grasses of La Pausa, at work together on *The Endless Enigma*, and also posed romantically reclining side by side in the painting *L'Instant Sublime* (*The Moment Sublime*). The text, which reads like an advertisement, bewitchingly chronicles Dalí as having painted Gala and himself "suspended in time," where they are caught inside their collective dream. This magical image, *Bazaar* tells its readers, can be seen in person alongside *Enigma* at the Julien Levy gallery. Dalí, it goes on to report, is currently working on a commissioned portrait of Lady Louis Mountbatten, whose blue eyes are painted as windows to a sapphire sea. In conclusion we learn that Salvador is not only excited about his upcoming ballet but "exploding with ideas" for his World's Fair pavilion.

Edward James agreed to underwrite half the World's Fair exhibition, but Levy had trouble coming up with backing for the other half, so it wasn't until May that the contract Gala insisted on having could actually be signed. Levy was in charge of publicity. Because the Dalís would miss the fair's debut in April 1939, he commissioned Eric Schaal to photograph Gala and Salvador working as fast as they could to complete the decorative details of a water-filled glass tank called *Dream of Venus*, which they planned to people with swimmers costumed as sirens.

The "other backer," an unnamed Midwestern businessman derisively described by Levy as "the rubber man from Chicago," wanted Dalí's installation to advertise his rubber products. This was not at all what the artist had in mind. In the wild conflict that ensued, the Dalís forced Levy to pay to have hundreds of copies of their leaflet "Declaration of the Independence of the Imagination and the Rights of Man to His Own Madness" dropped by plane all over New York City before sailing off to Europe in June. They left James behind to cope with the carnival.

On the preview night for *Dream of Venus*'s official opening, Edward threw a drinks party that turned into a revel where Levy got dead drunk on too much champagne.[22] Furious, the "rubber man," who insisted that he had "paid for publicity," which because of Levy's condition he hadn't received, blamed James for the debacle and cut him out of the deal. At the end of the day, none of this really mattered. In the eyes of the press and the public, the pavilion's mix of art, sex, and wizardry was simply breathtaking.

Vogue's June 1 issue effused, "Of all the amazing exhibits at the World's Fair, the most curious is Dalí's 'Surrealist Dream House.' Hundreds of thousands will see it and wonder . . ." Four subsequent pages of the magazine were devoted to crayon-colored sketches of a seaweed-fringed piano, an eye rimmed with "lashes that ended in telephones," and surreal beauties in sulfur-yellow, cyanide-violet, and alkali-green bathing suits "that will make splashes this season," all signed "Gala Salvador Dalí."

The following week, *Time* magazine could not contain its wonderment: "A writhing plaster castle on the outside, shrewdly combines Surrealism with sex, and proves that there is plenty of Broadway method in Dalí's madness. . . . but the real crowd-catcher [is] a long glass water tank filled with . . . living girls, nude to the waist and wearing little Gay Nineties girdles and fishnet stockings . . . these Lady "Go-divers," seen at close range and water-magnified, should win more converts to surrealism than a dozen highbrow exhibitions. . . . The 'Beach of Gala Salvador' exhibits [magnificent] exploding giraffes.

"Never publicity-shy, Dalí, who recently broke one of Bonwit Teller's Fifth Avenue windows because Bonwit Teller tampered with his display, is at present haranguing the Fair because it wouldn't let him exhibit, outside his nuthouse, a woman with the head of a fish. The Dream of Venus's press release is titled: 'Is Dalí Insane?!'"[23]

On September 3, a scant three months after the succès fou of their World's Fair extravaganza, Gala and Salvador, who by that time were back in Paris, learned that England and France had finally declared war on Germany. Leaving the capital as quickly as possible, they settled into Arcachon, near Bordeaux, where they rented a rambling colonial-style beach house on the Atlantic from a local named Henri Calvé.

With its delicate white pillars and elegant cupola, Villa Salesse was the oldest, prettiest dwelling in the community and a safe haven where they could entertain their like-minded houseguests: Coco Chanel, Marcel Duchamp, and Man Ray, who played chess in the garden. To relax a little and take her mind off current events, Gala read books about what she called "the facts of history,"[24] plotted a new escape route to the United States and did her best to quell Salvador's anxieties by feeding him foie gras, duck in orange sauce, and wonderful local oysters, which she paired with the red wines for which Bordeaux is famous.

When she turned a rabbit she had been raising for the purpose into her version of jugged hare (another regional specialty) for Sunday lunch with Jean-Michel Frank and Samuel Beckett, Leonor Fini, who had moved in next door with her clowder of kittens, accused Gala of murdering her pet.

Infamous for her love of orgies and multiple lovers of both sexes "Quand c'est Fini ça commence" (when it's Fini [finished] it begins), Éluard quipped whenever she walked into a party—Leonor was a rich, spoiled, voluptuously sensual Argentinian wild child with a mop of unruly hair, full lips, and disarming almond-shaped eyes. More important, she was a gifted and unwaveringly original, self-taught artist, and despite their differences, Gala really liked her.

In her brief essay "Portrait of Gala," Leonor, who knew Gala and Salvador from art openings in Paris, wrote that because the Dalís had no car in Arcachon, they often borrowed her housemate André Pieyre de Mandiargues's[25] large American one. She, Gala, and André frequently drove to Bordeaux together, and as they knew many of the same people, their conversations were "easy, entertaining, and sometimes brilliant." Salvador, she wrote, was a genial and flamboyant spectacle (although very self-involved and basically unapproachable). But Gala "was quick, lively, and down-to-earth and smart—but not at all intellectual." She loved to laugh, "opening her mouth wide in amusement or derision." As for her appearance, Leonor who couldn't understand why men found her sexy, described Gala as small and well-proportioned, with a strong, well-defined nose, thin lips, and glitteringly alert, tawny eyes that were placed "on the bias" across her face. But except for her large, very strong, sensual hands and her assured, masculine stride, Leonor found Mme Dalí visually unexceptional.

Of course, in Paris, there had been gossip about Gala's bitter childhood. But Gala herself never broached the subject, and since in Arcachon they were all living in a kind of untouchable bubble, there wasn't much discussion about the war either.

There were, however, many conversations about Leonor's painting. Gala asked her all kinds of questions about her techniques, and how, when she made highlights on bare skin, she managed such a smooth, glowing, sensuous surface, showing no brushstrokes. Although Gala was passionate about art, she didn't give a fig for the art scene, the fairs, or the critics, and Leonor, who echoed Gala's disdain, admired the direct, forceful, "cynical," effective, and "predatory" way her friend "seized" what she wanted.

Surprisingly, Gala did mention, if only in passing, that she might "take Leonor's career in hand" as she had Dalí's. Leonor refused to let herself take the offer seriously and would have had to think carefully about saying yes anyway, but she was ecstatic. Gala (who as "the mother of Surrealism" and Dalí's alter ego was considered *the* éminence grise of the art world) "never flattered anyone."

As usual, Gala focused on business. During one of her frequent visits to Paris to store some canvases with Tailleur Fils & Cie, she sold Peggy Guggenheim, whose London gallery had recently folded, *Birth of Liquid Desires*, a beautiful, sexually charged early Dalí, and gave her a lecture. In Gala's opinion, the American heiress needed fewer men and more money.[26] It is better, Gala told Peggy seriously, "to concentrate on just one."[27]

Leonor noticed that when Salvador was left by himself, stripped, as it were, of his wife's protection, he became helpless and timid. He insisted that Leonor walk him home across the street after dinner parties because he was afraid of the dark, and he inched closer to Coco, who welcomed his company.

One day, as Chanel told psychoanalyst Claude Delay, when Gala, who was anxious about having her papers in order, went to Bordeaux to get a last stamp on her passport, Coco coaxed Dalí away from his easel and down to the beach. They kicked off their shoes, which they lost in the sand dunes, and while Salvador did cartwheels to the roar of the ocean, Chanel imagined all their friends from the ballet, Nijinsky, and Serge Lifar floating down from the trees to dance after them.[28] Rumors that Coco and Salvador were having an affair spread like wildfire, but as Chanel, who was more than twenty years Dalí's senior, later conceded, these flirtations with the artist were really staged "*pour embêter*" (to annoy) Gala.[29] Dalí agreed. In reply to Buñuel, who had wondered if he and Gala were separating, Salvador wrote, not at all: "Gala is the only person I listen to. . . . She alone can say what my future will be."[30]

Bacchanale, which went on a tour of the United States, opened in New York on November 9 without Chanel's beautiful costumes. The designer thought it was too dangerous to let them cross the Atlantic by themselves. The choreography was credited to Léonide Massine. The libretto, costumes, and sets were all by Salvador Dalí, who chose the Venusberg from Wagner's *Tannhäuser* as the music. Venus herself, played by Nini Theilade[31] in a flesh-colored body stocking, caused a furor.

At the end of June 1940, just a few weeks after Paris had been invaded, a distraught messenger blew into town to announce that the Germans were coming to Arcachon, where they "would shoot everybody." The Dalís immediately ran off in their bathrobes, leaving, Leonor wrote, "*everything!*" They had their paintings and suitcases sent along later. Salvador was terrified. "He insisted Gala come with him."

Fini saw her friend just once after the war. By that time, Leonor remembered, Mme Dalí was very rich and living at Le Meurice in Paris. She refused to be a part of her husband's entourage. When she did show up at a party, it was for less than a minute. Tragically, Gala seemed so remote, so cocooned in the armor of her now-famous personality, that when they met again, Fini couldn't think of what to say.[32]

CHAPTER 18

EXILE

On August 6, just as Hitler was deploying Aldertag ("Eagle Day"), his futile attempt to destroy the entire British Royal Air Force, Gala and Dalí, who were by this time practically household names in New York, embarked on their third Atlantic crossing. Germany had been engaged in months of heavy bombing all over England, and war was raging from Russia to Africa, but the United States had not yet entered the fray. Thanks to Gala's careful planning, the Dalís were able to set sail for Manhattan from Lisbon on the American Export Line's *Excambion*, a cargo ship that had also been designed to carry 125 first-class passengers and had become famous during the war for its transportation of refugees. The couple had no return date in mind, and no idea of the length of their stay.

1940 had been a year of endings and separations. Their old world was in chaos. Chanel had closed up shop. With the exception of Paul and Louis Aragon, who had decided to stay behind, join the Resistance, and fight for their country, and Soupault, who had already been arrested by the Nazis for criticizing Hitler,[1] practically everyone they knew was fleeing Europe. The Surrealist coalition was over. Like Éluard, Ernst had stopped speaking to Breton. His personal life was also a mess. He had lost the love of his life, the painter Leonora Carrington, to the Mexican ambassador Renato Leduc, and was in the midst of a dysfunctional affair with Peggy Guggenheim, whom he would marry to stay in America. To make matters worse, even though he was by now a celebrated artist, Max was still having a very hard time selling his work. Breton, whom Peggy had helped escape to the United States with his family, had no aptitude for English and felt imprisoned in Manhattan. He had become a recluse, subsisting on Guggenheim's handouts and spending most of his time arguing with his current wife, Jacqueline Lamba, who would leave him in 1942 for a golden-haired, Adonis-like American photographer named David Hare. Man Ray had moved to Los Angeles, where he had relinquished photography for painting. To top it all, Marcel Duchamp, the father of twentieth-century art, claimed to have given up art altogether. He now spent his time playing chess.

As a result of wartime exigencies, the art market was crumbling. It was clear to both Gala and Dalí that in order to survive in the United States, it would be necessary to find a new solution to the old question of the meaning and purpose of cutting-edge art.

Building on the crucial endorsement from Surrealism's patron saint, Gala extended Freud's connection of Dalí to the Masters of the Renaissance as she helped her husband prepare a new speech for the admiring journalists who were sure to gather on the pier to greet their arrival in New York. Gala, who was as much a performer as her husband, had designed the moment in detail: Salvador would be wearing an immaculate pin-striped suit. She would stand demurely slightly behind him, smiling enigmatically, dressed in dove-gray Chanel.

It all went off as planned. Dalí began: "Surrealism is dead. I Dalí, its greatest exponent, am about to initiate a return to classicism. My upcoming autobiography, *The Secret Life*, will chart the pathway of my success, from enfant terrible to the *savior* of Modern Art." Clearly, he had not been named Salvador for nothing. As pencils scribbled and cameras lit up all around them, it was certain Dalí's words had the expected effect. Although the war was now foremost on everyone's minds, the *New York Times* hyped *The Secret Life*,[2] and the *Daily News*, which misunderstood the meaning of classicism, excitedly reported that Dalí would be working on "biblical painting."[3] Meanwhile, the *Pittsburgh Press*, under a headline that read "He'll Be Good," welcomed a newly well-behaved Dalí back to America.[4] Photos of the attractive couple appeared everywhere.

From New York, Gala and Salvador proceeded to install themselves chez Caresse Crosby, who was now living on an estate in Virginia that was twenty-five miles south of Fredericksburg and four from Bowling Green—a tiny town described by a Washington journalist as the size of two baseball diamonds sewn together. With the advent of the war, Caresse, along with the rest of her Lost Generation, had drifted back to the United States, where she was in the process of refurbishing Hampton Manor, which she had purchased as a place to which she could invite her European friends. The magnificent property, constructed in 1836 to designs by Thomas Jefferson, was already something of a tourist attraction. Situated on five hundred acres of fields and woodland, or, as Dalí described them, "ancient forests," serenaded by cricket song and whippoorwills, the house was extraordinarily comfortable, with a huge library, five servants, who lived in their own small houses on the property, two horses for riding, and a lake to bathe in.

When the Dalís arrived, "out of breath and still very depressed by the exodus from France and everything that had happened,"[5] the diarist Anaïs Nin and her lover Henry Miller, notorious for his sexually explicit, train-of-thought fiction, were already installed as fellow lodgers. In her memoir, *The Passionate Years*, Caresse describes the house as being divided among the guests. "Dalí [was] on one side of the Jeffersonian hallway painting from dawn 'til dusk, and Miller on the other side, completing *The Colossus at Maroussi*," the book he considered the best of his career.

In truth, Caresse's guests detested one another, and Gala, who still spoke little English, complained in her journal of how hard it was for her to get life back on track in Virginia. Simultaneously, Miller, who was particularly envious of Dalí's facile creativity, commented loudly and nastily that the Catalan's work was "the Styx, a river of neurosis that doesn't flow." In her widely read diaries, Nin described her own dismal first breakfast with the famous art couple:

> Both small in stature, they sat close together. Both were unremarkable in appearance, her in moderate tones, a little faded, and him drawn in charcoal like a child's drawing of a Spaniard, any Spaniard, except for the incredible length of his mustache. They turned towards each other for protection and reassurance, not open, trusting or at ease.[6]

Nin then went on to detail all the ways Gala eventually made it clear that Dalí was the chief guest, complaining that without ever raising her voice or appearing to be directorial, Gala managed to rearrange the workings of the entire household to the Dalís' convenience. On her end, Gala, who was vulnerable and defensive in a foreign environment, battled Nin's attempts to flirt with her husband. When Nin began speaking with Salvador in Castilian (high Spanish), which no one else understood, Gala announced firmly that Dalí would speak only French, and when Nin cooked a Spanish dish, "just for Dalí," Gala, losing her temper, remarked pointedly that she *hated* Spanish cooking.

In the long afternoons, Gala played endless chess games by the library fire with her husband, which, since Dalí's entire technique consisted of moving his king around the chessboard, she invariably won. She read to him, as was her habit while he painted; exhorted him when he was despondent and comforted him when his homesickness became unbearable. Sometimes they listened to classical music on the gramophone. And since Salvador usually stayed inside because he was afraid of the crickets, Gala took her long walks in the Virginian countryside with Caresse's proud, plumy Afghan hound named Ceilo and daydreamed about having a lover "like a strong, beautiful tree."[7] Most of her time, however, was spent working with Salvador to complete *The Secret Life*, the autobiography he had teased to the press on their arrival in Manhattan.

Caresse returned from New York with the Dalís' friend from the Villa Reale di Marlia, jewelry designer Duke Fulco di Verdura, and Caresse, Gala, and Dalí all had a good time tricking him into thinking he had been invited to stay at a haunted house. Soon recovered from the prank with the help of a bottle of Pol Roger, Verdura, Gala, and Dalí began work on designs for strange, beautiful jewelry to be shown alongside Dalí's newest masterpiece, *Daddy Longlegs of the Evening—Hope!*, at his upcoming show in Julien Levy's gallery.

At Gala's invitation, cameramen from the European newsreel Pathé-Journal arrived to check on the artist's progress and Caresse indulged Mme Dalí by prodding her prize heifer into the library, where she could be filmed. Gala also suggested that Caresse telephone *Life* magazine to photograph a grand piano dangled from a magnolia tree on a steel cable[8] and to Caresse's delight, she also was able to write in her diaries that the *New Yorker* magazine had noted, "a Virginia hostess finds it easier to swing a piano from a tree top than to make a fourth at bridge."

One windy September night, the actor Selbert Young, Caresse's soon-to-be-former third husband, turned up uninvited with his current girlfriend. They were both very drunk and, according to Gala, tried to get into bed with the Dalís, who actively resisted what they considered an assault. In a burst of inebriated fury, Selbert then threatened to destroy all of Dalí's paintings, at which point Salvador and Gala jumped out of bed, rolled up their canvases as fast as possible, and took flight.

After an overnight stay in Washington, they ended up seeking refuge with Edward James, who unsuccessfully tried to rent a house for them near the art patron Mabel Dodge's mansion in Taos, New Mexico. There James introduced them to the German-born Frieda Lawrence, a relative of World War I flying ace "The Red Baron" and a model for the heroine of her late husband's (D. H. Lawrence) scandalous novel *Lady Chatterley's Lover.* Gala, who was still off stride from fleeing both Europe and Virginia, took an immediate dislike to the widowed baroness when she wouldn't let them stay with her and accused Edward, who *was* the baroness's houseguest, of consorting with "leftovers."[9]

After a stop in Hollywood, where they visited their friend and patron Harpo Marx, whom Salvador had declared "Suralissimo" ("the ultra-Surrealist"), the Dalís returned to Hampton Manor and finished the manuscript of *The Secret Life*, which Gala personally delivered to Haakon Chevalier, an American translator highly regarded for his English renderings of French novels. Since Dalí stubbornly refused to learn English, Gala and Chevalier, who was teaching at Stanford, planned to work on the American version together when Levy's show reached California.

Dalí's final exhibition at the Julien Levy gallery opened on April 22, 1941. Gala ghostwrote the invitation, which read, "Salvador Dalí requests the pleasure of your company at his latest scandal, the beginning of his classical painting." The works were hung in antique frames, and the opulent catalog, which Gala had designed as a mini-advertisement for Salvador's upcoming autobiography, *The Secret Life*, began, "The two luckiest things that can happen to a contemporary artist are first to be Spanish, and second to be named Dalí. Both have happened to me."

Pointing out the cherub in the lower left-hand corner of a recent work *Daddy Longlegs of the Evening—Hope!*, the Dalís described the current paintings to a reporter from the *Virginia Times-Dispatch*[10] as having "more design, more balance; more precise technique." But they were not exceptionally different from Salvador's previous work, and amid the deep wartime art-market depression, the exhibition received mixed reviews.

Although he was unable to see much classicism in Dalí's new paintings, Henry McBride of the *New York Sun* loved everything about them. Calling *Piano Descending by Parachute* "on the order of Perugino," he wrote, "The one thing we positively know art mustn't do is to weary. Salvador Dalí doesn't weary anyone, even himself. Of all the refugees he continues to épater [amaze] les bourgeois over here just as well as he did there. He certainly 'épated' me. . . ." On the other side of the fence, Nicolas Calas, a leading American Surrealist, wrote an essay for the magazine *View*[11] in which he accused Dalí of being "a renegade who had changed sides for personal gain" before concluding in a nasty reprise of Breton's invective: "because [Dalí] is too frightened to be a poet, his pictures [are] lifeless."

The exhibit included society portraits, to encourage commissions, and the jewelry designed with Verdura. "In the period of the Renaissance, great artists did not restrict themselves to a single medium," Dalí noted.[12] An onyx-and-gold hoot owl and a spider caught in its own web of shimmering diamonds were especially beautiful examples. But the show didn't sell out. André and Jacqueline boycotted the opening. Max Ernst and Peggy Guggenheim were conspicuously absent as well.

In 1941, "business was not only terrible; it was nonexistent," as Levy later wrote in his book, *Memoir of an Art Gallery*.[13] To help matters, he decided to take the exhibition on a tour, which he described as "a caravan of modern art." The plan was to start at the National Arts Club in Chicago, where the Dalí exhibition ran from May 23 to June 13. Gala, who was wonderingly described in the *Chicago Daily Tribune* as very "Parisienne,"[14] wore a short black backless chiffon dress to attend her husband's vernissage with Fowler McCormick's[15] wife, Edith Rockefeller, who had lent her portrait to the show. Acting as Dalí's interpreter, Gala helped prospective buyers decipher the imagery in some of his most recent paintings, such as *Piano Descending by Parachute*, as well as very early masterpieces like *Honey is Sweeter than Blood*. From there, the tour, which was scheduled to end in Hollywood, proceeded to San Francisco.

The Golden Gate City was a disaster. Julien Levy's prime example of his experience there is the story he recounts in his memoir about a clearly moneyed woman who came into his gallery soon after the vernissage to ask him about the price of one of the canvases on display. She thought it was too expensive and inquired after the price of a drawing. When he told her what that was, she showed him her massive diamond wristwatch and said sadly, "Oh dear, if I hadn't just bought this, I would have considered it!" When Levy brought out a $15 etching, she grinned and whispered confidingly that her husband was not "really strong for art. But," she added brightly, "where did you get those attractive glass thumb tacks?" Levy just gave her one, hoping "she would take it home and sit on it."[16]

Gala and Salvador avoided San Francisco. Edward James, who was traveling with them, had suggested it might be more interesting to explore the Pacific's fabled coastline, and the Hotel Del Monte in Monterey, which was sure to be filled with interesting people. Although the Dalís didn't know anyone in the vicinity, "Night in an Enchanted Surrealist Forest," the wildly inventive, magical party conceived as a work of art Gala hosted there to benefit migrant artists, was attended by Gloria Vanderbilt, Clark Gable, Alfred Hitchcock, Bob Hope, and 996 other prominent partygoers, all of whom wanted to be part of a Dalí creation. Because the performance was filmed by several newsreels, it had enormous exposure and bewitched literally millions of filmgoers around the world. It was also a turning point for Gala, who, as she described herself, lived "as all artists do for talent's opportunity to express itself." She was beginning to realize just how vast that opportunity could be.[17]

Certainly the Dalís had made their mark on California. The

popular, instantly recognizable couple were now being shown to the best tables at Romanoff's and the Brown Derby in Los Angeles and invited to the most glamorous Hollywood parties. They rented a studio in Monterey, built of California redwoods and decorated by Gala with plain Sears, Roebuck furniture. She described it as looking "like a luxurious tourist cabin." Here, decked out in embroidered cowboy shirts, fringed leather jackets, and Native American–style moccasins, Dalí began to paint portraits of well-known bicoastal society women and, as reported by *Life* magazine, practiced saying the lone word of English that Gala had been able to teach him so far: "Connnnnnecticut." "Mrs. Dalí," the article giving Dalí's impresario a bit of well-earned credit, continued, "is self-effacing and shrewd. She pays the bills, signs the contracts, and otherwise acts as a buffer between Dalí and the world of reality. When he goes out, she carefully ties a tag to his clothing with his destination written on it so he won't get lost."

In Los Angeles, Julien's life had become "much more entertaining." He was introduced to the eminent mid-century art collectors Walter and Louise Arensberg, who lent him Marcel Duchamp's *The Bride Stripped Bare by her Bachelors, Even* for his exhibition, and was able to reconnect with Man Ray, who having returned to his first love, painting, complained that his clients only wanted photographs of themselves. Artist Tamara de Lempicka's husband, the wealthy Hungarian Baron Kuffner, provided the dealer with elegant catering inside a large circus tent in the parking lot next door to the Dalzell Hatfield Gallery, where Levy, who enjoyed watching Hollywood stars enjoy the buffet, was amused when an "outrageously drunk" John Barrymore urinated on a Max Ernst painting (but avoided the signature), and was thrilled to sell Salvador Dalí's *The Accommodations of Desire* to collector Wright Ludington, who had motored up from Ventura County, where he was one of the founders of the Santa Barbara Museum of Art.

At the end of November, it was time to go home. Levy drove across the country as speedily as possible, with his secretary, Lotte, following in a second car. By the time they reached New York's Penn Station, they could hear the news of Pearl Harbor booming out from loudspeakers all over the city. The United States was at war.

CHAPTER 19

METAMORPHOSIS

*L*abyrinth debuted at the premiere of the Ballets Russes de Monte Carlo's fourth season at Manhattan's Metropolitan Opera, on October 8, where, as John Martin described it,[1] "everybody was all dressed up on both sides of the footlights and apparently in fine fettle." Dalí's libretto was based on Theseus's battle with the Minotaur. Massine designed the choreography to music by Schubert, and Salvador contributed what Martin described as "two stunning settings" and "half a dozen mad moments." It was a perfect overture to his upcoming MoMA show.

A one-man retrospective at New York's Museum of Modern Art, whose status and size had by the end of the 1930s grown to "awesome proportions,"[2] was a singular honor reserved for less than a handful of modern and contemporary talents: Van Gogh, Toulouse-Lautrec, Matisse, and Miró,[3] all truly great artists. So it was that when the Salvador Dalí exposition opened on November 19, 1941, the prestige of being part of the Surrealist circle that had been so crucial to his success in Paris ten years earlier no longer mattered. The Dalís had become more than just internationally famous. Now that Salvador was sanctioned by MoMA, his place as a force majeure in art history was assured. It was the kind of apogee most artists work for their entire life and may never achieve. Salvador Dalí was thirty-eight.

In the thoughtfully worded introductory essay for MoMA's catalog, Monroe Wheeler, the museum's director of exhibitions and publications, addressed backlash from André Breton's vituperation. He excused Dalí's obsession with self-promotion and defined the importance of his work. "The fame of Salvador Dalí has been an issue of particular controversy for over a decade . . ." he wrote. "Dalí's conduct may be undignified, but . . . the art is a matter of dead earnest, for us no less than for him. . . . Salvador Dalí is particularly fitted for describing the tortured psychology of today."[4]

In "Dalí Goes to Town," his review of the show in *Art Digest*, Peyton Boswell Jr.[5] called Dalí "20,000 volts of uninhibited energy," observing that, "As newspapers continue to drain our nervous systems of the vitality necessary to normal living, it is peculiarly apt that The Museum of Modern Art should again bring surrealism into the spotlight. . . . [Dalí's] is a . . . nihilistic art expression, but undeniably it has the hypnotic gift for exciting even those who are surfeited with acres and acres of canvas. . . . The most voluble of Dalí's critics must credit him with these two virtues: a Dalí painting is never boring; a Dalí painting is never empty of thought. . . . Dalí," Boswell concluded, "is the voice of his time."

As soon as the retrospective closed in New York the following February, it went on to tour eight cities across the United States: Northampton, Cleveland, Indianapolis, San Francisco, Williamsburg, Utica, Detroit, and Omaha, where the exhibitions, which predictably generated mountains of newsprint, were jam-packed not only with aesthetes but with those who had never thought to set foot in a museum before. Many who knew Dalí from the popular press only were awed to discover he was also a very great painter.[6] One twenty-eight-year-old businessman in particular—A. Reynolds Morse, an enterprising Harvard Business School graduate from Denver, together with his fiancée, Eleanor Reese—headed straight for the show as soon as it reached Cleveland, in March 1942. They had read about the work in a 1939 *Life* article in which, among other images, *The Enigma of Hitler* had been reproduced. As Eleanor wrote forty years later, the combination of Dalí's superb draftsmanship, his deep, nostalgic perspectives, and his unreal subject matter amazed them. They were both entranced by his art, and, she remembered, their mutual enchantment drew them closer together. Salvador Dalí was someone they were determined to know.

The Black Star Agency[7] sent Philippe Halsman to shoot the 1941 installation at Julien Levy's gallery, and Gala immediately took to the young Latvian, who had made a name for himself as a lighting wizard with his photographs for *Paris Vogue* in the late '30s. While the MoMA show was on tour, she asked Philippe to photograph her and Dalí. The result was an image of Salvador painting Gala's forehead with a Medusa,[8] the Greek snake-haired goddess who could literally petrify enemies with her glance. It marked the birth of a collaboration that would last until Halsman's death in 1979 and the beginning of the Dalís' investigation into what Susan Sontag would express in 1973 as the "essential surrealism of photography."[9]

On March 9, 1942, *Click* magazine[10] published "The Secret Life of Dalí by Dalí: Salvador Dalí Sub-Conscious Editor for Two Pages," which began, "When the editors of *Click* decided to explore the subconscious mind with a camera they asked Salvador Dalí, to edit and stage this story." It "took two months, three photographers, the Museum of Modern Art, Madame Dalí, and a minor nervous breakdown" to get it in print. "Dalí has emerged as the first to bring the Surrealist approach to photography." *Click* boasted gleefully, "He has unlocked the inner door of the mind and thrown away the key."

The pages that follow are filled with Eric Schaal photographs directed by Dalí and combined by the artist into a montage representing his creative process. The mosaic includes a "visualization of Dalí's thoughts" rendered metaphorically through an image of Gala's profile, on which Dalí inscribes his ideas and expresses the passage of time in the form of a soft pocket watch."[11] The end note explains that Salvador's mornings are devoted to work on *The Secret Life of Salvador Dalí*, to be published in October. The collage was a trailer for the book.

The campaign to promote *The Secret Life*, which was published simultaneously in London and New York, was in full swing by September, with Gala directing it from the Beverly Hills Hotel in Los Angeles. The book itself was an exquisite object.[12] The hard covers were black cloth. Hundreds of drawings, photographs, and reproductions, including Dalí's 1929 portrait of Paul Éluard, illustrated the text. The front of the dust cover displayed a reproduction of *The Persistence of Memory*. Its verso was the sketch of a lusciously nude Gala with her back to the viewer astride a dinghy that glides through the water paddled by her bare feet. The little boat's prow is a buzzard's head sprouting a tree. Beneath the drawing a handwritten scrawl proclaims, "*Gala, celle qui avance*" ("Gala, who moves everything forward").

Praise for Dalí on the back flap included three quotations: "Dalí's imagination reminds me of an outboard motor continually running"—Picasso; "I have never seen a more complex example of a Spaniard. What a fanatic"—Sigmund Freud; and "Dalí's book is a strange picture, madly humorous, aggressive, offensive, provoking, yet unwillingly beautiful. Look for the conscious, you will find an intelligence respectful of tradition, and a heart craving for faith"—André Maurois.

It's uncertain that the last part of Maurois's endorsement has any bearing on reality. Although the Dalís were respectful of and exceptionally knowledgeable about artistic tradition, they were spiritual but never pious, and Dalí's religious interest appears to have had very little to do with what is commonly thought of as faith. Instead, it was centered on a deep curiosity about the power of religious iconography and its relationship to his personal experience: notably Gala and their life-changing love.

Similarly, although Gala collected Christian icons, frequently posed for her husband as the Madonna, and even made a pilgrimage to Santiago de Compostela Cathedral near the end of her life; she almost never went to Mass. She certainly believed in spiritual trancendance, but to quote Dalí expert Montse Aguer: "Gala was more mystical than religious."[13]

The Secret Life's fanciful beginning—"At the age of six I wanted to be a cook. At seven I wanted to be Napoleon. And my ambition has grown steadily ever since"—signals that it is not biographical in the traditional sense of the word. What it is, as was clearly intended, is a deeply amusing book filled with Cervantes-style irony, and humor that fluctuates playfully between self-aggrandizement and modesty. Reading it is a bit like having a famous dinner partner who spends the entire evening telling little stories about himself that are quirky and spellbindingly intimate, but probably not true.

Biographers have been quick to criticize its omissions: "There is not a single mention of André Breton in the entire text"[14] (which, by the way, isn't accurate, since Breton is mentioned on page twenty-one), and the occasional inexactitudes such as the (still unknown) day of Lorca's death. Meryle Secrest misses the point when she describes *The Secret Life* as the "deliberate construction of a false persona," but she hits the nail on the head when she concedes that it is "revealing" nonetheless.[15]

There is nothing false about *The Secret Life*. While, for example, it is unpalatable to believe that young Salvador actually bit into his dead pet bat to terrorize a little girl he had a crush on, it is easy to imagine and smile at the thought that he was the kind of little boy who, angry at having been ignored by the object of his affections, dreamed of doing something as outrageous as this.

Without dwelling on details of Dalí's daily existence, this "biography" is a winning mix of physical and psychical reality. It accurately paints Salvador in a way Gala knew readers would both understand

and appreciate: as a resolutely outrageous but lovable man who also just happens to be a genius. Because it's a novel masquerading as what is generally assumed to be fact, *The Secret Life* should be classified as auto-fiction, which in no way diminishes its charm or subliminal accuracy.

Crucially, *The Secret Life* shifts the focus of Dalí's story from his male colleagues Buñuel and Lorca, and his early, noir obsessions with alpha males (his father, William Tell, Hitler, and Stalin) to the women he has known: specifically, Gala. She becomes the personification of what is described as "the same feminine image that has recurred in the course of my whole love life."

Luckily Dalí's contemporaries understood that *The Secret Life* was intended as entertainment. As such, it was enthusiastically reviewed. Malcolm Cowley wrote humorously in the *New Republic* that *The Secret Life* would provide evidence "for the collapse of Western Civilization." James Thurber, who loved the theatricality of it all, noted in the *New Yorker* that Dalí had been born with "perfect scenery" and "perfect costumes" with which to stage his "small" rebellion. In the same magazine, Clifton Feldman cautioned his readers, "If you think bad boys should not be able to write their memoirs, you should not poke your nose into *The Secret Life*." The professional international hostess and syndicated columnist Elsa Maxwell praised it as "Baudelaire-ian" [*sic*], and an anonymous writer for *Time* called it "one of the most irresistible books of the year."

Although the publisher, Burton C. Hoffman, priced it extravagantly at $6 a copy,[16] *The Secret Life*, infinitely more affordable than fine art or even fine jewelry, was a little bit of genius almost everyone could own. When it became an immediate transatlantic bestseller, Gala could not have been more pleased. She had underscored Dalí's status as a great artist while rebranding him as an accessible, therefore highly marketable celebrity. In keeping with her meticulous nature, she began creating her own scrapbook of the book's reviews.

That December, while Enrico Fermi's team was initiating the first self-sustaining nuclear chain reaction below the bleachers of Stagg Field at the University of Chicago (a discovery that not only would change the world but would resonate loudly in Dalí's later art), *Esquire* magazine published a fold-out double-page spread of Salvador's most recent painting, *Nativity of a New World*. The companion article by journalist Raymond Gram Swing described this work as Dalí's homage to "America now, with its contours, canyons . . . redwood trees, and sloping hills. The central individuals," the text continues, "a cowboy and a Negro . . . are *the genuine representatives of the American of today*." All in all, the painting was, Swing concluded, "a call to courage" as well as a symbol of Dalí's own success in, and personal admiration of, the United States.

Gala did not show *Nativity of a New World* with Julien Levy, who was known exclusively as a dealer of cutting-edge art. Instead, she arranged for the opening of the next Dalí exhibition to be held in Knoedler's imposing Carrère and Hastings Beaux Arts town house at 14 East Fifty-Seventh Street in Manhattan. M. Knoedler & Co., as it was also known, was a distinguished institution dating back to 1846, when the French blue-chip print dealers Goupil & Cie opened a branch of their Paris gallery in New York. Michel Knoedler purchased the New York outpost in 1852. By the time Gala was born, the gallery had, under the direction of Charles Carstairs, who was also Henry Clay Frick's art adviser, developed a reputation as America's leading dealer of old master paintings at a time when these were understood to be blue-chip investments. Knoedler's roster of clients included Cornelius Vanderbilt Whitney, William Rockefeller, Walter P. Chrysler, J. P. Morgan, the Metropolitan Museum of Art, and the Louvre.

Nativity of a New World was only one of the works on display in the show, which ran for three weeks, from April 14 to May 5, 1943. Its real attraction was a top-class selection of Dalínean portraits from the late 1930s and early 1940s of celebrities, members of American high society, exiled European personalities, and friends. These were mounted, as would befit a Perugino, a Raphael, or da Vinci, in impressive antique frames.

Mythological references lent the work historical legitimacy. Cosmetics tycoon Helena Rubinstein (Princess Artchil Gourielli), festooned with her famous necklaces, was painted as though carved into a craggy cliff to remind the viewer of Andromeda chained to the rocks. She was hung next to Dorothy Spreckels, heiress to the Spreckels Sugar Company, sweetly seated, like a Nereid in a blue chiffon evening gown, on the back of a dolphin. Viewers could similarly admire the portrait of the famously beautiful Mrs. Harrison Williams (later Mona von Bismarck), voted the Best-Dressed Woman in the World,[17] barefoot and in rags. Mrs. Harold McCormick, trophy wife of the harvesting-machine millionaire, was portrayed as a sculpted bust on a rococo stand. And lovely Lady Louis Mountbatten, known for her handsome husband, aristocratic lineage, amusing lovers, and cozy friendships with kings, was rendered as a seductive Medusa with a crown of black hawthorn (*The Goddess Tree*) embellished with small jewel-like serpents. In contrast, Dame Judith Anderson, who played Mrs. Danvers, the mad housekeeper, in the 1940 film *Rebecca*, appears as herself.

Dalí also deployed artistic and literary allusions. In one of his few portraits of men, his patron the Marquis George de Cuevas, a famous ballet impresario, looks out past the sands of a foam-lapped beach where he is posed in front of a Cyprus tree/burial chamber underneath a green sky. The painting's setting references Swiss Symbolist Arnold Böcklin's *Isle of the Dead* (1880) and Charles Baudelaire's famous "A Voyage to Cythera" (1857).

One of Salvador's earliest, most heartwarming portraits, the little 1934 profile of Gala with olive-leaf locks, hung in the last room, rounding out a display whose virtuosic, deliberately head-turning iconography valorized his clients as timeless historical figures by positioning Dalí in the tradition of Raphael, Titian, and Ingres.

In a two-column anonymous review titled "Done the Dalí Way," *Art Digest*[18] commented, "Those who can forget *The Secret Life of Salvador Dalí* will find portraiture lifted to an unforgettable plane in these carefully charted and meticulously recorded studies of the Upper Crust, on view until May 5, together with a bewildering collection of Dalí's classical and strangely imaginative drawings. As usual anything goes."

Edward Alden of the *New York Times* agreed: "Those familiar with the exploits of this extraordinary Spanish artist (and who by now is not?) will feel safe in deciding even before [seeing them] that these portraits won't prove portraits in the traditional sense of the word."

When, as had become their habit, the Dalís arrived at the St. Regis that autumn, where they were given the presidential suite and an adjoining room for Salvador's studio free of charge, they found they were invited even more than usual by New York's upper crust. Now "everyone" wanted to sit for the great painter. One of their hosts was William I. Nichols, the former editor of *This Week* magazine, which had 1.5 million subscribers. At the suggestion of columnist Leonard Lyons, Nichols had put a photograph of a Dalí painting of bread on the cover. *This Week*'s covers were usually foliage or football players, so the editor remembered this as a "radical" move, and perhaps one of the Dalís' first experiences with a mass audience.

William's French wife, Marie-Thérèse, who thought it would be lovely to sit for the painter, invited the Dalís for dinner but found herself put off by the artist, whom she described as "too elegant." His relationship with Gala was equally distressing. She remembered: it was "just like the Duke and Duchess of Windsor." Marie-Thérèse had never seen a man so "much in thrall of a woman. In the middle of dinner one would observe him consulting notes on bits of paper she had given him. Or he would turn to her and ask: 'What do I say? What do I say?'" Gala, who did all the bargaining, "had a way of jabbing her finger at you. She said, 'We will give you a special price,' but she wanted cash on the line."[19]

Years later, in 1954, one of the portraits, for which Dalí charged approximately $25,000 (a little over $300,000 today), actually did backfire. When Ann Woodward, a former showgirl and the wife of William Woodward Jr., heir to the Hanover Bank fortune (Manufacturers Hanover) saw the icy, predatory gleam in the eyes of her likeness, she refused to accept the picture. Bill would have preferred to avoid controversy by simply paying for the work and hiding it in a closet, but Ann, panic-stricken by the accuracy of Salvador's image, was obstinate. During the ensuing media tsunami, Gala was obliged to sue for the previously agreed-upon price of the commissioned portrait, of which the Dalís recovered only $7,000, less than a quarter of what they were owed. When on October 30, 1955, in what the tabloids described as "The Shooting of the Century," Ann killed Bill with her rifle, Dalí's intuition about her character was proved accurate.

For the most part, however, Dalí's subjects were flattered to be associated with his famous Surrealist symbols. Amazement and outrage expressed by the press were welcomed by both subject and artist as intimations of fame, and by this time, fans and critics of the Dalís agreed on one thing: In Europe, Dalí's work had been supported by intellectuals, but in the United States, he had a wider appeal. Even if the public didn't understand all their nuances, the poetry and emotion of Dalí's paintings was attractive to them.[20]

Twenty years later, Andy Warhol would capitalize on Gala's idea. In search of a way to monetize the critical success of his controversial 1967 silk screens of Elizabeth Taylor and Marilyn Monroe, Warhol offered to make similar portraits for paying customers and was enthusiastically taken up by such influencers of their time as the Pop Art collector Ethel Scull, art-world doyenne Emily Fisher Landau, and fashion designers Carolina Herrera and Yves Saint Laurent.

By March 21, 1943, the now-married Morses had saved up enough money to acquire *Araignée du Soir Espoir* (*Daddy Longlegs of the Evening—*

Hope!), the first painting Dalí made in 1940, when he and Gala had just moved into Caresse Crosby's Virginia estate. They negotiated the purchase on the phone with art dealer George Keller even though they had never actually seen the painting, which they only knew from its photograph in *The Secret Life*. Eleanor remembered that the elaborately carved antique frame, chosen by the artist himself, cost twice as much as the canvas. When they bought *Archaeological Reminiscence of Millet's Angelus* (1934) just a few weeks later, Keller suggested they might like to meet its maker.

Eleanor wrote to the Dalís in New York, requesting an interview, and Gala answered in French from the St. Regis, inviting them to the hotel on April 13. The meeting, which marked a turning point in the lives of the Morses, took place at the St. Regis's King Cole Bar, beneath Maxfield Parrish's vibrant thirty-foot, 1906 Art Nouveau mural of Old King Cole and his brightly costumed, fawning attendants.

Eleanor knew nothing about Catalonia or, for that matter, any other region of Spain, and Reynolds, who couldn't speak French, had a horrible time decoding Dalí's idiosyncratic personal version of that language. Nonetheless, there was a lot of congeniality on both sides. An entente cordiale was rapidly achieved. Eleanor and Reynolds, who made a point of attending every Dalí vernissage, started to acquire more and more work. At first they found Gala's harsh Russian accent off-putting. Her habit of being affronted when someone suggested she might be asking too much for a painting was intimidating as well, but her intelligence won them over, and soon they were buying directly from her. Within five years the Morses, who began seeing Gala and Salvador frequently, were well on their way to forming one of the world's most outstanding collections of Dalí's work. In time they would replace Edward James as the Dalís' most important art patrons.

In its June 1943 "People Are Talking About" section, *Vogue* published a full-page Horst P. Horst portrait of Gala in her own dress in ers .Ga

front of a reproduction of Dalí's new painting *The Triumph of Tourbillion*. The accompanying article describes Mme Dalí as the force behind the Dalís' two most recent sucesses: *The Secret Life* and the Knoedler portrait show. Gala, the copy goes on to inform us, was a mover and shaker in Surrealist circles and is currently her husband's indispensable spiritual collaborator. It concludes, "Many of [Dalí's] works are signed with a curious square signature decipherable as 'Gala Dalí.'"

CHAPTER 20

EXPRESSIONS OF TALENT

By the time the June issue of *Vogue* hit the newsstands, Gala and Salvador, who had accepted John D. Rockefeller's granddaughter Margaret de Cuevas's invitation to spend the summer in Franconia, New Hampshire, were ensconced in her luxuriously minimal hideaway in the heart of the White Mountains, where it was surrounded by forests of beech and sugar-maple trees and serenaded by Flume Gorge's rushing rill.[1]

Margaret, the first woman accepted to study at Oxford, had been an original member of The Zodiac. Her husband, George, founder of the International Ballet, was producing Salvador Dalí's ballet *Mad Tristan*, and together the de Cuevases were ideally sympathetic, indulgent hosts.

Their closest neighbor, Robert Frost (who had just won his fourth Pulitzer Prize, for *A Witness Tree*), was plainly right when he wrote, "Literature begins with geography," because it took the Dalís just four months of fourteen-hour writing days to produce one of their most complicated works, a polygonal 413-page epic novel aptly named *Masked Faces*. As both Gala and Salvador adored mind games, they certainly had a wonderful time writing it.

Although it's much longer and more complex than Huysmans's *A Rebours* and Oscar Wilde's *The Picture of Dorian Gray*, *Masked Faces*, chockablock with multifaceted allusions, is clearly in dialogue with both these great works. It also owes much to Raymond Radiguet's succès de scandale, *Le Bal du Comte d'Orgel*,[2] and it makes frequent allusions to this classic 1930s novella.

Le Bal du Comte d'Orgel, which mocks the superficiality of the French upper crust, has been defined as *"un roman où c'est la psychologie qui est romanesque"* ("a novel in which psychology is the romance") because the real action in its narrative takes place in the minds of the protagonists.[3] The subject of the story is the powerful illicit attraction between a young nobleman, François de Séryeuse, and his beautiful Creole cousin Mahaut, who is married to the glittering Count Ann d'Orgel. This love is never consummated. And when, after an agonizing deliberation, Mahaut finally confesses her mental and emotional transgression to her husband, d'Orgel not only refuses to countenance its existence but complains that her silly conversation is making them late for the ball he's hosting that night.

Similarly, *Masked Faces*, which is often characterized as a roman à clef, details an unconsummated love affair and parodies the absurdly decadent crowd the Dalís frequented in Europe. Like Radiguet's novella, it is filled with acute and amusing caricatures of famous social and cultural figures who could easily identify themselves and enjoyed being a part of the work.

Thus in the Dalí's novel Count Hervé de Grandsailles, the wrongheaded, ultra-masculine protagonist who masterminds grand balls and can't resist trying to control everything, takes after both the fictional Comte d'Orgel *and* the flesh-and-blood art patron Étienne de Beaumont, who was famous for organizing his lavish parties "to annoy the uninvited." The rich American lesbian Veronica is modeled on the playwright Hoytie Wiborg, whose sister Sara and her husband, artist Gerald Murphy, were friends of F. Scott Fitzgerald and Jean Cocteau. Coco Chanel makes her entrance as the opium eater Cécile Goudreau, whose den is filled with pure-gold drug-smoking accessories and cluttered with chinchilla-upholstered banquettes. Cécile's supplier: costume and set designer Bébé Bèrard, who was Salvador's rival, has a cameo as himself. Solange de Cléda, the heroine of *Masked Faces*, who spends the entire four hundred–plus pages of the narrative in futile love with Hervé (who loves her back even more unsuccessfully), was a mix of Bettina Bergery and Roussy Sert. The latter, however, is more likely represented by a hapless copper-blond Polish aristocrat named Betka, who is loved by Veronica and introduced to heroin by the birdlike Goudreau. Finally, according to *Faces* scholar Esther Álvarez, Dr. Alcan, Solange's physician, is based on the controversial psychologist Jacques Lacan, best known for his identification of an "alienated imaginary" psychic order.[4]

If it all sounds complicated, that's because it is. Social satire is just one of the layers of *Faces*, which spans ten years, from 1934 to just before the resolution of World War II in 1944. The central theme of the novel, which, according to Alvarez, owes more to medieval allegories *The Romance of the Rose* and *Tristan* than it does to the nineteenth- and twentieth-century fiction obviously referenced by the Dalís, is LOVE.

In *Masked Faces*, the emphasis on psychological rather than physical love proffered by Radiguet is further refined. As in *The Romance of the Rose*, it is described in each one of its possible aspects. By the end of the book, it has morphed into a kind of tantric/psychic link between the two lovers, who can influence each other telepathically. The novel's finale reveals their physically unconsummated passion to be (at least for its heroine, Solange de Cléda) both deadly and revivifying. To please her lover, Solange dies by simply willing her own death. She is reborn as a tree in the cork oak forest that overspreads the Grandsailles ancestral grounds. Accordingly, this phoenixlike, eternal woodland becomes the Cléda (*clé*, "key," of Dalí/Gala.) Gala herself is depicted in the book's frontispiece as Solange, the oak tree nymph.

Masked Faces was published by Dial Press in 1944 and did not sell well in the United States. The tide of taste had turned during the war years, and aristocratic Europeans were out of fashion.

The *New York Times'* number one fiction bestseller in 1943 was *The Robe* by Lutheran minister Lloyd C. Douglas. Its subject is a Roman soldier who, after the Crucifixion, wins Christ's garment in a gambling game. In 1944, *The Robe* was replaced at the top of the list by Betty Smith's poetic *A Tree Grows in Brooklyn*, which charts an impoverished young American girl's coming-of-age in the slums of New York. Both these books are about as far as you can get from *Masked Faces'* arcane love potions: dabblings in devilry and other dissolute doings of Europe's entitled as mocked by Gala and Salvador. Reviews were mixed.

An anonymous writer for *Newsweek* suggested that if all Frenchmen were like Grandsailles, "It would be better not to send Americans to their deaths trying to liberate them from the Nazis."[5] And in the *New Yorker*, Edmund Wilson, who called Salvador a very clever fellow and admired the work's satire, still felt that it would be better for him to stick to his original métier.[6]

The novel's fascinating attempt to address age-old conceits in terms of modern history and the fact that the work's refrain is a dream of a post–World War II Renaissance[7] went straight over the reviewers' heads. None of this daunted Gala, who, probably accurately, concluded that as long as their novel was widely reviewed, it could be considered a success. Despite, or perhaps because of, its involvedness, *Masked Faces* is still studied today.

Writing was, of course, only one aspect of the Dalís' new broadening of artistic expression. As early as the mid-1930s, they had begun to diversify: designing clothing, furniture, accessories, and decorative objects. Expanding the practice did more than just broaden the Dalís' audience; it also informed and enriched their creative vision. Encouraged by the widespread appreciation of the American public (starting in 1940, they had been obliged to sign with a clippings agency just to keep up with everything published about them the length and breadth of America), Gala increasingly channeled their efforts into more commercially renumerative directions.

The result of all this diversification was that Gala soon found herself running an increasingly complex, very lucrative business. As she modestly explained to her stepfather, Dimitri Ilyich Gomberg, in a draft letter dated 1945, she handled "everything related to the practical part of our life because he, as you can see, is totally immersed in the creative world, in his work. He is not able to deal with these trifles."[8] By the mid-1940s, she was able to negotiate $2,500 ($54,000+) for one advertisement, $5,000 ($110,000+) for book illustrations, and $600 ($12,000+) for a magazine reproduction of one of Salvador's paintings. Although she claimed to be "not very good" at practicalities herself, Gala had a Midas touch, and Salvador renamed her "Soloizé": the Russian word for "my gold."[9]

In 1939, when André Breton invented the nickname Avida Dollars to describe Dalí's cupidity, he meant that Salvador was willing to debase his talent for cash. It's an opinion that, perhaps because of the catchiness of the anagram, has been widely parroted. As it turned out, however, a good deal of the Dalís' so-called commercial work negotiated by Gala was so exquisite and so perfectly thought out that, like the designs made in collaboration with Schiaparelli in the 1930s,[10] it actually elevated "design" to the level of "art." Some examples: A 1940 limited-edition seven-inch Steuben bowl of lead crystal takes on a double meaning when it is intricately hand-etched with the woman's body from Dalí's 1938 ink drawing *City of Drawers*. A 1945 advertisement for Bryan's Hoisery is really a portrait of Pegasus, whose wings are made of stockinged legs. Darling putti cavort on a raspberry colored Dalí lip sofa in the announcement for Schiaparelli's lipstick Red, while the 1957 poster for the American Silk Congress proffers a medley of exotic butterflies.

Gala also encouraged Salvador, as she had Max twenty years earlier, to design objects to sell. Among the first designs, three poetically titled men's ties, created exclusively for Marshall Field—"Symphonic Spring," "Birth of Knowledge," and "Gypsy Mandolin"[11]—were planned to be included, along with a sterling-silver lipstick case in the shape of a "bird in the hand" (the starling's head, which is the base of the lipstick, screws out from the body and wings) and designs by Alexander Calder, Juan Gris, Isamu Noguchi, and Georgia O'Keeffe, in MoMA's 1950 touring show "The Artist and the Decorative Arts," which was a celebration of contemporary industrial art.

In 1967, Air India was so pleased with a limited-edition ceramic ashtray in the shape of a shell wrapped with a serpent, designed by Salvador for their first-class customers, that they sent the Dalís a baby elephant as a thank-you present. (Dalí and Gala regifted the calf to the Barcelona Zoo.)[12] And as late as 1985, a crystal bottle with an elongated stopper for "Dalí perfume" was really a limited (5,000) edition small sculpture version of Dalí's painting of a nose in *Apparition of the Face of "Aphrodite in Cnidus."* It was priced at $3,000 a bottle.[13]

Gala had enjoyed meeting Jack Warner at a Beverly Hills lunch in the 1930s,[14] and, at her instigation, Dalí also made more inroads in Hollywood. He was commissioned to design the nightmare scenes in Alfred Hitchcock's 1944 psychological thriller *Spellbound* (for approximately $70,000 in today's dollars). He also collaborated with their friend Walt Disney on parts of *Fantasia*[15] and drew *Destino*, a seven-minute animated short about Chronos, the god of time, and his doomed infatuation with a mortal woman. This animation was not completed until many years later, but when the Walt Disney Company did finally release *Destino*, in 2003, it received an Academy Award nomination.

That Gala was *the* key player in all of these contracts was common knowledge. If Dalí, who still thought in terms of European money, quoted a price for a painting that she felt was too low, Gala would simply tell the prospective buyer he meant dollars, not pesetas (the exchange rate in the 1940s was approximately eleven pesetas to the dollar). The real bargaining never began before Gala entered the conversation. *Script* magazine, which chronicled celebrity contracts in the

1940s, described the conclusion of negotiations for Dalí's 1947 illustrations of *Don Quixote*: "The overall fee had been settled but the publisher suddenly asked: 'How many full-page color illustrations do you intend to supply?' Dalí, who speaks no English, at least during business hours, held up five fingers. The publisher picked up his hat and coat and said, 'Anyhow it's been fun.' Mrs. Dalí, who acts as her husband's agent, saved the day with her fast come-back: 'When Dalí says five he means ten.'"[16]

In a subsequent interview for the same article, Gala asserted her proficiency in public relations. *Script* asked Salvador to name the greatest living artist. The painter, who was clearly uncomfortable with the question, answered haltingly that he admired Pablo Picasso and Giorgio de Chirico. When the same question was put to Gala, she announced firmly, "Dalí is the very first and greatest of all." "I agree," snapped her clearly relieved husband.

Unlike Salvador, who never made the effort, Gala enjoyed being self-sufficient. As soon as she arrived in the United States, where everyone drove everywhere, she applied for a driver's license. By March 1944, the couple, who enjoyed spending the spring in California, had acquired a sleek black Cadillac, which Dalí customized with tinted windows and flowery Louis XVI door handles. In May, when Gomberg wrote to Gala to tell her that her mother was dying, Gala exorcised her sorrow by driving her limousine.

In the morning, after dropping Salvador at the studio, Gala sped along the precipitous coastline, whirring past wind-twisted pines and rocky inlets where the gulls cried and sea lions growled as they surfed the high waves of the Pacific. Driving gave her time to remember her childhood in Moscow and mourn the mother she hadn't seen for over thirty years. The mother she had always loved and who had always loved her was dying on the other side of an unimaginably vast ocean during history's most lethal battle: the siege of Leningrad.[17] The Cadillac was Gala's salvation. At five foot three, she was so tiny she could barely peer over the dashboard, but she was an expert driver. She felt in charge at the wheel and less like the stranger in a strange land she had been for most of her life.

Through it all, Gala was careful to keep up appearances. She had always had a unique, elegant figure and a talent for fashion, and she was gifted outfits from the most prestigious houses: Christian Dior, Elizabeth Arden, and her old friend Schiaparelli. Even Adrian, Hollywood's go-to designer, who featured Salvador's "rock print" in his 1947 spring collection, designed a one-of-a-kind dress for her. Like many Adrian designs, it was gingham, channeling his most famous costume: Dorothy's blue dress in *The Wizard of Oz*. But Gala, who had no interest in looking like a ten-year-farm girl from Kansas, refused to wear it.[18] In contrast, she loved luxurious, sophisticated simplicity, and the reopening of her friend Coco Chanel's couture house in 1954 was cause for celebration. In 1960, Gala had an evening dress, wittily decorated with Salvador's drawings for a new French edition of Cervantes's *Don Quichotte*,[19] specially made by the Alexandrian couturier Jean Dessès. She wore it in Venice to the opening of Maurice Béjart's ballet *Gala*, which was dedicated to her.

Just as Gala worked at being attractive, she enjoyed testing her powers. In his memoir *A Not-So-Still Life*, Max Ernst's son Jimmy recounts running into her in New York, where he was working for Julien Levy. At first sight, Jimmy thought Gala seemed rather like an "unchaste Diana." Suddenly overcome by what he describes as "an intense curiosity" about this woman who had destroyed his parents' marriage and changed his life so radically, he blushingly agreed to an afternoon of shopping and lunching with her. Gala took him to the Russian Tea Room, where she ordered in Russian and brushed his leg with her foot under the table. While Jimmy savored his blinis with sour cream and beef Stroganoff, Gala regaled him with stories of the Tyrol, where, as she said, Éluard and his father had become such close friends that they were willing to share any experience in the world.

Gala at about eight with her siblings, Lidia, Vadim ("Vadka"), and Nicolai ("Kola"), circa 1904. © *Fundació Gala–Salvador Dalí, Figueres*

Paul Éluard as a little boy, surrounded by his family, probably in Saint-Denis. He is holding a book prize for poetry recitation and standing next to his grandmother, who was known as an excellent cook. Behind him, to the right, are his mother and father. © *Succession Paul Éluard*

Éluard and Gala disguised as twin Pierrots for a bal masqué at the
Clavadel Sanatorium, Davos, Switzerland, circa 1913. Éluard dedicated
the picture to André Breton, writing, "Paul dressed as Gala."
© *Succession Paul Éluard, Musée d'art et d'histoire Paul Eluard–Saint-Denis*

Clavadel Sanatorium, Davos. Located in the sunniest part of the Davos region, this was the clinic where Eugène Grindel, the future Paul Éluard, and Gala first met in 1912. Still open today as a rehabilitation clinic, it is the same sanitarium described by Thomas Mann in *The Magic Mountain*. *Public domain*

Paul Éluard, Gala, and their daughter, Cécile, 1929. This
picture was probably taken by the Éluards' friend René Crevel
in Leysin, Switzerland, after a short stay in the sanitarium
in Arosa. © *Succession Paul Éluard/private collection*

Gala playing with a squirrel, photographed by
Man Ray, circa 1925. © *Succession Paul Éluard*

Portrait of Max Ernst, 1925–30. Berenice Abbott learned photography as an assistant in Man Ray's studio in Paris from 1923 to 1925. Max Ernst sat for her more than once when she was living there. © *Berenice Abbott*

The Dada Group, Cologne, Germany, 1922. *Left to right:* Gala,
Max Ernst, Jean Arp, Louise Straus, Johannes Theodor Baargeld
(a German Painter who founded the Cologne branch of Dada with Ernst).
Max and Louise's son, Jimmy "Minimax," is on Baargeld's lap. Gala is
wearing Max Ernst's Croix de Guerre, and the sexual tension between
them is palpable. © *Berenice Abbott/Musée d'art et d'histoire
Paul Éluard—Saint-Denis. Cliché: I. Andréani*

Dalí as a little boy in Pepito Pixtot's garden in Figueres.
Salvador loved this garden, which he described as
"one of the most marvelous places" of his childhood.
© *Fundació Gala–Salvador Dalí, Figueres/private collection*

The Parisian Surrealist group around André Breton, circa 1930, photographed by Man Ray. *Left to right:* Tristan Tzara, Paul Éluard, André Breton, Jean Arp, Salvador Dalí, Yves Tanguy, Max Ernst, René Crevel, and Man Ray. © *Telimages/Man Ray Trust/ADAGP/ARS*

Gala and Éluard in Cadaqués, August 1930. That summer,
Éluard, with Nusch and René Char, visited Gala and
Dalí on the Costa Brava. © *Succession Paul Éluard*

Gala wearing the *Shoe Hat* and *Lips Jacket,* which she inspired. They were designed by Schiaparelli in collaboration with Dalí in 1938. Photograph by André Caillet. © *Salvador Dalí, Fundació Gala–Salvador Dalí, Figueres*

Gala and Dalí fleeing the war in Europe and arriving in New York in 1940. The original caption reads: "Salvador Dali, the noted Surrealist artist, and his wife, Gala, are shown arriving in New York City, on August 17th, on the American export liner *Excambion* from Lisbon." *Getty Images*

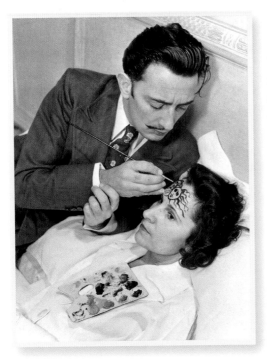

While Philippe Halsman was in New York in 1942, Gala asked him to photograph her and Dalí. The original *Toronto Star* caption to the picture, taken in their suite at the St. Regis in New York, reads: "On his wife's forehead, Salvador Dali paints the head of Medusa, one of the three snaky-haired Gorgon sisters whose glance turned into stone everything on which it rested. Mrs. Dali looks serious, as well she might, at the thought of carrying wherever she goes a threat like that." *Getty Images*

Gala and Dalí, sighted at the St. Regis in New York,
February 6, 1968. *Getty Images*

Salvador Dalí, *Galarina*, 1947. Of this famous portrait of Gala
at fifty, Dalí wrote, "Begun in 1944, this work was completed
in six months, working three hours a day. I called it *Galarina*,
because Gala is to me what *La Fornarina* was to Raphael."

Gala with her favorite Chanel bow, posing for Dalí's painting *Battle in the Clouds*, 1979. Photograph by Robert Descharnes. © *Descharnes & Descharnes sarl*

Salvador Dalí, *Portrait of Gala with Lobster*, circa 1933. Oil on plywood panel, 20 × 22.5 cm. Signed lower right at a later date "Salvador Dalí." This painting was made to be shown as an example of the kind of portraits Dalí could achieve. The lobster was to become one of Salvador's most famous symbols. Cat. no. 330. © *Salvador Dalí, Fundació Gala–Salvador Dalí, Figueres/ private collection*

Salvador Dalí, *Suburbs of the "Paranoiac-Critical Town,"* 1935. Oil on wood panel, 46 × 66 cm. Signed and dated lower right: "Gala Salvador Dalí/1935." Former collection of Edward James. Cat. no. P 434. © *Salvador Dalí, Fundació Gala–Salvador Dalí, Figueres/private collection*

Salvador Dalí, *Gala Nude from Behind*, circa 1960. Oil on canvas, 41 × 31.5 cm. Unsigned and undated. Cat. no. 769.
© *Salvador Dalí, Fundació Gala– Salvador Dalí, Figueres*

It was all wonderful until she suggested he might like to come back to the St. Regis, and Jimmy panicked, bolting out onto Fifty-Seventh Street. When he got up the nerve to tell Julien about his lunch with Mme Dalí, the dealer countered, "You should have gone with her. You don't know what you missed."[20]

Back in France, Éluard, who had clear memories of what he was missing, pined for Gala. He hadn't had any news of his ex-wife since their daughter had visited Arcachon just before the Dalís left for America, and it wasn't until May 1945, when the war ended in Europe, that he heard from her again. As soon as she could, Gala sent both Paul and Cécile care packages, which were very much appreciated, especially since commodities such as toothpaste and coffee beans were scarce in Paris.

During the Occupation, Paul and Nusch had gone into hiding. They felt lucky to have escaped the gestapo. Now, thanks to his subversive ode "Liberté," thousands of copies of which British bomber pilots had parachuted all over France during the Occupation, Paul had become "The Poet of Freedom," France's most famous author and a cultural ambassador for his country. He was very happy to report in his letters that, although Nusch was now dyeing her gray hair black, while he had become "very blond" and was so sick he had to stay in bed to do his writing, he had been getting "pretty good change" for his poems. In fact, since the Liberation, he had been making more than he ever dreamed he could earn. "According to our 1917 agreement," he wrote gleefully, "I owe you a fortune."[21]

The blow of the atomic explosions in Hiroshima and Nagasaki on the sixth and ninth of August 1945 shocked both the Dalís and reverberated in Salvador's art. His first work on this subject, *Uranium and Atomica Melancholica Idyll* (1945), attempts to render the power of the atom by using his characteristic soft shapes to illumi nate a reality beyond the images of airplanes, bombs, and explosions in the composition. *Melancholica Idyll* marks the debut of Salvador's mystical/nuclear exploration in which the disintegration of the atom is contrasted with religious icons. It was included in "Recent Paintings by Salvador Dalí," a show Gala opened with fanfare on November 20, 1945, in Midtown Manhattan at the Bignou Gallery, a branch of an eponymous Paris establishment known for its stable of major modern artists: Paul Gauguin, Henri Matisse, and Amedeo Modigliani.

The exhibition included eleven oil paintings, drawings, and watercolors and a selection of illustrations for Maurice Sandoz's *The Maze* and *The Biography of Benvenuto Cellini*, which were described as "miraculous" by Carlyle Burrows in the *New York Herald Tribune*.[22, 23]

The centerpiece of "Recent Paintings" was *Galarina*. This masterpiece is the indelible image of fifty-one-year-old Gala, devoid of makeup, in a partially unbuttoned plain oxford button-down shirt, with her beautiful left breast defiantly exposed.

Fulfilling the prediction made five years earlier, when the Dalís were disembarking in New York, *Galarina* pays homage to classicism and links the Renaissance to the twentieth century. Unlike the symbol-laden portraits the Dalís exhibited at Knoedler, however, in *Galarina* the sophisticated brushwork and the deceptive simplicity of image speak for themselves.

Dalí wrote that the portrait's light play comes from Vermeer's photorealistic painterly technique (chiaroscuro), where effects of brightness and shadow allow the artist to highlight minute details and focus the work on just one moment.[24] The rest of the story is supplied by the viewer's experience.

The Latin-sounding title, which ends with the Italian suffix "*rina*," blurs the border between Spain and Italy. According to Dalí, the name *Galarina* is directly indebted to *La Fornarina*, Raphael's erotic portrait of his mistress Margherita Luti, which also highlights its subject's bare left breast.

The three-quarter-length compositions of *Galarina* and *La Forna-*

rina both reference da Vinci's enigmatic *Mona Lisa*. As in Raphael and da Vinci, the real force of Dalí's painting is the contradiction in the image itself. In *Galarina*, the silky, delicate curve of Gala's nurturing breast clashes with her tight, determined lips and the commanding intensity in her close-set eyes. As in da Vinci's androgynous portrait, it's *Galarina's* mismatches that mesmerize.

Describing his own work, Dalí told Edward Alden Jewell of the *New York Times*,[25] "Gala has become my basket of bread." According to the artist, Gala's breast was the bread, and her interlaced arms form the basket. This insight contains a kernel of mischief. In *La Fornarina*, the artist's signature wraps his mistress's upper left arm like a bracelet, but in *Galarina* an opulently jeweled serpent, which was Edward James's gift to Gala following a night spent with her husband, is entwined around her left wrist.[26]

"Recent Paintings" also marked the debut of the *Dalí News*, a spoof newspaper whose name was an intentional and immediately recognizable pun on the *New York Daily News*. Above the title, a crown with a scroll read, "GALA FIRST." The four-page publication, which chronicled Dalí's deeds, projects, and miracles, included an article called "The Gala Names," which lists Salvador's various loving descriptions of her many iterations, such as Olive, Olivette, Lionetta (for "little lion"), and Galushka, a term of endearment both Dalí and Éluard liked to use. *Dalí News*, which humanized the deific Gala, was a great hit, and according to the "Tales of Hoffmann" column in the *Hollywood Reporter*,[27] people were lining up to purchase it at 25 cents a copy (a little under $5 today).

Suddenly, that November, without supplying a reason, or perhaps because they both had become so very famous, Paul uncharacteristically decided (and hoped Gala agreed with him) that "we should avoid leaving any hint of our private life behind us. Thus I'm ripping up your letters."[28] He did in fact destroy the entirety of his ex-wife's correspondence, or at least no trace of anything she wrote to him after their marriage remains. Luckily, Gala as usual kept her own counsel *and* Paul's letters, which she in turn passed down to Cécile.

Six days after Paul's missive to Gala about obliterating their personal correspondence, Nusch suffered an unexpected brain aneurysm and died, leaving the poet so distraught he considered suicide. It wasn't until the following March that joyful news finally arrived to distract him. Cécile, who had married the Swiss Surrealist painter Gérard Vulliamy (Éluard describes him as "no genius but he loves her deeply"), gave birth to their first grandchild, a "gorgeous," tiny, blue-eyed girl named Claire, who laughed a lot and appeared "very intelligent."

"If you want to send me some clothes for the baby," Cécile wrote to her mother, "I've heard that in America they make a sort of one-piece suit, for when the child goes out, that covers feet, legs, and arms as well as the body." "Your boxes," Paul—who cherished the books and sweets Gala also included in her care packages—added longingly on the same page, "are very helpful to us. I'm often alone at mealtimes."[29]

Gala's French family was not the only recipient of her generosity. She often thought of her old friends the Tsvetaeva sisters. Marina was dead. She had hanged herself on August 31 in the Yelabuga political prison in Tatarstan Russia, where she had been imprisoned by the Stalinist government because, like all Russians who had spent any extended time in Europe, she was considered suspicious by Stalin. But Marina's sister was alive. Anastasia had been sentenced to ten years' hard labor in 1937 for supposedly being a member of the Rosicrucian Order.[30] In 1947, she was still incarcerated at Amurlag, a corrective labor camp that was a subdivision of the Gulag.

Although there was nothing she could do to help Anastasia or her other old friends directly, in 1947 Gala began funding needy Russian writers stranded in Europe through her new ally Maria Zetlina, who had been famous in prewar Paris for her literary salon and collection of works by Russian artists.[31] In 1942, Maria and her husband, the poet Mikhail Zetlin, who had narrowly escaped the Nazis, founded the *New Review* magazine to subsidize and publish Russian writing in New York. Gala regularly sent extra funds to the writers they published.[32]

Like Gala, Salvador kept up with his family. Just a few days before leaving for New York in 1940 he had made a whirlwind trip to Cadaqués to say goodbye to his father, and they were now on much better terms.

For eleven years, since Lorca's disappearance in 1936, Salvador had avoided spending any time in Spain, and one has only to look at the paintings he made during his exile, almost all of which are set on the Costa Brava's seashore, to understand how unendurably homesick he must have been. A case in point is his image of Gala floating kinetically above a pedestal beside Zeus, disguised as a swan. In this sketch for *Leda Atomica*, exhibited at the Bignou in November 1947, Cap Norfeu, near Cadaqués, is the location of the mythical, world-changing rape.

In *Art Digest*, Alonzo Lansford wrote that Dalí's version of Leda and the Swan was "a lovely nude portrait of his wife Gala," which despite Salvador's "traditional landscape" was a significant example of the artist's awareness of "what was going on in the world."[33]

Look magazine's coverage of the Bignou exhibition reproduced four of its highlights: *Dream Caused by the Flight of a Bee around a Pomegranate a Second before Waking, Portrait of Picasso, Leda Atomica*, and Dalí's small nineteen-by-eleven-inch *St. George the Dragon-Killer* a single ear of golden wheat against a black background, now in the collection of Coco Chanel. The artist had refused an offer of $12,000 for the painting (approximately $170,000 today) from an unidentified buyer.

As usual, the vernissage itself was a happening. Under the headline "Some Came to Look," *Look* devoted two pages of party pictures to the "mad mixture" of people who attended the opening. These included the best-dressed Mrs. Harrison Williams; Cecil Beaton; Dr. Gregoire, a Belgian scientist at the Rockefeller Institute; and Mme Pierre Cartier, described in the magazine as "wife of jewelry head."

René Crevel's old friend The Zodiac member Countess Tota Cuevas de Vera, who already owned four of Dalí's paintings, had flown up from Argentina expressly to admire the illustrations for Salvador and Gala's soon-to-be-published new book, *50 Secrets of Magic Craftsmanship*. Tellingly, Secret #16 of this self-help grimoire for aspiring artist/magicians not only advises would-be painters to fall irrevocably in love with one geographical location, but categorically dictates, "Your studio must be close to the spot where you were born."[34]

CHAPTER 21

HOME

By keeping Spain out of World War II, Francisco Franco had ably preserved both his country and himself. In the late 1940s, the dictator's power was still intact, but now that the war was over and Spain's economy and politics had stabilized, there was no chance, as there had been in 1936, that Salvador might be murdered in Spain "for reasons of personality." There was even a faint glimmer of hope. Though Franco remained the Caudillo ("leader") and Juan Carlos de Borbón would not be selected as the head of state until 1969, Spain had been proclaimed a kingdom through the Law of Succession and La Jefatura del Estado ("States Leadership").

Although he was nominally nonpolitical, Salvador, who adored all the pageantry of his country's rich history, could not help being emotionally attached to the symbolism associated with its crown. The possibility of a parliamentary monarch made his heart leap with joy.

Nineteen years after he had first glimpsed Gala in her little bathing suit, Dalí was blessed with a wonderful homecoming. When he landed at Le Havre with Gala's big American car and all his other worldly belongings in numerous crates, there was no question that the promise of his talent had been realized. Owing to Gala's artistic guidance, emotional support, practical good sense, and business acumen, the Dalís were the richest, most famous art couple in the world. Dalí y Cusí had every reason to be beaming with pride.

Gala and Salvador headed straight to Cadaqués, where it had been arranged for them to stay with Dalí y Cusí, Anna Maria, and Tieta while their Portlligat residence was being renovated. Gala hid in the street while her husband knocked on the door of the family home, but when Salvador's father, who knew how vital she was to his son's accomplishments, saw his daughter-in-law lingering in the background, he opened his arms to give her a big, welcoming hug.

Ignacio Agustí, a reporter from the Catalan journal *Noticias*, had traveled from Barcelona to interview Dalí and was waiting for them by the gate with his photographer. A few days later, a large-scale picture of Salvador sitting next to his father, reading his new book *50 Secrets of Magic Craftsmanship*, appeared on the front page of the capital's most widely distributed newspaper. The return was further celebrated by the *Noticiario Cinematográfico Español*, which printed a photograph of Gala, Salvador, and his father walking arm in arm in Cadaqués.

The cover for the *50 Secrets* as seen in the Noticias photograph was a beautiful image of Gala's back next to a detail from *Leda Atomica*. Two of *Magic Craftsmanship*'s secrets were also dedicated to her. Secret #12: "The secret of why Gala loves painting and why painting loves Gala" describes Gala being as busy as a honeybee. Constantly feeding Salvador's works in progress with wonders, she finds ways to make them even better. In Secret #13, "The secret of the form of an olive by virtue of which the painter may be guided in choosing the woman he must marry" explains that in order for a painter to create genuine works of art, he first must marry Gala, who will then give him everything he needs to develop his talents.

"Without Gala, Salvador would have ended up under a Paris bridge," Dalí y Cusí confided to his friend the painter Doña Roser Villar as they were looking through newspaper clippings together.[1]

Most of the Dalís' belongings were shipped straight to Barcelona, where the gleaming Cadillac caused a commotion when it was unloaded at the port. In the late 1940s and early 1950s, there were still only a few cars in Spain, and those that were there tended to be small and rickety, so the Cadaqués citizenry was amazed by the luxurious vehicle. Dalí y Cusí in particular was thrilled with this car. He loved being driven through the countryside by Gala and had a wonderful time showing the limousine off to his cronies as they whooshed past Figueres's outdoor cafés. According to the set designer Isadoro Bea, who later helped Salvador paint some of his larger canvases, if any motorist got in their way, Gala, turning into a miniature menace, would speed up, cursing the offender in her best Catalan.

That fall, the Dalís stayed with Giuseppe Roi at the marquess's magnificent villa, sixty kilometers west of Venice. There they worked on costumes and sets for Luchino Visconti's production of William Shakespeare's *As You Like It*. For two weeks before the play's opening on November 26 at the Teatro Eliseo in Rome, Gala spent all her time scouring the twisted streets of the Eternal City for images of sheep that could be used for the play's single setting.[2] The result was the now-famous backdrop of the heroine Rosalind's country cottage surrounded by a herd of spindly-legged elephants. It received its own standing ovation.

The Dalís were back in Rome one year later on November 23, for an audience with Pope Pius XII, at which His Holiness approved Salvador's newest work: the 19.3-by-14.8-inch *The Madonna of Portlligat*: an iconized portrait of Gala as the Virgin. A local fisherman's baby was the model for the painting of the Holy Infant where Mother and Child are outlined against cerulean heavens that conjure Gala's rapturous description of a sky that "opens its generous arms to All with profound blueness . . ."[3] As in *Leda*, everything is motion. Gala, the fisherman's child, and his cushion, all animated by mystical energy, float through the heavens. What makes this painting of Wonder especially poignant is Dalí's choice of such personal models.

At the first sight of her father hugging Gala, when she was just back in Spain with Salvador, Anna Maria was overcome with such bitterness that, according to legend, she spat on the floor. The baby of the family, she had grown up adoring her brilliant, handsome older brother, with whom as a toddler she shared a bedroom. When Salvador went to art school, she had been thrilled and proud to serve as his model. She had welcomed and admired his gifted friends Luis Buñuel and the charismatic Federico García Lorca, who played the guitar beautifully and was so witty and amiable that he made the entire family laugh all through dinner, turning the evening into a celebration. It had always been Salvador who brought color and excitement to his sister's claustrophobic small-town life. When Gala arrived, joy disappeared. Salvador had escaped to glory in lands Anna Maria could only dream of, while for years and years now she had been left alone to look after her bearlike, overbearing father and neurasthenic stepmother/aunt. Now she was forty, too old to marry, and Gala, a hateful, full-blown witch who had magicked Salvador into abandoning his only sibling, was the source of all of her pain. Anna Maria began to craft her own book.

As soon as Dalí got wind of this project, he sent his sister a long letter begging her to consult with Gala as "the writer in the family" before doing anything on her own. Anna Maria ignored his request. *Salvador Dalí as Seen by His Sister* was published in December 1949 with a foreword by Salvador Dalí y Cusí that invoked his sainted dead wife and praised the truthfulness of his daughter's reminiscences. For Gala and Salvador, who were in New York for the season, it was a very nasty Christmas surprise. The thesis of Anna Maria's seventy-five-page treatise was that Surrealism in general, and Gala in particular, had destroyed Salvador and his family. As she described it, "The ruinous ideas of Surrealism reached Cadaqués with the force of a storm, and striking with its hatred and perversity destroyed the peace of our home, making us victims of this malevolent movement that unfortunately engulfed Dalí."[4]

The delicate entente Gala had worked so hard to build with her in-laws was shattered. Now, if anything happened to Salvador, she would have no support from his family. To make matters worse, in

the 1940s the French civil marriage of a Spanish citizen was not recognized by the Spanish government, so Gala was in a particularly
precarious position.

The hypocrisy of it all made Salvador furious. He wrote directly
to his first cousin, Monserrat, a close friend from childhood, saying
that it was *vile* of his family to capitalize on his fame by publishing a
book about him without his knowledge or permission. He demanded
that every painting he had left in his father's home be returned to him
immediately. He also printed an "autobiographical note," which he
distributed widely to everyone he knew or had access to. It read:

MEMORANDUM:

I was expelled from my family in 1930 without a single cent to my
name. I have achieved my entire worldwide success solely with the
help of God, the light of the Emporia, and the heroic daily abnega-
tion of a sublime woman, my wife, Gala.

Once I became famous my family accepted reconciliation but my
sister could not resist speculating materially and pseudo-sentimentally
with my name, selling paintings of mine without my permission and
publishing absolutely false accounts of verifiable facts of my life.

For which reasons I feel it is my duty to warn collectors and biographers.

—Salvador Dalí, New York,
January, 1950

On January 30, 1950, Dalí y Cusí made his third new will, in
which he reiterated that Anna Maria would be his sole heir. He also
signed the Cadaqués beach house over to her for an annual stipend of
approximately $5 in today's money. When his father died, just eleven
months later, Salvador received precisely $57.50 (sixty thousand pese-
tas) . He had been disinherited for the last time.

CHAPTER 22

A MADONNA IN PORTLLIGAT

While Salvador was fighting with his family, Gala and the builder Emilio Puignau, with whom she had been in constant contact since 1948, worked to make the Portlligat villa habitable. By 1950, they had succeeded brilliantly.

Now the Portlligat House Museum, this unique, unpretentious whitewashed dwelling, sited directly on the town beach, was created by building winding stairs and narrow passageways to connect a group of adjacent fishermen's huts. It has become a major tourist attraction, so crowded that timed tickets are necessary.

Simultaneously very public and exceptionally private, the property is a cross between an alluring maze and a cozily chic Hobbit hole that invites interior exploration while remaining remarkably open to its surroundings. Starting in the entrance hall and through all the adjoining areas, a multitude of windows, each deliberately a different height, shape, and size, offer a diversity of perspectives on the majestic seashore.

In the rooms themselves, which are defined by souvenirs and personal mementos, Gala's taste is visible everywhere. A seven-foot polar bear garlanded with tastevins on long silver chains holds up a lantern to greet visitors at the front door, where the lip sofa, reimagined in green-and-white chintz by Mme Dalí, encourages guests to rest in the reception room. Three stuffed white swans perched on the top of the library bookcase raise their wings as if preparing for flight. The old fashioned deep-sea diver's suit famously worn by Dalí to his lecture in London leans jauntily against a wall in the artist's studio, where it looks out at the ocean. Gala's collage of photographs— Edward James, the Dalís, and Walt Disney; Salvador on the porch of the Cadaqués house beside his father, who dwarfs him; Salvador on the covers of *Time* magazine, *Mundo Hispánico*, and *Town & Country*; and a reproduction of Gala as the Madonna of Portlligat—papers the walls of the dressing room and conceals the door to her own private retreat: the oval room.

This famous egg-shaped meditation space was completed in 1961. Gala decorated it with her fabled collection of religious icons and hundreds of colorful little pillows, clearly acquired through many travels, which brighten the banquette that wraps around its curved walls.

The bedroom, built on two levels, is the largest room in the house. A sitting area with bookshelves, an armchair, and a welcoming fireplace designed by Dalí connects through a small flight of stairs to the higher level, where twin beds with matching wrought-iron headboards and blue canopies are placed beside floor-to-ceiling windows.

Entertaining was outside. For large parties, guests usually gathered underneath the cypress trees around the long penis-shaped pool that was added by Salvador in the late 1960s to startle and amuse. It is guarded by a macho stuffed lion and equipped with a splendid outdoor chef's grill. On more intimate evenings, friends were invited to relax on the lavender-skirted patios that faced the Mediterranean's glamorous horizon. All visitors were booked at a neighboring hotel. No one was invited to stay the night.

Gala transformed the abandoned olive terraces on the parched hummock above the house into a garden that became, under her loving surveillance, her version of a mythical Greek knoll, dotted with cliff roses, anemones, daisies, and lupines. A white stone path—"The

Via Lactia," or Milky Way, as she named it, edged with rosemary and pomegranate trees—meandered down from the hill to a small, secluded bay where Gala and Salvador liked to swim naked.

All summer, when she wasn't combing Girona for antiques or exploring the Mediterranean coastline in her little yellow dinghy, Gala spent her time collaborating with Salvador. He was working on a second, larger-than-life twelve-by-eighteen-foot version of *The Madonna of Portlligat*.

The Eucharist, visible through a window in the Christ Child's chest, is at the heart of *The Madonna of Portlligat*, where it creates the composition as a visual Communion. Here Gala, who was by now firmly established as the many-splendored Goddess of Salvador's personal iconography, personifies adoration. She appears twice in the work. She is the Madonna and can also be seen in the background of the painting, where she materializes as an attendant angel with cuttlefish-bone wings who represents the spirit of change. As in Dalí's previous Madonna, the entire composition lives in a state of suspended animation. Salvador explained this condition as follows: "Modern physics has increasingly revealed to us the dematerialization which exists in all nature and that is why the material body of the Madonna does not exist and why in place of the torso you find the tabernacle 'filled with Heaven.' But while everything floating in space denotes spirituality it also represents our concept of the atomic system that is today's verbalization of divine gravitation."[1]

When Gala and Salvador returned to New York that winter, the painting, which had taken five months to complete, was exhibited at the Carstairs Gallery at 11 East Fifty-Seventh Street, where it attracted a great deal of press coverage, including two articles in the *New York Herald Tribune*. The second of these was careful to note that a previous version of the *Madonna* had been presented to and accepted by Pope Pius XII.[2]

To celebrate Christmas, Gala curated an installation at the Alemany and Ertman gallery, on Manhattan's Upper East Side. It included all the jewels made by Dalí to date and opened at the same time as an overview of nearly three hundred Fabergé objects in the neighboring Hammer Gallery, widely known as the recognized expert on Peter Carl Fabergé. The shows were reviewed together in *Art News*, which praised the exquisiteness of the two troves of "fantastic" jewelry, whose virtuosity "rivaled that of adornments crafted by Renaissance masters."[3] Gala wore a white silk Christian Dior dress richly embroidered with black vines and sunflowers enhanced with pearls and silver sequins from the 1949–50 haute couture collection to the festive Alemany and Ertman gallery opening where she was photographed with Salvador by Marvin Koner, who specialized in images of the distinguished for *Look* and for *Life*.

By 1950, the Dalís, who had given up the Paris apartment Éluard looked after for them during the war, had settled into an annual rotation. Autumn and winter were divided between New York and Paris, where they invariably stayed at the same hotels: the St. Regis on Fifth Avenue and the Le Meurice on the rue de Rivoli, overlooking the Louvre Museum and the Jardin des Tuileries. Spring and summer found then in Portlligat.

It was at Portlligat that their old friend Christian Dior, who they had first known when he was Pierre Colle's assistant in the 1930s, visited them in June. Since his introduction of the New Look three years earlier, Dior had become the world's most influential couturier, and the Dalís were collaborating with him on designing their costumes for Carlos de Beistegui e Yturbe's Ball of the Century. The ball was the first big postwar costume party, to be held September 3 in Venice's Palazzo Labia's ballroom, whose arched ceilings were decorated with Tiepolo frescoes depicting Cleopatra and Marc Antony's star-crossed love.

Beistegui, who had purchased the palazzo in 1948 and restored and refurbished it with priceless tapestries and antiques, was a fabulously rich Frenchman, with equally fabulous taste. His wealth derived from inherited silver mines in Zacatecas, Mexico, but Beistegui had been born in France, and educated in England. He had visited his family's country of origin only twice.

A discerning and prodigious art collector, Carlos thought of the Dalís and Dior as close friends, and they were at the top of his 2,100-name guest list, which included half the *Almanach de Gotha*.[4] Invitations had been sent out early, at the beginning of March, to allow everyone enough time to prepare their costumes and choreograph their entrances. These were usually rehearsed for days in advance with a dancing master.

In the early 1950s, a journey to Venice was more of an expedition than it is today. Gas was still rationed, and travel was slow. When the day of *le Bal du Siècle*, ("the ball of the century") finally arrived, the partygoers' easiest option was to sail from the lagoon down the wide Cannaregio Canal into the Grand Canal, where they could wave regally at the gaping crowds who were lined up on the banks to greet them.

The costumes were various and magnificent.

Collector Arturo López-Willshaw, disguised as the emperor of China, arrived with his wife and their retinue from the Chinese embassy in an authentic Chinese junk. Jacques Fath's Sun King costume was so tight that the couturier was forced to stand up in his gondola because he could not sit down. The lovely Lady Diana Cooper, wife of Duff Cooper, the former British ambassador to France, made her entrée as Cleopatra. Surrealist painter Leonor Fini alighted as a black angel, and Singer sewing-machine heiress Daisy Fellowes was an African queen in yellow robes designed by Dior adorned with her Cartier Tutti Frutti necklace.[5] Everyone, from the Aga Khan to Orson Welles, and Gene Tierney, who was at the peak of her Hollywood career, was there. Cecil Beaton roamed the palazzo taking snapshots for *Vogue*.

Gala and Salvador, who had spent the summer designing their looks with Dior and his assistant, Pierre Cardin, made the most unusual entrance of them all. Cheered on by passersby, the little troupe, which also included Victor Grandpierre, Dior's famous interior decorator, and *Harper's Bazaar* editor Marie-Louise Bousquet, walked to the palazzo on foot, crossing bridges and meandering through the narrow streets of the Doge's city camouflaged as masked giants in black military tricorners. Their identical costumes were long, phantasmagorically white, narrow robes decorated in the Spanish tradition with rows of delicate black bows. Dior's was exactly the same, except in miniature. He came as a dwarf.[6]

Posed majestically at the top of his sweeping marble staircase, Carlos greeted the revelers with aristocratic aplomb. He was coiffed like Louis XIV in an eighteenth-century sausage-curl peruke, and his bespoke buskins had five-inch platforms, which made him much taller than everyone else in the room. As Dominick Dunne, who profiled de Beistegui for *Vanity Fair* in the 1990s, noted, "On this the most important night of his life, he had made sure to see and be seen."[7]

Taking a philosophical view of the festivities, *Time* magazine reported that at least one guest "found time to reflect that the wasteful rich might be facing oblivion: 'I don't know,' the Aga Khan mused, toward the end of the evening, 'that we will ever see anything like this again.'"[8]

While Gala was working with Dior on the costumes for the Venetian masquerade, the German photographer Ricard Sans had been busy taking informal pictures of her. Dalí appropriated some of these candid portraits to use as models for his "Atom-ical" rendering of his "most mystical" wife in his latest work: *Assumpta Corpuscularia Lapislazulina* (*Bodily Assumption in Blue*). Here Gala appears as an elongated sunburst of transparent atomic corpuscles who gazes heavenward as she floats over the waters of Portlligat.

Time magazine deconstructed the work simply: "Dalí believes the two deepest preoccupations of mid-century are religious mysticism and atomic physics. His picture combines them to show: the Roman Catholic dogma of the Virgin Mary's bodily assumption to Heaven as seen by an age newly aware of nuclear physics."[9]

Gala Placidia, in which Gala's face is a composition of nuclear atoms, is a different expression of the same philosophy painted during the same period.

After spending the fall preparing for their trip to England, Gala and Dalí attended the December opening of Salvador's exhibition at the Lefevre Gallery, in London, which had hung the second version of *The Madonna of Portlligat* with *Assumpta Corpuscularia Lapislazulina*, *Gala Placidia*, and *Christ of Saint John of the Cross*, purchased for a little under a million dollars today by the Kelvingrove Art Gallery and Museum, in Glasgow's west end. *Christ* is an image of St. John of the Cross's vision of Christ in ecstasy. Dalí's version is painted looking down on the figure of Christ, so that all we see of him is the top of his head. The vast floating cross is cantilevered over the beach of Portlligat, where Gala's little yellow dinghy has been stranded at sunset.

In direct opposition to Grünewald's Christ for the sixteenth-century Isenheim Altarpiece, where our Savior's flesh is shown mottled and diseased, Dalí's *Saint John* emphasizes the majestic splendor of the crucified deity.[10] In its "Letter from London," the *New Yorker* reported that, while the English press was less than enthusiastic about Dalí's "classicism," which they criticized as "Victorian," the show attracted huge, very appreciative crowds.[11]

Later that month, in a speech celebrating the publication of his illustrated treatise *Manifiesto Místico* (*Manifeste Mystique*) in Castilian, Dalí described Gala as the "wave and corpuscle of my Mysticism."

CHAPTER 25

TURNING A PAGE

The last letter from Paul that Gala saved is dated February 21, 1948. It was written when he was still in deep mourning for Nusch and very lonely. As he was writing it, Paul's hand started shaking so badly that Cécile had to finish the page. The letter begins, "Little Galotchka I dreamt of you last night. We were in the country," and ends, "I've been invited to spend some time in Algeria but don't think I can leave my home again . . . Nusch's absence. *Little Galotchka! How I would like to see you.*" On November 18, 1952, at nine in the morning, Paul Éluard died of a heart attack in his modest apartment at 52 avenue de Gravelle, in the southeast suburbs of Paris, near the Zoological Park. He was fifty-six years old.

Ten days later, his elaborate funeral was attended by, among others, Louis Aragon, Henri Cartier-Bresson, René Char, Jean Cocteau, Yves Montand, Pablo Picasso, Simone Signoret, Paul's daughter, Cécile, and his wife of eleven months, Dominique Lemort.[1]

The ceremony was organized by the Communist Party, but a crowd of thousands gathered spontaneously and followed the casket to the Père Lachaise Cemetery, where Molière and Marcel Proust were also entombed. "That day," the poet Robert Sabatier remembered, "the whole world was mourning."[2]

Although Gala, who hated funerals, did not attend his interment, Paul's death was a critical loss. Paul had been her first love, her first lover, and, as she remembered, "the best lover" she ever had. He was also her family. They had been divorced for nearly twenty years, but he had remained her consistently close ally and admirer through all the difficult times since her wild, ambitious teenage years at Clavadel. He was one of the few people she could trust and confide in and perhaps, since Salvador was so dependent, the only one to whom she could fully unburden herself. A page in her life had turned.

If Gala avoided Père Lachaise, she made sure to keep up with Cécile and her grandchildren, whom she visited regularly whenever she was in Paris and liked to spoil. Her granddaughter, Claire Sarti, remembers Gala as a tiny, chic, and formidable woman who hosted the whole family at long Sunday lunches in an old Russian restaurant called Au Cochon de Lait (Suckling Pig), where she would order an entire coulibiac of salmon with mushrooms and lemon sauce "so big it almost stretched the length of the table." After the meal, she would carefully instruct the staff to wrap up all the leftovers. There were always presents: wonderful dresses from Best & Co. in far-off Manhattan, suits for Claire's brothers, and beautiful books and envelopes crammed with cash for Cécile.[3]

The war had been over for seven years now. Prosperity had slowly returned to Europe. Salvador was recognized as a great artist all over the world, and Gala's busy life had settled into a calmer routine of travel and interesting projects. In November 1953, the Dalís returned to Italy, where they toured Turin before motoring down to Rome so that Gala could oversee the printing of Dalí's 102 watercolor illustrations for Dante's great epic poem *Divina Commedia*, which traces a soul's pilgrimage from the inferno to heaven. Since Salvador, by his own admission, had never read Dante, Gala, who initiated the project, devised the ideas for all the illustrations. The book was published by the Istituto Poligrafico e Zecca dello Stato. At the same time, Gala helped her husband prepare for his upcoming exhibition at the Palazzo Pallavicini-Rospigliosi, a splendid building that was once the home of Pope Paul V's nephew, the historic art collector Cardinal Scipione Borghese. In 1611, Scipione had commissioned Giovanni Vasanzio and Carlo Maderno to build the palace and its gardens on the Quirinal Hill at the center of Rome, where its magnificent view of the city overlooks the Trevi Fountain. Here Gala had arranged for Salvador's work to be hung in the company of paintings by Botticelli, Carracci, Van Dyck, Rubens, and Guercino, who is famous for his rendering of Saint Sebastian (circa 1930).

Dalí's luminous first retrospective in Italy opened in the palazzo's courtyard on May 14 of the following year with a performance piece during which he improvised his own death and rebirth inside a "metaphysical cube" made of paper, from which he "magically" emerged like a fledgling from an egg. Afterward, Salvador delivered a short, emotional speech describing Gala as the inspiration for the exhibition, which included one of his most unusual works: *The Royal Heart.*

As recounted in *Manifeste Mystique,* this was a present Salvador had made for Gala when she wished for "a ruby heart that beats."[4] Effectively, the jewel is a hollow, crowned, ten-by-five-inch eighteen-karat-gold heart, whose diadem is set with pearls, diamonds, sapphires, emeralds, and amethysts. In its center, camouflaged by a rectangular net of small, cabochon-shaped natural rubies, an ingenious mechanical mechanism literally makes the heart beat.[5] "Without Gala I would no longer be Dalí," Salvador told the Catalan magazine *Del Arco.*[6]

Meanwhile, the Dalís' domestic expansion was ongoing. Since they were now constantly either mobbed by press, surrounded by collectors, stalked by worshipful hippies who pitched their tents on the beach to be close to the Dalís, or gawked at by curious tourists, Gala wanted a more private space for her personal use. The Dalís purchased, redesigned, and began to renovate a large sailing boat moored in the Cadaqués harbor, which Salvador named "Gala's Farmyard." He filled it with antique architectural elements and decorated it with ornate doors and Baroque mantelpieces. *The Farmyard*, which remains unfinished, was frequently used for parties and performances.[7]

By 1955, Salvador, who had begun his career making small-scale paintings, was deep into his investigation of enormous canvases and needed help laying out his grand new work. Gala, who as usual scouted for her husband, interviewed Isidoro Bea, a forty-five-year-old scenery designer from Lleida,[8] who had studied art and scenography in Barcelona. Bea was well-known in Northern Spain as a reliable, discreet, and highly respected painter of theatrical backdrops with a sure eye for perspective. Gala hired him to be Dalí's studio assistant on a large nine-by-five-foot painting of the Last Supper. It was the beginning of a relationship that would last for thirty years, during which time Bea, who often painted the backgrounds to the larger works, would continue to assist Salvador with his paintings. From the beginning, Isidoro, who was eventually given his own home on the property, was expected to work as zealously as Salvador. Sunday was the only day of the week he had for himself.

The Sacrament of the Last Supper was purchased that June by the famous American investor Chester Dale, who visited the Dalís with his wife, the painter and art critic Maud Murray, in Cadaqués. He donated the masterpiece to the National Gallery of Art in Washington, DC, the following March.

At the same time, Sir Alexander Korda, the British filmmaker responsible for such triumphs as *That Hamilton Woman* (1941), with Vivien Leigh, and *Cry, the Beloved Country* (1951), starring Sidney Poitier, was in the midst of producing Shakespeare's *Richard III*, directed by Laurence Olivier, who also starred as the humpbacked king. Korda and Olivier decided it would be brilliant publicity to have the actor's portrait in costume as the murderous Richard painted by Salvador Dalí, who, in the resulting *Richard III*,[9] wittily portrayed the Laurence Olivier/King Richard personality with two faces. Gala, who kept one of the couple's bank accounts in Rome, had asked that the fee of £10,000 (approximately $500,000 in today's money) be delivered in lira to take advantage of the exchange rate and avoid customs. So Korda sent Salvador to see his "man in Italy," an ex–army captain named Peter Moore.

Handsome and dashing, Moore was an Irishman with a sociopath's genius for verbal mimicry. He had an impeccable upper-class British accent and was conversant enough in French to be habitually mistaken for a Parisian. During the war he had worked in counter-intelligence, where he proved so skillful that he sometimes reported directly to Winston Churchill, who liked him, made him a captain, and wrote a recommendation for him to Korda's enterprise, London Films.

When Salvador went to meet Moore and collect his remission, the captain, who was lunching with Orson Welles, agreed to arrange a second "unofficial" visit with Pius XII for the artist, who wanted to petition the pope for a dispensation to marry Gala. Dalí was grateful for the favor. He was also impressed by the Irishman's military background, elevated connections, and worldly demeanor. After Alexander Korda's death in 1956, the Dalís kept in touch with Moore, who would soon play an important part in their lives.

Later that year, Gala and Salvador had a second consequential encounter. At the Knickerbocker Fete, a society charity ball chaired by Mrs. Cornelius Vanderbilt Whitney[10] in Manhattan, Dalí introduced himself to Maria Fernanda Kalashnikov, a statuesque blonde in an impeccable red dress he couldn't help noticing from across the dance floor. It turned out that her father was José Maria Carretero, who, under the pseudonym El Caballero Audaz ("Bold Knight"), had been a famous bestselling erotic novelist in the 1920s and was one of Salvador's favorite authors. Born in Madrid, "Nanita" was married to Michael Kalashnikov, a jeweler at Harry Winston, with whom she had three beautiful daughters. She was working with the hat designer Lilly Daché, who, following Elizabeth Arden's lead, had in the late

1940s expanded her business to include clothing, cosmetics, and salon services.

Nanita's distinguishing physical characteristic was a wonderful Roman nose that resembled that of France's famous Sun King, and Salvador affectionately renamed her "Louis XIV." He immediately invited her to visit Portlligat when she was in Spain. Nanita became one of his closest friends. In his last years, "Louis XIV" was the only one allowed to cut Salvador's hair.

The stream of visitors to Portlligat was now so consistent that in March, when *Harper's Bazaar* published a story about the villa with photographs by Brassaï, the piece began by noting a few of Gala's world-famous visitors: Serge Lifar, Philippe de Rothschild, the bullfighter Luis Miguel Dominguín, and the Greek tycoon Stavros Niarchos (who glided into the port on his two-hundred-foot yacht, the *Creole*). Walt Disney and his wife, Lillian, would follow suit in a yacht of their own, the following year.[11]

It was only after detailing Gala's guest list that *Bazaar* went on to also admire the Dalís' "magnificent bedroom"; praise the candelabras designed by Dalí, placed on a sixteenth-century refectory table in front of a frieze of starfish, and make special mention of Salvador's *objets d'étonnement* ("surprising knickknacks") displayed on shelves in the sitting room.[12]

Two months later, Giuseppe and Maria Albaretto, a wealthy couple from Turin, were vacationing on the Costa Brava half an hour by car from Portlligat, where they met and befriended the art critic Rafael Santos Torroella and his wife, María, who were among Gala and Salvador's closest friends. When Santos invited the excited young couple along on one of his calls to the famous beach house, it took Gala exactly one hour to sell them a painting. The Dalís also found Christina, the Albarettos' eight-year-old daughter, beguiling, and everyone was invited to come again the next day. Within six months, the Turinese had become major collectors of Dalí's work. They acquired some early paintings: the 1926 still life *Invitation to Dream* and a 1925 portrait of Dalí's sister from a Barcelona dealer named Sala Gaspar, who got them from Anna-Marie. But chiefly, they bought directly from Gala, who always set the price. "When we first met the Dalís," Maria Albaretto remembered, there was "no dealer promoting [Dalí's] art . . . he was far better known in America than in Europe. We were lucky to meet him when we did. We had no serious competition, and his work was reasonably priced."[13] In addition to the Albarettos, the Morses remained passionate collectors and immediately purchased the latest portrait of Gala, *Saint Helena at Portlligat*, when it went on display at the Carstairs Gallery that December.

It was twenty-four years since Gala and Dalí's civil wedding in Paris, and Paul Éluard had been dead for more than six. The new pope, John XXIII, graciously granted the Dalís their long-sought dispensation. At last, Gala and Salvador could be married in the eyes of the Church (and the Spanish government).

On the morning of August 8, 1958, Gala drove Salvador and the three clerics who were their witnesses in her midnight-blue American limousine to the isolated hilltop Santuari de la Mare de Déu dels Àngels in Sant Martí Vell, Girona. Here, in the vaulted, immaculately white, unadorned chapel, the simple ceremony was performed under the loving gaze of the chantry's only sculpture: a tenderly smiling giant Madonna who dominates the entire altarpiece. Francesc Vilà i Torrent, the parish priest of the township of Fornells de la Selva, officiated. There were no guests, reporters, or photographers.

The following afternoon an old friend, Meliton Casals, took the official wedding pictures on Gala's *Farmyard*. Salvador, all dressed up in a pearl-colored vest and a dark cravat, looks prosperous and quite serious, while Gala, who is partially hidden by the vast bouquet of white flowers she is clutching, smiles as shyly as a schoolgirl on her first date. The Dalís celebrated for a third time with their best friends, Marcel Duchamp and his wife, American artist Alexina

"Teeny" Sattler, at the *Farmyard*. "See, I am the contrary of everybody," Salvador, who called marriage "a stimulus to the imagination," told Leonard Lyons proudly. "While everybody is divorcing; Dalí marries."[14] That May, Gala and Salvador made a point of returning to Rome to personally thank Pope John XXIII for their dispensation and receive his blessing.

Dalí's December show at the Carstairs Gallery was dedicated to Gala, whom he described as his "Sistine Madonna." She was represented in the exhibition's centerpiece, *Cosmic Madonna*, and appeared again in the show as the Virgin Mary on the ship's banner in the foreground of Salvador's thirteen-by-nine-foot *The Discovery of America by Christopher Columbus* (1958), which was a commission for Reynolds and Eleanor Morse.[15]

Gala was delighted with Salvador's new work and her images in it. She described his artistic growth as "spreading out like a vigorous ramified tree"[16] and could not help but be thoroughly amused by the flurry caused by *Cosmic Madonna* when, in November 1960, Marcel Duchamp included it in a show he curated for the D'Arcy Galleries in Manhattan.[17] André Breton, who had personally expelled Dalí from the Surrealist circle more than twenty years earlier, was so indignant over Duchamp's effrontery that he published the manifesto *We Don't EAR It That Way*, whose cover was the reproduction of a fragment of Dalí's *Assumpta Corpuscularia Lapislazulina*, in which Gala's Madonna face is defaced with the same mustache Duchamp had painted on the Mona Lisa. Below the image, the printed Duchampian initials L.H.O.O.Q., which stand for *"Elle a chaud au cul"* ("She's in heat"), constituted a highbrow French version of "YO MOMMA."

CHAPTER 24

NEW FRONTIERS

After the armistice and Baba's death,[1] Jean-Louis de Faucigny-Lucinge visited New York, where his old protégé Salvador invited him for a boys' night on the town. "He gave me a bit of a shock when I first saw him," the prince told Meryle Secrest with a smile. "He had developed those enormous mustaches and a cane. I thought to myself, 'How can I walk around with this figure of fun?' But I found that I couldn't have been more wrong. He was instantly recognized and welcomed everywhere."[2]

Fifteen years later, Salvador's appearance was even more dramatic. His black hair was longer, dyed and pomaded. He affected gold waistcoats and leopard-skin capes, which Gala picked out for him, and he had acquired a collection of walking sticks with different handles. One was carved amethyst; another was Russian enamel. The stick he most enjoyed twirling had an elaborately embossed silver handle. It was a precious antique once owned by the "divine" Sarah Bernhardt, who had been France's greatest stage actress at the turn of the last century.[3]

Although she was determinedly less extravagant than Salvador, Gala's persona had altered as well. In the Spanish newsreel of the Disneys' visit to Portlligat in 1956, she appears on the beach to welcome her friends in a trending back-combed hairstyle, stylish Capri pants, and ballet slippers. Gala, who always took excellent care of herself (and may in fact by that time have had a first facelift) had become an unquestionably chic, worldly woman whose gracious demeanor makes it clear without saying it that the Disneys are being received by "art-world royalty." This stately, soignée, mid-century Gala was worlds away from the opinionated, bare-breasted daredevil who had turned the heads of France's intellectual Who's Who in the 1920s.

Dalí charmed, amused, and provoked. Gala played the straight man. It was her job to impress. On August 12, 1960, a "comical, Surrealist bullfight" organized by Marcel Duchamp,[4] who commissioned the endearing bull—a self-destructing construction of paper and plaster covered over with gold plates sculpted by Niki de Saint Phalle and her partner Jean Tinguely—was celebrated in Dalí's hometown, Figueres. It honored the artist and the new museum he and Gala planned to build in place of a grand old 1850 theater that had been burned to the ground during the civil war. Commemorative press photos show Salvador animated, laughing, and leaning forward to throw his hat in the ring. Gala, beside him, stands regally erect and immobile in the front tier of the corrida. She is chastely arrayed in the impenetrable sunglasses of the famous, and a dignified skirt suit.

Ten days later, Gala was in Venice at the premiere of Maurice Béjart's ballet *Gala*: a tribute to her as mystical Earth Mother, danced with electric sexuality by Ludmilla Tchérina. Alessandro Scarlatti composed the score. The sets and costumes were by Dalí. As the guest of honor, Gala spent almost all her time off in a corner of the Teatro La Fenice, being photographed for the morning papers in her bespoke Jean Dessès ball gown decorated with Dalí's illustrations for *Don Quichotte*.[5] During the interval, Salvador, in a gondolier's costume, warmed up the theatergoers before the performance with a new "magic trick." Imitating Lord Berners, he slashed the large canvas he had been painting on the balcony facing the audience and released a loft of pigeons into the auditorium.

Gala's public persona was impeccable. Still, her disparate, often conflicting identities as the "adult" of the Dalínean partnership in which she played wife, tigress,[6] lover and mother, fashion influencer and model, art-world royalty and art critic, muse, collaborator, dealer, business/licensing manager, hard-nosed negotiator, welcoming hostess, bill collector, nurse, and always the recurring mystical centerpiece of her husband's work—were becoming difficult to juggle without help. On January I, 1961, Salvador sent Peter Moore a first-class ticket to Manhattan, where the Dalís had been ensconced at the St. Regis for more than a month.

Alighting at New York's Idlewild Airport the "Captain," as the Dalís now liked to call him (with a capital "C"), arrived just in time to profit from a burgeoning, heady new age. Russian Yuri Gagarin was about to become the first man to travel in space. Handsome John Fitzgerald Kennedy, at forty-three the youngest-ever elected president of the United States, was promising America a New Frontier. Meanwhile, what *Vogue* editor in chief Diana Vreeland called "the Youth Quake"—a brash, bright, and adventurous cultural revolution led by the Baby Boomers[7]—was in full swing.

In New York City, long-locked British rockers—the Beatles, the Animals, and the Rolling Stones—were overwhelming staid Ed Sullivan on Sunday-night TV and setting music on its ear with their rhythmically driven acoustics. In London, a twenty-one-year-old British designer named Mary Quant was making the first miniskirts, while in Paris, André Courrèges accessorized his models with white space helmets. On Seventh Avenue, Rudi Gernreich had just invented the famous breast-baring "monokini," a new version of the topless bathing suits Gala wore in 1929, while three hours north, in Millbrook, New York, psychoanalyst Timothy Leary was advocating psychedelics and echoing André Breton's dictum *Lâchez tout* ("leave everything") when he called on everyone under thirty to "turn on, tune in, and drop out" of their parents' jaded, bourgeois society.

The cutting-edge art world was now centered in Manhattan and id=page212

also experiencing a generational shift. The Abstract Expressionists of the 1950s, such as Pollock and the Dalís' friend Willem de Kooning, had produced uninhibited, gestural, seemingly spontaneous canvases that were philosophically in a direct line with the unconstrained automatic writings pioneered by Breton and Philippe Soupault. Now they were making room for Pop and Op artists like Bridget Riley and Roy Lichtenstein. Interestingly, even though their pictorial styles were totally dissimilar, Riley, who toyed with optical illusion, and Lichtenstein, whose personal paranoiac reality was cartoon art, both shared intellectual communality with Dalí's trippy mind games and highly imaginary, interiorized ways of viewing reality. Or as Dalí, who described Lichtenstein as "a romantic," explained to Carlton Lake: "Most Pop Artists admit they are descended from me and Marcel Duchamp."[8]

GALA AND SALVADOR, at the height of their fame, delighted in novelty. They embraced all these changes, not in the least because many of them corresponded to their own ways of working and thinking. For the Dalís, in the early '60s anything and almost everything seemed possible.

The arrangement Gala negotiated with Peter Moore was mind-bogglingly generous. He would be their "business manager" and Dalí's strategic adviser. While he would not receive a salary, he could take 10 percent commission on all deals he generated. His sphere was everything except original paintings and drawings, the sale and marketing of which remained Gala's exclusive territory. In other words, any business connected to licensing or reproduction was Moore's domain. Moore accepted the offer immediately. Although he later bragged that he made $500,000 (over $5,000,000 in today's dollars) in his first weekend with the Dalís,[9] he took an instant dislike to his benefactress. Gala was the only one who stood between him and Dalí, his perceived pot of gold.

Moore began by complaining unconscionably that Gala was a terrible dealer who sold to unsuitable people at mistakenly low prices because she had alienated important art galleries with her anti-Semitism.[10] The last bit is particularly difficult to stomach, especially since Gala enjoyed telling anyone who would listen that she had been taught all she knew by her brilliant Jewish stepfather, who was a very great lawyer, and Dalí himself liked to say that she had Jewish blood.[11]

Having sunk his fangs into the hand that fed him, Moore's next step was to expand his position in the Dalínean universe. Observing that Dalí editions were an underexploited source of income, he maneuvered Salvador into endorsing a declaration stating that if Dalí signed a reproduction of one of his images, the copy became equal to the image it was derived from. This clearly could never be. However, the affirmation is so close to Duchamp's thought-provoking refusal to make a distinction between one of his original artworks and its facsimile that it's easy to see how Salvador could be seduced into agreeing with Moore's fallacy. The tragic difference, of course, was that while Duchamp was claiming copyright to any and all derivations of a Duchampian invention, Dalí would (in Moore's hands) end up giving away much of his artistic credibility.

For the time being, however, the show went on. For Gala, this meant a continual stream of debuts and public appearances. On December 19, 1961, she attended Dalí's lecture on his latest work in progress, *Galacidalacidesoxiribunucleicacid* at the École Polytechnique in Paris. Otherwise known as *Hommage to Crick and Watson*.[12] This ten-by-thirteen-foot, hazily atmospheric painting shows Gala who is the only distinct and easily recognizable figure, kneeling with her back to the viewer. Her gaze, which Dalí described as a kind of Communion, is fixed on the blood dripping from the arm of Christ, who is being raised up to Heaven by Our Father. The color of her hair is the color of a loaf of bread, which, as Salvador, referencing *Galerina*, noted, he had always thought of as Eucharistic.

To Gala's right, a double helix, now transformed by the artwork into an iconic proof of immortality and therefore God's existence, stretches up beyond the horizon, mirroring the movement of Our Father's right arm. "The more I studied the sciences, the more I realized that everything religion tells us is true," Dalí elucidated.[13]

Through the Knoedler Gallery, Gala was beginning negotiations for *Hommage*'s sale to New England Merchants National Bank who wanted to hang it in their new headquarters at the Prudential Center of Boston. The price, $150,270, was exceptionally high for that time.[14]

When the ballet *Gala* traveled to Belgium the following April, Gala modeled her Don Quichotte dress once more at the performance. The Dalís reached Paris the following week to attend the launch party for the book *Dalí de Gala*, hosted by their old friend Marie-Laure de Noailles at her famous town house on the Place des États-Unis. The first luxurious photo book about the Dalís' work and life, *The World of Salvador Dalí* (its English title), was assembled by Gala, Dalí, and their soon-to-be secretary, the photographer Robert Descharnes.

Gala played nurse to Salvador at a May book signing in the window of the Doubleday bookstore at Fifty-Second Street and Fifth Avenue in New York, to honor *The World of Salvador Dalí*'s debut in America. Here Dalí was hooked up to an instrument for registering heartbeats. As each buyer came forward, he handed them an "oscillogramme" [*sic*] signature, which expressed his personal cardiological response to that dedicatee. Philippe Halsman photographed the performance with his "fish-eye" lens.

In the midst of this bustle of public appearances, Gala somehow also found time for new friends and private memories. On August 18, 1962, she lent her name and presence to a festival organized by a woman she liked and admired: Carmen Amaya, Spain's most celebrated flamenco dancer, who was raising funds for the illumination of the ruined sixteenth-century castle in Begur, a tiny hamlet sheltered in the foothills of the Pyrénées at the northernmost point of the Costa Brava. It was the last public appearance of the great gypsy dancer, described by art writer Sebastián Gash in *El Mirador* as "soul pure soul; feeling made fresh."[15] Although the fifty-year-old Amaya could not complete the performance, she received a twenty-minute standing ovation. She died a few months later, on November 19, of kidney failure.[16]

Gala made a second, very special, contribution later that year to the Picasso Museum in Barcelona. This time her gift was in memory of her first love, Paul Éluard. Paul and Pablo Picasso had been best friends. And on October 12, Gala presented *Head* (1913)—a linear, lyrical charcoal-and-collage work on paper by Picasso, which she had acquired during her first marriage—to Picasso's museum in honor of the man who'd stood by her husband until the end. In his syndicated column "The Lyons Den," Leonard Lyons commented mockingly that it was now *Picasso's* turn to give a present to the soon-to-be-opened Dalí museum in Figueres.

CHAPTER 25

NEW LOVE

Cozily installed toward the back of the legendary Half Note jazz club on Hudson Street in Manhattan, William Rothlein, a twenty-year-old aspiring actor from a modest, Conservative Jewish family in Brooklyn, was enjoying a Christmas-week cocktail with Nico, the almost-six-foot blond superstar of Andy Warhol's film *Chelsea Girls*, when Salvador Dalí ambled over, introduced himself, and chatted briefly before moving on. That Rothlein was unforgettably attractive is attested by the poet John Giorno in his account of his first encounter with Gala and Salvador, over red wine and diet sodas in the King Cole Bar, on January 10, 1964. Rothlein wasn't present on that occasion, but Giorno, who met Will months later with Gala and had a crush on him, makes a point of describing how magnetic the "beautiful" dark, fine-featured Will Rothlein was for both women and men, including himself.[1]

These "drinks" were organized by Salvador's former studio assistant Ultra Violet so that Warhol and Giorno could persuade the Dalís to attend the opening of *Sleep*, Andy's just-finished film of John sleeping for five hours. The get-together turned out to be a victory for everyone. After the briefest of flirtations, Gala, whom Giorno describes as "art world royalty," "charming; gracious: a modest princess" with "the seeming self-confidence of the very famous," pronounced the concept of a film about one man sleeping for five hours and twenty-one minutes *"merveilleux."* When she promised Giorno that she and Salvador would attend its January 24 premiere[2] and presented Warhol with a Sioux chief's war bonnet, Andy was thrilled and his admiration for Gala was sealed.[3] Giorno's coda to this success story is that Dalí, whom he describes as "a great artist of the 20's, 30's, and 40's," and Warhol (who had been emulating the Dalí's salesmanship for years) soon became close friends and marketing coconspirators. They both knew how to make "huge amounts of money through art to support their luxurious lifestyles."[4]

Two days after his March 16 birthday, twenty-one-year-old Rothlein and Ruth Kligman, the lone survivor of the 1954 car crash that had killed her boyfriend Jackson Pollock, were standing in line for *Two Nights with Cleopatra*, starring Sophia Loren, at the Apollo on West Forty-Second Street when Dalí and Gala came out of the theater. Salvador recognized Rothlein immediately and suggested they meet again. There was a new project he wanted to discuss with him. Gala took down Will's information and rang up a few days later to invite him to Sunday lunch at the Russian Tea Room. Will arrived early and ordered a Bloody Mary at the bar. When he saw the Dalís walk in with Sophia Loren and Peter Ustinov, he nearly fell off his stool. From that moment on he was mesmerized by them.

Gala and Salvador had been discussing making a film about Dalí's youth with Luchino Visconti and had decided that William's dark hair and striking, angular features made him a perfect candidate for the lead role. Naturally, the twenty-one-year-old found this idea thrilling.

As the winter wore on, when Salvador was throwing one of his "high teas" at Trader Vic's for friends like Ultra Violet and Mia Farrow,[5] or off at one glitzy event or another that Gala, who preferred more intimate evenings, did not care to attend, she and Will began spending time together. Over the course of many dinners at some of Manhattan's best restaurants, where she would always quietly slip him money for the bill under the table, Gala and William got to know and like each other. Gala was curious and open to anything new particularly if it was pertinent to the art world. She loved meeting William's loft-mate, artist Wynn Chamberlan, and Will enjoyed visiting artists' studios with her. He appreciated the care with which she looked at the work she was shown and was impressed by her thoughtful, sharp questions.

On March 22, the Gallery of Modern Art at 2 Columbus Circle opened to great fanfare. It was headlined by the *New York Times* as "A&P heir Huntington Hartford's Palatial New Museum" and described by the Pulitzer Prize–winning architectural critic Ada Louise Huxtable as Edward Durell Stone's "die-cut Venetian Palazzo on Lollypops."[6] As the Madonna on the banner of Columbus's caravel in Dalí's *The Discovery of America by Christopher Columbus*, Gala was the star of the exhibition's centerpiece. She was viewed by 4,277 visitors on the museum's opening day.[7]

Although Rothlein did not attend the opening, his photographic portrait by Philippe Halsman was on display in one of the galleries. When the Dalís left for the April 15 vernissage of the *Surrealist Retrospective* in the Parisian Galerie Charpentier, Gala and William wrote and telephoned.

In Paris, the Dalís were, as usual, in room 108: the Alfonso XIII Suite at the Le Meurice, from which the eponymous deposed king of Spain had run his government-in-exile until his death of a heart attack in 1941. The apartment was decorated in eighteenth-century-style gilt, cream, and red brocade, and the toilet in Salvador's favorite bathroom had a gold leather seat. There were three bedrooms and two sitting rooms with walls of French windows overlooking the Jardin des Tuileries and the Louvre, with a view of the Eiffel Tower and Notre-Dame in the distance.

In this setting Dalí held court for a variegated entourage. It included several French television crews; assorted photogenic twenty-something blondes who were either models or script assistants; Carlton Lake, who was writing a book about Dalí; and a sculptor named Rutsch, with whom Salvador was creating a work to replace a possibly fake Dalí titled *Homage To Immanuel Kant.*[8] This controversial object was currently on display at the Galerie Charpentier, where it had already been viewed by the more than five thousand people, who jostled one another at the Surrealist show's opening.

The new *Homage* was a tribute to Duchamp's self-destructing bull. As soon as the statue was completed, it was publicly demolished by Rutsch for the delectation of the press, who were so baffled by the performance that they mistook it for vandalism and reported it incorrectly.

Ducking out of these melees as much as possible, Gala worked behind closed doors, organizing their upcoming summer in Spain. She emerged only rarely: to chat for a minute with her old friend the painter Leonor Fini, who had come for a visit, or to make sure her husband had his lunch on time. The second that Salvador ran out the door to an appointment, she would aggressively shoo all the reporters out of the suite. "That's the press for you," she muttered bitterly to Lake, who was watching her: "You're nice to them and look what happens!"[9]

True to character, when the Spanish magazine *Garbo*, generally dedicated to high-voltage film stars such as Jane Fonda and Brigitte Bardot, wanted to profile her for their September issue and requested an interview, Gala declined. Her "personal rule," she explained to *Garbo*'s editor, had always been "to never make any statements to the press."[10] "I intend," she amplified mysteriously, "to go down in history as a legend." Dalí agreed with this ambition. In his *Journal d'un Génie (Diary of a Genius)*, published earlier that year by La Table Ronde, he described Gala as more than a "genius." "She is," he wrote, "the unique mythological woman of our time."[11]

Film and television cameras were much in evidence that August, when William Rothlein arrived in Portlligat to join Gala as a model for a humorously titled painting: *Apotheosis of the Dollar*, which Dalí was making especially for the planned museum in Figueres. A visual résumé of Dalínean myths and obsessions, the work includes a portrait of Marcel Duchamp as Louis XIV, a reproduction of Watteau's *Lute Player*, Salvador himself painting Gala, and William as Hermes, the messenger god of thievery.

On the twenty-eighth, a French television crew arrived at the villa to make another documentary. Salvador, now wearing a black curly-haired wig, requested a "family portrait" of Gala and himself with William, whom he introduced as the mirror image of himself at twenty. William was to play Dalí *jeune* in a film collaboration with Visconti, tentatively titled *The Last Surrealist*.

A few days later Will, who had been sleeping across the street from the Dalís at the Portlligat Hotel, got very sick from drinking local tap water. Gala drove to see him every day for several weeks in the Figueres clinic, where she would sit for hours by his bedside, telling him jokes and stories about her childhood in Russia. At the end of his stay, Salvador also came to visit and made Rothlein's heart sing when he pronounced him "Adil": García Lorca's special anagram nickname for Dalí during the time of their closest friendship.

In the heady days of Indian summer that followed his recovery, Will and Gala spent magical mornings navigating the coves and inlets of the Costa Brava in one of her small yellow boats, returning in the early afternoon to lunches of just-caught seafood prepared by the Dalís' houseman Arturo and washed down with pink champagne. They had frequent visitors. Aristotle Onassis stopped by with Greek movie star Melina Mercouri, who was filming Juan Bardem's *Les Pianos Mécaniques* with James Mason in Cadaqués. Mercouri and Mason soon became regulars at the house. Sometimes they would all go out to dinner in one of the neighboring towns.

Gala spent her evenings with Dalí, but she went out of her way to make Rothlein feel important. The sexual tension that had been mounting between them intensified when William breakfasted on his hotel-room balcony with whomever he had slept with the previous night. Gala, who could see everything from her terrace, didn't like that.

In October, Gala and Will were driven to Rome by Ricardo, the Dalís' chauffeur, for several meetings organized by the Albarettos, who provided introductions to a corps d'élite of Italian filmmakers, including Vittorio De Sica, Michelangelo Antonioni, and Federico Fellini. Their leisurely route took them through the South of France, where they telephoned Picasso, who was in bed with a cold. They stopped off in Monaco for a heady evening of baccarat and chemin de fer at the legendary Hôtel de Paris, where their suites were contiguous. On the way back to their rooms, Gala looked at Will with such unabashed endearment that according to Rothlein, after a moment of wavering, he decided to "just let it happen." Gala and William became lovers that night.[12]

From Monaco, they made their way through Tuscany to the Etruscan mountain town of Volterra, where they enjoyed a wonderful dinner of wild boar, red wine, gossip, and laughter with Luchino Visconti. Unfortunately, Visconti was unable to take enough time off from *Sandra*, the movie he was currently making with Jean Sorel and Claudia Cardinale, to organize a screen test for Will just then.

They spent two nights with the Albarettos in Turin, before driving to Rome, where Federico Fellini was casting. After several hours of shooting Rothlein violently spreading paint on canvas, Fellini offered him a part in *Juliet of the Spirits*. "In my films, everyone is a star," he told the overjoyed actor.

Gala, who was hoping that Visconti, with whom Dalí had an excellent working relationship, would come through, hesitated. "There will be something better. Wait. There will be something better," she kept telling her twenty-one-year-old protégé, who could not imagine anything better than a role in Fellini's new film.

Rothlein was deeply attached to Gala and wanted to keep his friendship with both the Dalís intact. He finally gave in and turned the part down—but not without feeling both angry and regretful. For him the affair had become a Gordian knot of mixed emotions.

Alexander's sword fell swiftly. One evening, after a slightly tipsy dinner in a five-star restaurant, Will kissed Gala on the street in front of some Roman journalists who spent their life stalking the well-dressed and possibly famous in search of a scandal. The paparazzi went mad with excitement.

Salvador, who now called himself "*le divin*" ("the divine one"), was in Madrid receiving the Cross of the Order of Saint Isabella for extraordinary services to Spain, where he was generally viewed as half-god, half-hero, or, as Picasso's mistress the artist Françoise Gilot put it, "at the right hand of God and the pope."[13] When he saw the resulting photos in a local newspaper, Gala was summoned home.

The Albarettos, who had to buy up all the unpublished images to prevent further publicity, got William a first-class ticket to New York, where he received many worried letters from Gala and an affecting poem from Salvador that reads like a telegram: "LOWE YOU STOP" repeated thirteen times and signed with a little crown over the pointed "D" of the artist's signature.[14]

There was a tepid three-way reconciliation at the St. Regis that December, and as late as April 1965, Dalí was still hoping to make a movie with Will.[15] But Rothlein had fallen in love with someone his own age: a beautiful film star, Arabella Árbenz, whose father, Jacobo Árbenz, was the exiled president of Guatemala. At least from William's point of view, his affair with the fascinating woman who had introduced him to a world he'd only dreamed of was done.

Years later, long after he lost Arabella,[16] Will was traveling through Paris. He decided to stop by the Meurice, where, since it was springtime, the Dalís, who had been such a poignant part of his life, were surely in residence. When he rang up their suite from the lobby,

Gala answered the phone. "I remember you," she told him severely. "You're the one who likes to tipple. Well, you can't come up here without an appointment. And if you do anything to disturb or upset Dalí, I'll give you a piece of my shin in your back."[17]

When her affair with Rothlein was over, Gala immersed herself in the details of the Dalí enterprise. At seventy-one, the constant pressure of her jam-packed lifestyle was making her irritable. "We've got to have more free time," she told Carlton Lake at the Salon de Mai, which had just opened on May 16.[18] "I don't want to see Dalí working more than anyone else on this Earth. . . . I'm beginning to rebel. I'm being turned into a businessman. I might as well be on Wall Street."

A joking suggestion that she should buy some horn-rimmed glasses failed to amuse her: "I don't buy anything, neither glasses nor shoes, not even an appointment at the coiffeur, because I don't have time. I'm going to cut off a lot of people because Dalí just has too much to do. He will have to get more and give less and do the things he wants to do, whether they are things to sell or not—but do them of his own will," she retorted irately.[19]

Sadly, slowing down proved impossible. Gala posed for a photo montage of herself, Dalí, and Picasso for the back cover of the *Paris-Presse* issue announcing the Salon's opening. Then she attended a fashion show in the Meurice's lobby, organized by Peter Moore to celebrate the debut of a swimwear collection by Dalí for Jack A. Winter, a clothing manufacturer from Milwaukee. There, she watched disapprovingly as the elegant Irishman, with his pet ocelot draped over one shoulder, poured water on Salvador's head. Gala accompanied her husband to a "daytime discotheque" called "La Locomotive" ("The Locomotive"), stationed at 82 boulevard de Clichy, where Peter had arranged for Dalí and Andy Warhol to be "co–masters of ceremonies" at a performance by the British rock group the Zombies. (The band's latest hit, "She's Not There," had recently topped international charts.) And as she was packing up for the trip to Cadaqués, she

disdainfully observed Moore, who would later collect $5,000 (approx-
imately $48,000 in today's money) from the Beatles for a weed that
he claimed was one of Dalí's head hairs,[20] try to sell her husband's
priceless mustache to the industrial designer Raymond Loewy.[21]

August found Gala happily back in Italy this time as the guest of
Castrense Civello. In his teens, Civello had been a protégé of Filippo
Marinetti, one of Italy's great poets and the author of the *Futurist Manifesto*, but by 1965 he was chiefly focused on promoting the splendid
architecture of his native Bagheria, a densely populated port on the
Tyrrhenian Sea, eight miles northeast of Palermo. He had asked Salvador to make a sketch for the cover of a book he was writing about
the fabled Villa Palagonia, otherwise known as the Villa of Monsters.

Older than Rothlein, but still more than twenty years younger
than Gala, Castrense was tall and well-built, with wavy hair and dark
eyes. She was charmed by the inventive, unconventional word juxtapositions of his neo-Futuristic outsider poetry[22] and impressed by his
deep love for his country. Villa Palagonia, in particular, had a definite
allure. The Baroque mansion, built in 1749 by Francesco Fernando II
Gravina, the tenth Prince of Patagonia, was famous for its winding,
mazelike exterior staircase and the sculptures of human-faced ogres
that live in its gardens and decorate its walls. These lovable monsters had a long history of captivating discerning travelers like Henry
Swinburne, Alexandre Dumas, and André Breton. For Gala, the visit
to Sicily was a welcome escape.

She was back at work in Zurich, reviewing the Dalís' bank accounts a scant month later, when Amanda Lear,[23] a stunning blonde,
decked out in the tiniest of miniskirts over heavy work boots, arm in
arm with Brian Jones of the Rolling Stones, made a head-turning entrance at Castel, the famously fashionable private nightclub on Paris's
rue Princesse. They were invited to join Dalí's table.

Amanda was attracted by what she knew of Salvador Dalí's work
and intrigued by his cult-figure status. The swinging generation con-

sidered him "psychedelic," or, as she phrased it, "one of us." Brian, who found Salvador "crazy! Completely crazy!," was thrilled to be near him. And although the maestro had to leave almost immediately, he invited Amanda to lunch the next day at Lasserre, a hip, Michelin-starred restaurant near the Champs-Élysées.[24]

The introduction to Salvador was easy, but Amanda's debut with Gala was the definition of difficult. In her memoirs, dedicated to "Gala the loving wife," Lear details her first nerve-racking meeting with Mme Dalí. It was at the Meurice, where Gala, whom Lear describes as "tiny with narrow shoulders and broad hips," wore a stylish red pantsuit and a sparkling, chunky, colored-glass necklace. Her hair was tied back with her trademark black bow, which had been Chanel's welcome-home present to her in 1948. When Salvador introduced them, Gala greeted Amanda with a formal handshake, a guttural "*bonjour, chère,*" and the long stare of her "little bright eyes," which gave Amanda the impression that hiding anything from Mme Dalí would be impossible.

Because Gala refused to tolerate the "chic trendies" at Lasserre, the trio had dinner at nearby Pavillon Ledoyen, another Michelin-starred restaurant housed in a graceful neoclassicist mansion right on the Champs-Élysées, where Gala, who declined to order anything more than a clear consommé because everything else on the menu was too expensive, was the focus of Salvador's rapt attention as she coughed her way through the meal, complaining incessantly. The restaurant was airless. It was drafty. The Cadillac needed repairing. The chauffeur was too pricey. She had called Cadaqués. The heat wasn't working. During the entirety of this litany, which lasted throughout dinner, Gala completely ignored Amanda, who was made to feel totally invisible. The following day, Dalí reported that his wife, who was "an infallible judge of character and never made a mistake," had decided that Amanda was a "narcissist." "She says you never stopped looking at yourself in the mirror," he informed his horrified new protégée.[25]

By December 17, Amanda was modeling in London, and Gala was with Salvador at the preview of his three-hundred-work retrospective, "Salvador Dalí 1910-1965,"[26] at Huntington Hartford's Gallery of Modern Art at New York's Columbus Circle. John Canaday's half-page review in the *New York Times* was titled "Dalí's Postnatal Retrospective" and illustrated with a photograph of the artist's 1954 *Crucifixion (Corpus Hypercubus)*. Canaday felt the show needed editing, but praised Salvador's "flawless brush," and speculated that the exhibition would be "so crowded you will have to wait on line to see it." He went out of his way to mention that the room devoted to early works from Gala's personal collection was a proof of Dalí's notable, wide-ranging, and "eclectic" abilities.

The preview party itself was a black-tie charity event for Letters Abroad, an organization devoted to finding pen pals for American troops overseas. Here Gala, who was photographed for the *Times* society section next to Dalí's portrait of her, was trailed by Peter Moore, carrying his "snarling ocelot," and a thousand other art lovers, including the Morses, Mrs. George Vanderbilt, Mrs. Chester Dale, and chemical manufacturing heir Lammot du Pont III.[27]

On February 23, just two months after the ferment at Columbus Circle, Gala performed with Salvador in a mixed-media concert titled "Super Gelatinous Melting Silly Putty Happening," organized at Lincoln Center by the New York Philharmonic.

The performance had been announced in September at a Midtown Manhattan manhole by Dalí, dressed in a gold lamé jumpsuit. "Underneath Manhattan are the activities which give the city life," Salvador, stroking Babou, Peter Moore's ocelot, proclaimed to the assembled newsmen, soundmen, and photographers, who were invited to accompany him forty feet underground in a primitive cable car to the construction of a new sewer line. "[It's] a real happening when no one knows what's happening," the artist explained.[28]

Over three thousand people packed the opera house to watch Gala as Isolde and Salvador as Tristan on the Celtic seashore. Surrounded by undulating dancers from Sarah Lawrence College who represented the swell of the ocean, the lovers bade each other farewell with a passionate kiss before Dalí crawled into a large plastic bubble and was carried offstage by the "waves." In the next morning's *New York Times*, Grace Glueck, who found the dancers "athletic," was unmoved by the narrative. She tetchily described the sold-out "Super Gelatinous" as a mix of "Metro-Goldwyn-Mayer and Bohemian cliché."[29]

The conclusion of Carlton Lake's *In Quest of Dalí* quotes Salvador as saying, "My painting is the least important thing about me." There was an iota of truth in this improbable declaration. Performance had long been a part of the Dalínean practice. In fact it can be argued that the Dalís invented performance art. By the mid-1960s, however, the great creator had sadly become as Lake further describes it: "a High Priest of *Showmanship* as the ultimate Fine Art."[30] Gala herself had done much to cultivate this state of affairs, but Moore was pushing everything too far. She now deeply resented the "Captain" for greedily propelling her husband over the edge of the dangerous tightrope between excess and genius that she had always been so careful to help Salvador navigate. She feared that her husband was becoming a parody of himself.

It wasn't until June, when Gala was working in Portlligat on Jean-Christophe Averty's film *Soft Self-Portrait of Salvador Dalí*, which traces her life through Dalí's oeuvre, that Gala met up with Amanda Lear again. This time it was for dinner at the villa. Salvador had done the inviting, and as usual, Gala's menu was superlative: chorizo followed by lobster in chocolate sauce, washed down as always with the excellent local pink champagne. The combination of the sweet and the savory was so delicious that Amanda gratefully accepted seconds. "Mon petit Dalí," Gala commented as Amanda took her third helping. "It's unbelievable how much she consumes. We're going to have to lock up the larder each time she comes, or we will be eaten out of house and home!" When Amanda answered that she had been trying to be polite, Gala was amused. "Politeness," she said, "has nothing to do with it: Your skirt is so short I can see your knickers. How long are you planning to stay?" Amanda didn't know. "What do you mean, you don't know?" Gala retorted. "I have to know so I can make my plans. It will soon be the Feast of the Assumption, and I intend to leave for a few days at the beginning of September. I shall lend you Dalí! You can come here in your miniskirts. But I advise you to eat a little less. Otherwise you will end up as fat as that rhinoceros on my dining-room wall."

"She likes you," Salvador whispered to Amanda on the patio, where they were all sitting out under the stars after dinner, listening to a recording of *Tristan und Isolde*. "If she didn't, she would have said so by now."

CHAPTER 26

PETER MOORE'S SCANDAL

When Gala was off on her trip, Amanda flew to Barcelona. Salvador had his driver pick her up at the airport and installed her in the guest bedroom of the Dalí suite at the Ritz. She was given a minute to wash up in the exquisitely mosaicked Roman bath with gold taps before being whisked off to a Pertegaz Couture defilé.[1] After the show, where he was photographed by an engaging young journalist named Enrique Sabater for the Girona newspaper *Los Sitios*'s social column, Dalí bought a green silk evening dress decorated with pink rosebuds for Amanda and a bejeweled gold lamé gown for Gala, which he thought would make his wife look like a queen. Before driving up to Cadaqués, Salvador and Amanda dined at the Via Veneto, a "chichi pink restaurant of the kind Dalí loved, with waiters in velvet waistcoats and lace vests."[2]

The next morning, on her way to the beach, Amanda came upon a lean-to on the grounds of the villa, where she was surprised to see Salvador seated at a small table rapidly signing blank sheets of paper. It was, she said, just like an assembly line on which Moore, who stood beside the artist, handed Salvador a new sheet just as soon as he had finished marking the old one.[3]

Dalí's faithful assistant-cum-butler, Emilio Puignau, had similar, equally vivid recollections of that shack near the villa where Dalí kept boxes of blank sheets next to a small table. "I remember well those whole days that Dalí would spend signing in a totally automatic manner. . . . It was like a printing shop," he reminisced unhappily.[4]

According to Moore,[5] this practice began in 1965, when Pierre Argillet, one of Dalí's French publishers, suggested he sign some sheets of blank paper. That way, if for some reason Salvador could not turn up as planned to approve the prints when they were made, Argillet could still put the contracted-for work on sale. Moore negotiated for Argillet to pay Dalí an extra $10 per signature, and since the artist was able to sign one thousand sheets in one hour, this meant he could earn money with amazing rapidity. In the first instance, according to the Captain, Dalí signed ten thousand sheets in ten hours. This earned him $100,000 (approximately $963,000 today) in Gala's preferred method of payment, which was $100 bills.[6] Gala was not involved with this arrangement. According to Peter Moore's agreement with Gala, all multiples were his domain. Since Salvador never signed her name to the blank pages, her consent to this scheme was considered unnecessary.

A proponent of Duchamp, who acknowledged no distinction between a prototype and its reproduction, Salvador had been manipulated by Moore into imagining that if he signed a copy of one of his works, it became the original's equal. From there it was the smallest of steps to saying that anything, even a forgery, could be art if the artist signed it. Exclusively Peter Moore's concoction, this line of reasoning became a Pandora's box of misfortunes for Salvador, who had never bothered his head about business.

Meanwhile, the market for Dalí prints was soaring. According to Mark Rogerson's book *The Dalí Scandal*, as late as 1987, one New York gallery alone had a turnover of over $100 million in Dalí limited editions.[7] According to Moore, thousands of clean pieces of Archer and Japan paper bearing Dalí's signature were stored in dark places as far apart as Paris, Barcelona, and New York with which result low-quality works and/or forgeries were being palmed off on unwitting collectors for tens, sometimes hundreds of thousands of dollars.

Peter Moore and the Dalís were becoming richer and richer. Gala, who like many upper-class Europeans of her generation was ever worried about the possibility of another world calamity, squirreled away currency in multiple accounts and safety deposits throughout Europe and America without telling any one person about all of them. She alone knew how much money there was.

Moore, who was aware of only some of these stashes, estimated that by 1974 (when the cracks in his scheme became public knowledge), the Dalís had at least $200,000,000 cash in today's money. Mark Rogerson believes they were billionaires. That summer, a small truck transporting forty thousand undeclared Dalí signature sheets from Andorra to Paris was stopped by French customs officials. Although the owner of the papers in question, Jean Lavigne, a Parisian art publisher who lived in Palm Beach, was able to argue successfully that he was not breaching the law, press on both sides of the Atlantic had a field day with the news. The incident became, as James Markham described it in the *New York Times*, "an international scandal."[8]

A year later, when the law governing taxation of green-card holders in the United States changed, Gala was investigated by the IRS for failing to report all her bank accounts. She hired Michael Stout, a thirty-year-old lawyer from Wisconsin, to straighten things out. By 1976, Stout was able, with the help of international counsel, to secure an IRS refund of more than $200,000 or more than $1 million today, for the Dalís, and a delighted Gala sent him to Zurich to examine the bank account there. Unsurprisingly, the lawyer found that money was missing. Michael Stout questioned Moore, who responded, "When you are called a thief over and over, you eventually become one. Gala is a mean, stingy old woman who refused to pay me what I'm worth. So I paid myself."[9]

Gala dismissed the Captain. But the evil he did lived after him. When he no longer worked for the Dalís, Peter Moore stayed on in Cadaqués, where, to Salvador's enduring dismay, he sold art said to be by his former employer from his own "Dalí museum and gallery." Meanwhile, all over the world, fake Dalís were being hawked to the unwary. Robert Descharnes, who became Dalí's press secretary, claimed that forgers in Germany had discovered a way to photograph small sections of Dalí's paintings, blow them up, and sell them as "new works" by the artist. A lithograph edition of one hundred produced in this way for about $50 could be sold off at approximately $5,000 per print. In 1986, Reynolds Morse, Dalí's biggest collector, told Rogerson that he was being offered "at least ten Dalí fakes a week."[10] Gala, who had had nothing to do with Moore's chicanery, was nonetheless deeply affected by this outrage, which harmed Salvador's reputation and damaged the market for his genuine work.

John Peter Moore lived to be eighty-six. When he died, in December 2005, his obituary in the British daily the *Guardian* noted that in October 2004, he had been accused of "dramatically altering" Dalí's 1969 *The Double Image of Gala*, which was stolen from the Knoedler Gallery in 1974 and hunted by Interpol and the FBI for many years without success. In 1999, it was discovered in the Peter Moore Art Center in Portlligat, where Moore and his wife continued to run their gallery yards from Dalí's studio. Moore had cut down the original work and renamed it *Dalí Painting Gala*. A subsequent search of Moore's home revealed ten thousand fake Dalí lithographs. It was decided that Moore and his wife, Catherine Perrot, were too old to be incarcerated, but they were ordered to pay compensation estimated at $1.2 million to the Gala-Salvador Dalí Foundation, which is charged with looking after the painter's heritage.[11]

CHAPTER 27

AMANDA BECOMES A ROCK STAR, GALA IS ISHTAR

By the late 1960s, partially as a result of the now-active friction between herself and the Captain that climaxed in 1976, Gala had begun to spend more time on her own. And the friendship between Salvador and Amanda deepened.

Almost every excursion with Dalí was a small adventure for Amanda. In Paris, she dined at Maxim's with Salvador and beautiful Nanita, aka Louis XIV. At the Meurice, she traded jokes with Isabelle Adjani and Catherine Deneuve when they came to audition for a new play Salvador had started writing. At Lasserre, she chatted with André Malraux and Maurice Chevalier. When the handsome Alexis de la Falaise[1] began courting her, Dalí, who was a friend of his sister Loulou, Yves Saint Laurent's indispensable muse, suggested Amanda invite him to the villa. "He is exactly the kind of chevalier you need," the painter exclaimed. Ill-advisedly, instead of choosing Alex, Amanda became entangled in a nightmarish affair with the playboy millionaire race-car driver Rikky von Opel. When Rikky abandoned her as soon as she moved in with him both Gala and Salvador were there to console her.

She was also Dalí's frequent official escort. Amanda accompanied the artist to a private lunch with Prince Rainier and Princess

Grace of Monaco in December 1968 at the Le Negresco in Nice. The following year, she was the maestro's "show date" to Alexis de Redé's lush Oriental Ball at the seventeenth-century Hôtel Lambert in Paris, where she sat next to Audrey Hepburn at dinner and was photographed with the Begum Om Habibeh Aga Khan III and Salvador, who was wearing his Cross of Saint Isabella on a wide blue satin ribbon tied across his chest.

By the early 1970s, Amanda, who had modeled for high-fashion names including Paco Rabanne[2] and Ossie Clark,[3] and also for the chic speciality store Biba,[4] decided that she wanted a singing career. Her debut single, "Trouble," was released unsuccessfully by Creole Records in 1976. Dalí was nevertheless proud of Amanda's accomplishment. He adored Elvis Presley, who had first performed "Trouble" in 1958, and encouraged Lear to persevere.[5] Fortunately, Amanda's subsequent 1978 album *Sweet Revenge* sold in excess of four million copies.

When Gala's sister, Lidia, asked Gala if she minded reading about Amanda and Salvador in the society papers, Gala's response was characteristically pragmatic: "You know," she answered, "it doesn't bother me. Amanda's not my friend, but she is a good friend to Dalí."[6]

While Salvador basked in the glamorous glow of the international jet set, Gala, who came alive when she was nurturing young talent, was on the lookout for protégés. One such disciple was Michel Pastore, otherwise known as Pastoret or "little shepherd" in Basque dialect. A student from a ranching family in the western Pyrénées, Pastore was completing his studies in music and philosophy before becoming a novitiate. He described his impressions of Gala in his poetically fragmented essay, "Letter to My Brother."

What struck Pastore when he first saw "Dalí's wife" on the beach with the Albarettos was her almost ferocious intensity; it occurred to him that perhaps she was on drugs. As a matter of fact, he wrote, "she was not drugged. She was a Russian who bowdlerized the superfluous." Her life, which she lived with "the pomp of wild freedom," was, he discovered, "uprooted, segregated, and asocial." She followed her own rules, always wondering if the world would forgive her for "making the sound of being free."

Gala's anxious and frequently unhappy childhood was, according to Pastore, a paradoxical reason for the incandescence of her laughter, the fact that she treated life as though it were "one of the endless games of childhood," and the chariness of her love—which, however, she gave freely to all the stray dogs in the village and all the wild doves, which she called her *macou*.[7]

She lived in the present tense only. Her past existences—as a young exile and wife; a Parisian muse; a thin fashion plate; Salvador's Gravida or even the Madonna of Portlligat—meant nothing to her now.

She would, she confided, have liked to be a man because then she could have "accomplished great things." Was this why, Pastore wondered, she insisted on giving men she loved "the destiny she wanted for herself?"

"Gala was burdened," he wrote, "with the twin weights of hope and lucidity. She wanted to influence others so she could understand who they were." At the same time, "Her lovers were a load that was almost too heavy to bear. Were they really her friends? 'At war as in war [*sic*]' was one of her favorite mottos."

A devotee of simplicity, Gala, was true to her Russian roots. She came from the land of "the Siberian wolf" and the "lonely cowherd." "Uncomplicated peasants, taciturn fishermen and always animals" were her preferred company. She liked only fresh, very plain food. She ate her slice of country bread with grilled fish slowly, elegantly, with her fingers, carefully piling the small bones on one side of her plate.

"If, like me, you are neither a brain nor a beauty,"[8] she enjoyed repeating, "creating is the only antidote to self-betrayal." For her, the act of creation was mystical.

There is a wonderful photograph of Gala from the time of her friendship with Michel. She is seated on the floor at the foot of her grand piano. As she leans back against a wall, listening to him play favorite music (perhaps Wagner), she is radiant with joy. For Pastore, Gala was Isolde because "above everything she was faithful to her husband and their work." Gala was the "little soldier," intensely devoted to her art.

In March 1971, as he was finishing up his doctorate, and just before he started the process of becoming a monk and "took his retreat," Gala and Michel made a farewell journey to Athens.[9] Although they both knew the friendship was ending, when they said their final goodbyes Gala was furious—as Pastore put it, "beautiful in her anger"—at the thought of having to "continue her mission alone."[10]

In 1968, Reynolds Morse published his own *Ode à Gala Incognita*, a slim book that includes Morse's brief essay on Gala and a collection of unsigned poetry about her. The book is dedicated "To Gala Dalí / Daughter of Dada / Mother of Surrealism / and Ageless Queen of Dalínean Enigmas." Mirroring André Breton's *Nadja*, its conclusion reads, "Is Gala real? Or is she a phantom to be seen but never expressed?"[11]

Salvador began work on his most mythical image of Gala that spring. He named it *The Hallucinogenic Toreador*.

Bullfighting, for which Spain is historically famous, is rooted in prehistory. The Minoans, who inhabited Crete, practiced bull dancing as early as the Bronze Age (3300–1200 BC). In "Gilgamesh and the Bull of Heaven,"[12] the Mesopotamian hero fights the Sun Bull to avenge Ishtar, the goddess of war and sexual fertility. The beast seems unconquerable until Gilgamesh, dancing in front of him, lures it with his cape and bright weapons while his partner, Enkidu, plunges a knife into its neck.[13] For ancient Mediterranean civilizations like Greece and Crete, where Poseidon's emblem was a white bull, the bull represents the sea, which destroys and gives life, as well as the sun, which sets to rise again the next day. The sacrifice of the bull ensures rebirth. It's the ritualized link between love and death. Salvador said his inspiration for *Toreador* was the reproduction of the Venus de Milo on a box of colored crayons he discovered in a Manhattan art-supply store. When he saw the bullfighter's face in the shadows of Venus's midriff, *Toreador* was conceived.

Even though the bullfighters always gave her their little black caps when she and Salvador attended the fights in Figueres, Gala, who disliked watching animals being killed, had no love for corridas. *Toreador* was dedicated to her because for Salvador she was the icon of Ishtar. In this role she is the focal point of the composition. Her stern, otherworldly visage appears on the steps of the ring. Bowing to her divinity, a youthful Dalí salutes Gala, whose sacred face is encircled with a halo of radiant red-gold. To the bottom left of the composition, a rectangular burst of color steers the eye toward the shape of a bull's head with blood dripping from its mouth. The blood pools form the seascape of Cap de Creus, where Gala appears for a second time floating on the blood pond in her little yellow raft. The work is a mirror of art as magic and magic as art. *The Hallucinogenic Toreador*'s progress was carefully documented through the year and a half of its making. John Lennon and Yoko Ono admired a 1969 version of it when they made a pilgrimage to Portlligat as part of their honeymoon that March, and Reynolds Morse snapped up the finalized version of *Toreador* from Knoedler in 1970 before the gallery even had a chance to put it on display.

CHAPTER 28

A CASTLE IN SPAIN

Enrique Sabater, in whose *Los Sitios* society column Salvador had appeared frequently by the late '60s, was interested in writing about *Toreador*. A jack of all trades, Enrique was both multitalented and ambitious. Before becoming a journalist, he had worked in public relations for the Ampuriabrava tourist development near Rosas. He was also an excellent pilot and a gifted photographer. He arrived at his interview with Dalí in the fall of 1968 carrying a slew of photographs with which he hoped to impress the artist. Among the images he brought with him were aerial shots of a crumbling eleventh-century walled manor near the parish of Púbol, named for the silvery poplar trees that grew through and around it.

For more than thirty years, since the days of their first love, Salvador had been promising to grant Gala's childhood wish to be the queen of her own castle, but the right property had been nearly impossible to find. Dalí needed something secluded enough to give Gala a feeling of independence and privacy and close enough to be an easy drive from the villa. At forty miles southwest of Portlligat, Púbol's situation was ideal.

Salvador was painting in his studio when Enrique arrived with his prints. "Dalí dropped everything and started to say, 'Gala! Gala! Gala' Right away he was in love already just to see one photograph. I never understood that," Sabater, who would soon replace the Captain as Salvador's representative, remembered.[1]

Dalí and Amanda drove to inspect the domain, which turned out to be a huge house of ancient stones surrounded by acres of tangled rose gardens where wild pigs roamed at will. Past a great courtyard, an imposing flight of steps led up to a landing surmounted with Gothic reliefs and an escutcheon whose coat of arms was a regal black crow spreading wide wings. As they peered at the once-fine interiors through a gap in the crumbling wall, a large bird of prey appeared, like an omen fluttering out of the shadows.[2]

Gala received her gift with grace and severity. "I accept the Castle of Púbol, but on one condition: that you will come to visit me there by written invitation only," she told Salvador, who for his part was delighted with his new role of Gala's gallant knight suitor in their modern-day feudal romance.

The builder Emilio Puignau, with whom she had worked so closely on the Portlligat villa, was hired for the restoration, which Gala monitored vigilantly. "So far, we have always triumphed in our work together," she wrote to Puignau. "The little house in Portlligat is famous . . . everywhere. Now . . . we will have a grand new success . . ."

Gala gave Dalí six commissions: 1) A fifty-foot ceiling with a fresco representing a nocturnal hole in the Mediterranean sky from which Surrealist treasures would fall; 2) Chairs that do not touch the floor; 3) Six stork-legged elephant water spouts to lead the way to her swimming pool; 4) Twenty-seven ceramic heads of Richard Wagner to decorate the pool; 5) Radiator covers painted with trompe l'oeil images of radiators; 6) Solid-gold showerheads and water taps for her bath.

Even only half-finished, the restoration was arresting. That September, Salvador and Amanda received a little engraved card that read, "Gala invites you to the castle of Púbol on September 18th at 4:30 P.M." The chatelaine walked her guests through the garden to the pool, which was almost completed. "Here I want you to design a bench in the shape of a flower," she said to Dalí, as he looked for the right spots to place his elephants. Walking up the stairs to the manor, Amanda noticed that the crow coat of arms still guarded the front door.

In the reception room, a long white table covered with religious icons held the place of honor under a vast candelabrum. High-backed chairs upholstered in white linen stood against the wall. The salon was distinguished by its large fifteenth-century tapestry, and a hand-somely carved antique walnut door. The tall windows afforded a view of the sky. In front of a long red divan where Gala served her guests fresh orange juice and tea cakes, an oval ostrich-legged glass-topped table was placed over a hole in the floor. When one looked down, through the table one could see the stable below. "I want it to be mo-nastic," . . . "With Dalí there is always too much of everything," Gala whispered to Amanda.

"Come back soon, Galushka. 'I'm waiting for you baby. Come back,'" Salvador sang, parroting a 1960s recording by the Equals as he and Amanda left for Portlligat.[3]

By April 1970, work was almost completed and Dalí wrote joy-fully that Gala had finally become "the impregnable castle she had never ceased to be. The fact is," Gala countered modestly, "that at best I might be a small tottering tower which, out of decorum, cloaks itself in thick ivy to hide its derelict walls—and find a little solitude."[4]

More than half a century later, Púbol is now, like the Portlli-gat villa, a much-trafficked museum on a small street that has been renamed Gala's Way. From its high perch forty miles from the sea, the manor has a bird's-eye view of La Pera's rocky, romantic coun-tryside, sprinkled with medieval townships and shining towers that guard every steep hill. A gathering of everything she found beautiful and desirable, this re-creation of Gala's childhood dream offers a rare glimpse into its chatelaine's extraordinary imagination, and a privi-leged view of her richly imagined personal life.

To dramatize her castle's interior, Gala enlarged spaces by demolisihing walls and removing parts of the second floor to create two-story ceilings. The result is a sequence of spacious rooms that are both simple and grand.

A taxidermied white Lusitano stallion[5] with a graceful neck and finely chiseled head stands proud in the center of the wide stables to greet new visitors to the castle. He may also be viewed by looking down through the ostrich-foot glass-topped table in the room above. In the adjacent garage, Gala's midnight-blue 1970 Coupe DeVille Cadillac, with leopard-print cushions and license plates from the principality of Monaco, is parked in front of a wooden nineteenth-century peasant's cart. In the Room of the Escutcheons, as Gala renamed the reception room, a long table draped with a white cloth adorned with a crucifix is placed under Púbol's coat of arms with its blazon of two crows.

The Escutcheons room's vaulted ceiling does not, as Gala had originally requested, represent a hole in the night sky spilling Surrealist treasures. Instead, the entire space, which was painted in 1969, is occupied by an eyelike circle that fades behind a crescent moon. Dalí called this fresco an homage to the current events of 1969, which was the year it was painted. It was on July 20, 1969, that Americans first walked on the moon. That same day Franco put the monarchy into orbit.[6]

The seats Gala had covered in white linen are now flanked by one of Salvador's oddities, Chair of Spoons, an old bronze stool to which Dalí attached ten wooden spoons and lion's-claw feet. Gala's "throne": a gold rococo cathedra whose back frames a circular Dalí painting of sunrise over the desert stands up three stairs, where it is guarded by two carved beechwood lions.

Past the lions, a life size portrait of an adolescent Gala[7] hovers in the air like an apparition, and points guests to the Lady of Púbol's personal chambers.

The first of these is the music room, whose grand piano Michel Pastore played for his lady's pleasure and where she first served tea to Amanda and Salvador. The walls are blanketed with two outsize fifteenth-century tapestries, the larger of which is signed "D. Eggermans" and pictures a wrestling match. Hung over the low strawberry-colored sofa, the second needlepoint, of a hunter on foot, is about half the size of the first.

On the west wall, Dalí's 1971 *Path to Púbol* reveals a narrow, dark path winding through a field of tall grasses past three tall poplars, where the white stallion pauses, turning his head to look back at the town and its church. In the sky, far above Púbol's steeple, a heavenly Gala floats in the sunset of a celestial landscape where minarets of a pearly Orthodox basilica gleam through copper-colored cumuli back-lit by the fading sun's last rays.

The spare, white-and-blue master bedroom is an example of Gala's talent for making the minimal luxurious. A wide canopied bed with turquoise curtains, two sofas, a table, and a large mirror with a wide chased-silver frame from Birmingham are its only furnishings.

To the side of the bed, a nearly invisible door leads to Gala's two favorite chambers, her private bath and her dressing room. Until her death, Mme Dalí, who was a devotee of facials and had had plastic surgeries as well as "youth injections" in Switzerland, did everything she could to preserve her appearance.[8] Although she socialized infrequently at Púbol, she refused to go out without makeup and never attended a party or a public appearance without first visiting her hairdresser. Gala's cozy, bright dressing room, warmed by a generous domed fireplace, was characteristically furnished for beauty and comfort. Its ample makeup table is cluttered with bottles of Chanel No. 5 and small jars of Oil of Olay. A spray of wheat in a small, curved vase was placed near the mirror for good luck.[9]

Gala's bathroom is exquisite. Andalusian tiles with Renaissance motifs of gold- and apricot-colored phoenixes, a gift of Ignacio de

Medina, Duke of Medinaceli, who had acquired them from the Carthusian Monastery in Seville, decorate the walls. And as Gala requested, the taps of the bath and washbasin are gold.

The guest bedroom, or Red Room, is all white, but the few carefully selected furnishings—a canopied bed, a small tufted banquette, and an oval draped table—are all covered in crimson. A little engraving of a guardian angel by Salvador Dalí hangs over the bed.

Down the back stairs in the silver-and-white kitchen, a parchment-colored rectangular table has been set for breakfast with porcelain dishes delicately and humorously decorated with reproductions of Millet's *L'Angélus*.[10]

The Three Glorious Enigmas of Gala Christ after "Pieta" and the Persian Sibyl by Michelangelo in the Sistine Chapel (1982), Dalí's last homage to his wife, was painted in the adjacent dining room where he worked from an easel set next to the long table between the fireplace and the door.

The cellar, or *delme*, where in the Middle Ages the inhabitants of the county came to pay their tithes (10 percent taxes due the lords of Púbol for anything grown or tended in their domain), is where Gala entertained the townspeople.

When she moved into the castle, the mayor of Púbol had asked Gala if on rainy days she could hold the local summer-solstice festivities in her *delme*. Gala not only agreed but paid all the expenses of the events. When she was in residence, she also enjoyed hosting weekend teas there for the village children. Now the *delme* is a crypt where, below the marble chessboard designed by Dalí as her tomb covering, Gala was buried in 1982.

Púbol's idyllic garden is its hallmark. Just past its gate, a long pathway edged by oleanders, medlars, and blackberry bushes that intertwine to create a green ceiling leads to the delicate marble statue of Venus guarding a bower overgrown with ivy and jasmine. This was, as Gala described it, her "place for heart-to-heart talks." On the other side of the arbor, Salvador's cement elephants on long gawky storks' legs sprout elegant sprays from their sinuous trunks as they ramble through the cypress on the way to the swimming pool, which is fed with a fall of fresh water through the mouth of a monstrous stone anglerfish. Surrounding this fountain, reproductions of a bust of Richard Wagner in different shades of varnished ceramic pay homage to the castle's romantic persona.

From the end of the '60s, wherever she traveled, Puból stayed in Gala's thoughts. It was her protection and her emblem of freedom and privacy.

Gala took a break from her gardens in November 1970, when she traveled with Salvador to his anthological exhibition at the Boijmans Van Beuningen museum in Rotterdam. It was the first time Dalí's work had been shown in Holland, and the opening was attended by more than two hundred thousand fans. Organized by the museum's first head curator of modern art, Renilde Hammacher-van den Brande, the installation juxtaposed Dalínean works from the 1930s and 1940s, including *Visage of the War* (1940) and Dalí's 1939 portrait of *Shirley Temple*, where she is painted as a child Sphinx, with fifteenth-century works by Hieronymus Bosch and Pieter Bruegel's dizzyingly detailed *Tower of Babel* (1563). There was, as Mrs. Hammacher-van den Brande later noted in a television interview, a real "communication between the images."[11] Dalí wrote a short preface to the catalog, in which he praised the art of his friend the Dutch-American painter Willem de Kooning and both Gala and Dalí were grateful to revisit works they hadn't seen for several years. *A Couple with Their Heads Full of Clouds* (1936), from Edward James's vast collection, made Salvador particularly nostalgic.

The publication of the December 1971 issue of French *Vogue* later that month was cause for a celebration at the Meurice. Dalí had been commissioned to create a special, luxurious commemoration of the monthly's fiftieth anniversary. The cover he chose was a photograph of Marilyn Monroe by Philippe Halsman, that he had "Mao-ized" by giving Marilyn's face Chairman Mao Zedong's trademark bald head. Below the Mao/Marilyn, a dedication to Gala is handwritten and signed "Salvador Dalí."

The magnificent issue features a double-page spread of the Gala photograph *Tête à Château* and the famous Man Ray image of Gala's "wall-piercing" eyes, covered with Salvador's handwritten endearments. These are followed by David Bailey photographs of a "Mao-ized" Veruschka, a nude Jean Shrimpton wrapped in sumptuous Léonard ribbons, and Amanda Lear, stretched out on a cream-colored cement cross in her formfitting Pertegaz green satin dress with pink rosebuds.

A cache of enticing views of the Púbol interiors by Marc Lacroix includes one image in which Michel Pastore plays the grand piano while Gala, seated in a small white chair behind a golden curtain, listens attentively from the room beyond. Party pictures of Dalí's outdoor cocktail party in honor of Marcel Proust, who is represented on a large poster hung by the swimming pool in Portlligat, round out the photographs.

Salvador personally contributed text in the form of an article titled "Le Point de Vue de Dalí" ("Dalí's Viewpoint"), and a short story by Ronald Firbank[12] as well as a review of Les Princes restaurant, newly opened in the Hotel George V. A breathtaking sequence of advertisements for gifts from Chanel, Nina Ricci, Guerlain, Jean Patou, Givenchy, Lanvin, Baccarat, Porthault, and Hermès that are either drawn by Dalí or designed by the artist and shot by Halsman round out this special Christmas edition.

CHAPTER 29

DARKNESS AND LIGHT

Four thousand miles across the Atlantic, Jeff Fenholt, a twenty-year-old who had grown up "tough," as he described it, in Columbus, Ohio, was being propelled to international stardom as Jesus Christ in Andrew Lloyd Webber's rock opera *Jesus Christ Superstar*, at the Mark Hellinger Theatre in Manhattan.[1]

Fenholt's astronomical ascent at the start of this new decade coincided with the dawn of a period in which contemporary art was neither well understood nor deeply appreciated. From 1970 to the early 1980s, the Museum of Modern Art's purchases of works by unknown artists slowed to a trickle. Simultaneously, with the exception of a 1970 Frank Stella retrospective, which left some critics grumbling that the thirty-six-year-old artist had already lost his edge, MoMA's major shows of the decade were Barnett Newman (1971), Marcel Duchamp (1973), Robert Rauschenberg (1977), and Sol LeWitt (1979), all artists who had risen to prominence in the 1950s or, in Duchamp's case, well before that.[2]

During this time of worry and indecision over the Vietnam War, student protests, the Watergate scandal; the energy crisis; and stagflation, rock music became the universally accepted language of cutting-edge expression. Led Zeppelin ("Stairway to Heaven"), the Who, (*Tommy*: a rock opera about a messianic deaf, dumb, and blind pinball genius), Elton John ("Candle in the Wind"), and Pink Floyd ("The

Great Gig in the Sky"), to name a handful of examples, were the real artists du jour. So although it is certain that she genuinely cared for him, Gala's attraction to Jeff Fenholt when she met him after one of his performances that January in New York was, to say the least, timely.

According to his 1994 "Testimony" *From Darkness to Light*,[3] Jeff's first memory was of being physically abused. When he was three years old, his mother amused herself by pouring a pitcher of ice water on his head while he was sleeping. It was the middle of the night. "Naturally," he wrote, "I was filled with hatred. Wouldn't you be?"[4] When Jeff turned twelve, his mother had him arrested for no apparent reason. The psychiatrist who interviewed him in the juvenile detention center where he was taken after the arrest reported that he found the child, who may have had a borderline personality disorder, to be "abnormal" and "incapable of love."

After almost three years of juvenile delinquency precipitated by this traumatic episode, Jeff stole a sound system from a neighboring church and managed to start his own band. He moved out of his mother's house, and by his fifteenth birthday, he had cut a single with a local rock group called the Fifth Order. Its title was "Goin' Too Far," and it hit the Top 40 on the Ohio pop charts.

By the time Jeff met Gala, he had already been on the cover of *Time* magazine,[5] and his latest recording, the cast album of *Jesus Christ Superstar*, was about to sell twelve million copies worldwide. He was also married to a beautiful convent-school-educated born-again Christian named Maureen (Reeni) McFadden from a prosperous Irish-American family. Jeff and Reeni had two children, a son named Tristan and a daughter named Shaye. Unfortunately, Jeff was also inextricably involved with whiskey and cocaine. His on-again-off-again relationship with Reeni frequently turned violent, and on at least one occasion, their fights landed her in the hospital.

Fenholt, who was extremely attractive, with long, thick auburn curls that fell past his shoulders and a mad, bad, sexy glint in his deep blue eyes, quickly became Gala's confidant, protégé, and show date, in which guise he was the perfect counterpart to the head-turning Amanda on Salvador's arm.

Over the next decade he was also a welcome guest at Púbol, where he spent several months every year being pampered, encouraged, and liberally subsidized while he made recordings that were never quite hits. By all accounts, Gala, who no doubt had great sympathy for Jeff's hard-knocks childhood and was deeply impressed by his raw talent and the successes of his early career, did everything she could to promote him to the ranks of musical genius. Fenholt, who admired both Dalís, also grew close enough to Salvador to call him "my best friend."[6] And while Mme Dalí's ongoing generosity, including a one-hundred-pound chocolate Easter egg for Jeff's daughter Shaye[7] and a lavish country house on Long Island for his entire family,[8] may very well have enabled Jeff's drug habit, it's a good guess that her motherly solicitude probably also saved the singer's life. To his credit, Fenholt, who denied ever having had a sexual relationship with the seventy-seven-year-old Gala, kept his promise to her and refused to discuss their life in her castle with the press.

After Gala's death in 1982, a short, acrimonious stint with the heavy-metal band Black Sabbath while they were recording their *Seventh Star* album, and a brief flirtation with occult practices, Jeff Fenholt abandoned rock music. Teaming up with Reeni, with whom he had had four more children and who dutifully went on tour with him, he become an evangelical preacher. At the time of his death, in 2019, Fenholt was a high-profile personality on the Trinity Broadcasting Network,[9] from which, according to his son Tristan, who is also a pastor, he "touched the lives of hundreds of thousands of people."[10]

Although the contemporary art world of the '70s was critically underappreciated, it was anything but dead. The conservative regimes of Richard Nixon and Gerald Ford proved paradoxically to be an exceptionally fertile time for unbridled artistic innovation, and the Dalís' practice was very much in step with the times.

By 1970, performance art, long pioneered by the Dalís, had sky-rocketed from its beginnings in the '60s. The Chilean Surrealist Roberto Matta's son Gordon Matta-Clark's 1972 restaurant FOOD, on the corner of New York's Prince and Wooster Streets, was a social/artistic experiment that became a soup kitchen, a salon for creatives, and a new way to integrate life and art into living sculpture.

Gala and Salvador followed suit the following year, when they published a bountifully illustrated cookbook—cum—art multiple, *Les Diners de Gala*, as their testimonial to food as an art form. The book also pays homage to Gala's famously artful dinners, which she populated with an ever-changing assortment of Fellini-like figures: film stars, writers and painters, transvestites, Spanish magistrates, French state ministers, locals, socialites, and beautiful young things from the modeling agency owned by Dalí's friend Jean-Claude Vérité, aka the Count du Barry.[11] The book was filled by the Dalís with observations about the synergy of food and art that accompanied and augmented their Surrealist recipes tested by Michelin-starred chefs from Lasserre, Maxim's, and La Tour d'Argent.

In January 1972, Vito Acconci performed "Seedbed," where, taking a leaf from Dalí's famous 1929 painting *The Great Masturbator*, he masturbated in Ileana Sonnabend's gallery, out of sight of the visitors who came to view his art. At the same time, Marina Abramović continued to blur the line between the body and the canvas, and art historian John Richardson, who was both a Knoedler vice president and the gallery's liaison to the Dalís, complained vociferously about being forced to cover nude girls in paint and roll them on sheets of paper for a March 1972 Dalí show. "Amazingly," Richardson exclaimed, "the stuff sold."[12]

Meanwhile, environmental artists like Robert Smithson (*Spiral Jetty*) and Walter De Maria (*The Lightning Field*) and installation artists such as Yayoi Kusama (*Infinity Mirrors*) built three-dimensional, site-specific works designed to transform the perception of space. Holography, a scientific method for generating *real* three-dimensional images, was one of Dalí's contributions to this prevalent artistic exploration of four-dimensional art.

On May 4, 1972, the first holograms ever shown were exhibited at Knoedler. They were based on the latest optical technology, and were created by Salvador in collaboration with Dennis Gabor, who had won the Nobel Prize for Physics the previous year.[13] Exhibited work included a holograph of a room in the Figueres museum containing a painting of Gala, and baseball players becoming angels, which was published by the Italian magazine *Bolaffi Arte* that June. The following April, Knoedler exhibited Dalí's cylindrical hologram *First Cylindric Chromo-Hologram Portrait of Alice Cooper's Brain*, which was dedicated to the flamboyant rock star, who Gala met through Jeff Fenholt and whose most recent album, *Love It to Death*, still hovered near the top of the charts.

Gala, who turned seventy-nine in September, was suffering from arteriosclerosis. Her heartbeat had become irregular, and she was frequently dizzy and out of breath. As always, she looked toward the future. It was time, she decided, to make peace with her death. She paid a pre-Christmas visit to the vast eleventh-century Santiago de Compostela Cathedral, where Saint James the Apostle's remains are interred.

The first Christian martyr,[14] Saint James was, even more importantly, one of only three disciples who were chosen to witness the Transfiguration. His basilica is the destination of an 800-year-old pilgrimage that covers 490 miles from Saint-Jean-Pied-de-Port in the Basque Country and crosses the Pyrénées. It's a journey on foot that is undertaken yearly by thousands of penitents, who heap stones on the cathedral's altar as a symbol of their desire to relinquish their sins and grievances in preparation for the afterlife. The church was consecrated in front of King Alfonso IX in 1211, after Master Mateo added its most spectacular feature, the Pórtico de la Gloria, in 1188. Famously decorated with two hundred sculpted figures representing the Apocalypse, the entry is surmounted by the figure of Saint James welcoming the faithful at the end to their journey.

Safely back from her penitant expedition that August, Gala turned her attention to her legacy and agreed to a very rare interview with Jordi Ballester of the Barcelona daily evening paper *Tele/eXpres*. Its subject was the Dalí Theatre-Museum in Figueres. "The collection of Dalí works which will be exhibited [in the museum] is mine because I have been putting it together year after year, setting it aside from the market to make sure to have something kept for tomorrow. I am giving [this collection] as a loan on the condition that I can dispose of it as I wish. . . . It is my obligation to make provision for the future," she told the reporter.

From then forward, Gala's focus would be her last great collaboration with her husband: the Teatro-Museo Dalí in Figueres.

CHAPTER 30

JACOB'S LADDER

Unlike most museums, the Teatro-Museo, which is really as much an integrated artwork as it is a museum, remains deliberately incomplete: "If it is ever finished, I will die," Dalí, who believed that all art is a quest for immortality, explains in *Dalí's Last Masterpiece*, the documentary film about the museum's creation. Each space within the Museo represents one of the artist's own specific obsessions. The building itself is a cohesive environment, containing a series of theatrical installations that connect the varied facets of Dalí's vision into the one world of his mind. The result is a composite portrait of Salvador. Within it, Gala is everywhere.

Beginning in the courtyard of the theater, now transformed into an open-air garden, a totem pole[1] is surrounded by four "G"-shaped flower beds. The base of the sculpture, one of Gala's old Cadillacs, is surmounted by the alchemical artist Ernst Fuchs's statue of Queen Esther pulling chains.[2] A pillar of tires representing a triumphal column for the Spanish-born Roman emperor Hadrian; a marble bust of François Girardon, the French Baroque sculptor famous for his works in the gardens of Versailles; and Dalí's treatment of Michelangelo's *Slave* complete this tower. The crown of the pile, Gala's small golden dinghy, drips the blue waters of the Mediterranean. Described by Salvador as "the biggest Surrealist monument in the world," the totem is a paean to art's infinity.

The triple themes of "Gala," "freedom," and "limitlessness" carry through to the stage of the old theater, which is surmounted by a huge geodesic dome designed by Emilio Pérez Piñero in the tradition of Buckminster Fuller. The dome's interior installation includes the famous *Hallucinogenic Toreador* and Dalí's Cubist portrait of the face of Abraham Lincoln. When the viewer squints his eyes, the American president transforms into Gala's naked back.

Gala's personal collection is housed in the Treasure Room, which is lined in red velvet like a box for precious jewelry. Here, the masterworks she carefully assembled over more than forty years include the poetic/hermetic *Basket of Bread* (1945), which links daily life and the Eucharist with art to create a transcendental experience; *Gala Nude from Behind* (1960); *Gala Laughing*, in which she actually smiles (1969); *The Spectre of Sex-Appeal* (1934); and a lyrical 1923 plein-air painting structured around the rose window in the Cadaqués church titled *Port Alguer*. This astonishing work, in which the buildings are Cubist and the sea is painted impressionistically, also displays Dalí's early mastery of a dazzling range of painterly techniques. After the museum opened, Gala's trove, which featured both acclaimed work and gems that had never been seen, was internationally praised. As the *Pittsburgh Press* reported, Salvador "publicly thanked his Russian wife for setting aside two of his paintings every year to become part of the museum. . . ."[3]

The Mae West Room, indirectly inspired by *The Ladder of Love*, Gala's 1930s maquette for a Surrealist living space, is a portrait of the iconic film star. It contains the lip sofa first designed for Edward James. Twin photographs of the Seine River in Paris represent the Hollywood star's eyes. And from a distance, the trees along the riverbank look like her eyelashes.

The Palace of the Wind is the room where Dalí's first exhibition, a group show in the old theater, was mounted when he was nineteen. It is named for the fierce tramuntana, the mountain wind said to drive men mad, which Salvador liked to "conduct" with a small baton from the top floor of his family house in Figueres when he was a little boy. Fittingly, this, one of the loveliest (and most amusing) installations in the museum, is all about the heavens. Here the sky is painted on the ceiling in the style of a Baroque cathedral, where it is flanked by the two suspended figures of Gala and Salvador, who hover between heaven and Earth so that all the viewer can see is the soles of their feet. The sky in the painting is really a reflection of the sky in the waters of the bay of Rosas,[4] where the sea merges seamlessly with the heavens and the Spanish inventor Narcís Monturiol's prototype submarine emerges from the center of the sun.[5] As in Gala's fantasy for her ceiling in Púbol, on either side of the sky the magic chests of Surrealism have fallen open to spill their largesse of golden coins, whirling wheels, and stars on their audience.

In the reception room, Gala and Salvador are tenderly represented in a Watteau-like image of the journey to Cythera, the island where Aphrodite was born. This leads to the bedroom, which displays, among other treasures, Dalí's portrait *Galatea of the Spheres* (1952), where Gala's face is a fusion of atomic theory and Renaissance art.

An opulent bed in the form of a shell was purchased by Dalí from the famously luxurious Parisian brothel Le Chabanais.[6] The bed itself is said to have belonged to "the most beautiful woman in Europe,"[7] the blonde Italian Comtesse de Castiglione, who was a spy for her country at the court of Napoleon III, where she became the emperor's mistress and an artist in her own right.[8]

The Torre Galatea, named in honor of Gala, is the last room of the museum. It is devoted to one of Salvador's lifelong fascinations: the hallucinatory experience of optical illusion, which he believed to be a bridge to infinity.

In this category, Gala is especially visible in Dalí's stereoscopic images of the 1970s,[9] including *Gala's Foot* (1974), *Dalí Seen from the Back Painting Gala from the Back Eternalized by Six Virtual Corneas Provisionally*

Reflected by Six Real Mirrors (1973), *Dalí Lifting the Skin of the Mediterranean Sea to Show Gala the Birth of Venus* (1977), and *The Chair* (1975).

Perhaps the most successful of these paintings is *The Chair*, in which a left and a right image are combined by means of mirrors to achieve a three-dimensional effect. Here, two separate portraits of Gala, seen from the back observing a chair hovering in the air in front of her, are combined by looking through a stereoscope.[10] Observed together with the help of properly placed mirrors, the images coalesce. Enhancing the trompe l'oeil, Dalí's hand, painting Gala's hair in the foreground, is reproduced in exact detail, including warts.

In these and in all her collaborations, as the scholar Estrella de Diego indicates,[11] Gala, like La Castiglione, acts as an artist and a performer who carefully plans her own images to inflect and define the work where they are reproduced.

The opening of the Teatro-Museo dedicated to the quest for life eternal was conceived as a birthday present to Gala. Scheduled to take place on September 23, 1974, a handful of days from her eightieth birthday, it was, as Amanda remembered, covered by journalists from all over the world.

The first guests to arrive, a few days in advance of the opening, were Reynolds and Eleanor Morse. As owners of about 10 percent of Salvador Dalí's output, they now had the largest collection of his work in the world and had opened a Dalí museum in their hometown of Cleveland, Ohio. They wanted to be the first to congratulate the Dalís in Portlligat.

When the great day finally dawned, Gala drove with Jeff Fenholt in her Cadillac to meet Salvador and Amanda. She wore a vermilion-and-gold dress by Elizabeth Arden, with a Russian-style bodice, full sleeves, and toggle closures. She had wound a double-strand necklace of huge, lavishly mounted turquoise drops, which Éluard had given her in 1928, around her neck.

The city itself was overflowing with locals, tourists, and a pack

of hippies who, to be as close as possible to their idol, had camped
out on the beaches near the Dalí house. Television cameras were everywhere. As the foursome made their spectacular entrance to the
opening ceremony, musicians and dancers, majorettes and elephants
performed in the streets for more than one thousand invited guests.
Spain's deputy prime minister, José García Hernández, presented
Dalí with the Gold Medal of Figueres in the square in front of the
town hall. When the speeches were over, Salvador and Gala, carrying
a spray of sweet-smelling white spikenard, which is the symbol of
eternal love,[12] led the throng through the thirteenth-century capital
to the Teatro-Museo.[13, 14]

A few weeks after the Teatro-Museo celebration, Gala received another priceless present. Anastasia Tsvetaeva had finally been released
from the Gulag, and a copy of Воспоминания, her just-published and
soon-to-become-famous *Memoirs*, was delivered to Gala's doorstep.
The handwritten inscription read, "To my dear Galushka, as Marina
called you, to my friend from adolescence, here is the book of our
young and old Moscow: With tender affection, Anastasia Tsvetaeva
(in the year of my 80th birthday)."

CHAPTER 31

A TIME TO REAP

Although her health was clearly in decline, the last seven years of Gala's life were as peaceful and rich as such years can be.

Together with Salvador, she was the recipient of the Prix Montesquieu de la Sommellerie Française for *Les Vins de Gala*. A sequel to *Les Diners de Gala*, published in October 1977 by the Parisian house Draeger, this 291-page artist's book/oenophile's bible lists twenty wine categories: ten each by Gala and Salvador.

Dalí's are classically organized by region, e.g., the Wines of Shiraz, King Minos (the historic winery of Crete), the legendary Lacryma Christi (from the slopes of Mount Vesuvius), Châteauneuf-du-Pape (the Rothschild winery in the Rhone Valley, with an essay by Philippe de Rothschild), Great Bordeaux Wines, Romanée-Conti (Burgundy), Château d'Yquem (The Gironde), and Wines of California.

Gala's classifications are all experiential. Her categories are of Joy, People, Aestheticism, Dawn, Sensuality, Light, Generosity, Frivolity, Veils, and "The Impossible." Dawn, for example, includes Chianti, Vino Verdi, Merlot, and Muscadet. Each is chosen for its own reason, and each addresses its own aspect of the hour before sunrise.

The 140 illustrations Gala selected are all by Dalí and range from religious (*The Sacrament of the Last Supper* [1955]) and surreal (*Suburbs of a Paranoiac-Critical Town* [1935]) to *Cabaret Scene* (1922), a quasi-Cubist painting he made of a debauched night spent drinking in Madrid as a student with his friend García Lorca. The illustrations are accompanied by such Dalí-isms as "I've always thought that a grape held close to the ear should make music."[1]

A perennial "objet de collection," *Les Vins de Gala* received a Gourmand World Cookbook Award in 2018. Together with its companion volume, *Les Diners de Gala, Les Vins de Gala* is still in print.

Another book, *Andy Warhol's Exposures* (1979), whose subject, according to its author, is the rich, the powerful, and the beautiful "people at the top,"[2] paid its own genre of homage to Gala, who in fact turns out to be the real subject of the section on Salvador Dalí. Here Warhol reveals that Gala, who always dressed in black and invariably referred to herself in the third person as "Gala," was "the most beautiful, the most fascinating, the most imaginative wife an artist like Salvador Dalí could have." She could also, he adds ruefully, be "tough as nails," and he admits, she "scared him to death."[3]

The chief reason for Andy's fear of Gala was that every time he tried to take her picture, which, given his obsession with snapshots of the very famous, must have been constantly, she hit his arm hard, firmly declaring, "Gala pose only for Dalí." Andy never had the courage to say anything, let alone to retaliate, but Bob Colacello, the editor in chief of Warhol's magazine *Interview*, certainly did.

Colacello had organized a small, elegant lunch at New York's best and arguably most expensive French restaurant, Lutèce. The guests were Gala and Dalí, Fereydoun Hoveyda, the Iranian ambassador to the UN, and his German wife, Gisela; Paulette Goddard, who had risen to fame as a Ziegfeld Girl and starred in Charlie Chaplin's last silent film, *Modern Times*, before briefly marrying him; and, naturally, Andy himself.

According to Warhol, everyone at that lunch was trying to sell something. Gala and Dalí wanted to sell a painting to the Museum of Modern Art in Iran, and Andy wanted to sell Gala on the idea of letting him take her picture. "Please let me take your picture, Gala," he wheedled. "Gala charge very high modeling fee," she answered gruffly. Then the maître d'hôtel arrived and "reeled off every incredible gourmet dish one can imagine." Gala ordered poached eggs on dry toast. Suddenly, she noticed that Andy was tape-recording without her permission and threw his little machine into a vase of flowers. At about the same time, Colacello brushed her leg with his foot, and Gala, who thought he was trying to kick her, punched the editor's arm. Bob hesitated a moment. Then he punched her right back. Warhol couldn't believe what was happening—Goddard muttered, "Go to it, Bob," and Dalí laughed, but all Andy could think was "Now she will never let me take her picture." When Gala reached over and kissed Colacello on both cheeks, his jaw dropped. Gala left the party before the dessert course because she hated sweets, and while Salvador was accompanying her to their limousine, everyone began to talk about her amazing behavior; everyone, that is, except Andy, who was too busy trying to fish his recorder out of the flower vase.

Perhaps it was because she was simultaneously so famous, so unattainable, and so very nonnative that even "pushing 90," as Warhol expressed it, Gala reminded him of "Greta Garbo in her prime."[4]

For others, Gala's perennial appeal was her personality. Beniamino Levi, who observed and interacted with her over many years, was an Italian gallerist who is now director of the Dalí Museum in Paris and president of the Dalí Universe in Montmartre, which houses his personal collection of Dalís and is visited by hundreds of thousands of Dalí fans every year. With Gala's help, Levi was able to start a lucrative business making approved and carefully monitored sculptural multiples in the 1960s, a time when most collectors were only interested in either paintings or works on paper by the artist. Without Gala, Levi says, his business would never have existed. She persuaded Salvador to accept commissions to create a series of bronzes based on the artist's most famous Surrealist images. The three worked closely on the bronze-sculpture projet, and according to Levi, while Salvador was fond of demanding the impracticable, Gala usually found a way to make the improbable possible. Gala was, Levi remembers, "very talented at visual translation, and visual translation is what these sculptures are."

Thanks to Gala's approval, Levi was also able to create the seven-foot bronze Menorah Hashalom at the Ben Gurion Airport in Tel Aviv. Based on a sketch by Salvador, it was finally erected in 1998. Levi fondly remembers Gala receiving him at Portlligat in the 1970s in black pants and a loose peasant blouse, with her espadrille-clad feet up on a table, looking for all the world like a miniature tough guy from a 1940s American film noir. He believes that, while not everyone considered her beautiful, her intelligence was irresistible. Surely, he says, "Salvador was in love with her mind."[5]

In August 1978, Gala and Dalí experienced the singular honor of a royal visit. To Salvador's huge joy, Juan Carlos I had been crowned on November 22, 1975, replacing Franco at Spain's helm as the head of an increasingly democratized monarchy. The king sailed to Cadaqués on the royal yacht the *Fortuna* with his wife, Queen Sofia, and their children, Elena, Cristina, and Felipe, to Girona. After lunch with the Dalís at their home in Portlligat, all seven boarded a helicopter flight to Figueres and the Teatro-Museo. Ever the provocateur, Dalí had wanted to put on a Catalan *barretina*, a short red stocking cap habitually worn by northern Spain's peasants and a symbol of Catalonia's independence, to greet his cherished monarch, but Gala, who still had control of Salvador's wardrobe, snatched it from his head as the royal entourage arrived.[6] Press photos show a happy, bareheaded Dalí giving the royal children a tour of the museum, while Gala, sparkling, in her famous Chanel bow, a silk jacket, and pearls, chats with Queen Sofia, who is wearing a head scarf.[7]

Two days before his seventy-fifth birthday, May 11, 1979, Salvador was invested as a foreign associate member of the Académie des Beaux-Arts Institut de France in Paris, which had been founded as the Royal Academy of Painting and Sculpture a century earlier by Louis XIV's court painter Charles Le Brun. Gala accompanied her husband to the induction ceremony. Carrying an enormous gold Toledo sword of his own design, whose hilt featured a swan surmounted by Gala's head, Salvador mounted slowly to the stage. He began his acceptance speech, *"Gala, Velázquez et la Toison d'Or"* ("Gala, Velázquez, and the Golden Fleece"), by thanking Gala and Paul Éluard for being his first supporters. After praising figurative painting and quoting Michel de Montaigne, he extolled art as a connection between the local and the universal and concluded, "Long live Gala and la Gare de Perpignan."[8]

That October, Gala and Salvador jointly presented *The Very Happy Horse*, their new four-by-eight-foot golden painting, to the Teatro-Museo, augmenting Gala's recent, much-publicized promise to donate another twenty-five works from her own collection to that institution.

The most comprehensive retrospective of Dalí's work to date, which ran from December 1979 to April 1980, at the two-year-old Centre Georges Pompidou in Paris, was toured privately by Gala and Salvador, who did not attend the opening. The presentation, impressively spread out through the entire fifth floor of the museum, included 120 paintings, 200 drawings, more than 2,000 documents, and a special room filled with soft sofas for lounging while viewing *Un Chien Andalou*. Some of the best pieces, which came from Gala and Salvador's personal collections of the haute Surrealist period, had never before been publicly displayed. When their exhaustive tour of the monumental exhibition was finally over, Dalí commented archly, "I never knew I made so much work."

The retrospective was a huge success. It attracted over a million visitors before traveling to the Tate in London, where Michael Shepard wrote in the *Daily Telegraph* that it was vital "for all of us to see for ourselves the work of this important figure." The ultimate accolade came seven months later. Alexander Iolas, the storied Egyptian art dealer who advised the Menil Collection in Houston and had once danced for George de Cuevas in the Ballet de Monte Carlo, bought Salvador Dalí's *Sleep* (1937) from Edward James for £360,000, setting a world record for the highest price ever paid for work by a living artist.

CHAPTER 32

A TIME TO REST

In February, while Parisians were still thronging the Pompidou to admire the richness and breadth of the Dalínean oeuvre, both Gala and Salvador caught a terrible flu. Unable to get out of bed, they stayed on in New York at the St. Regis for a month longer than usual. Dalí, who had never had a protracted illness, became so agitated and depressed that he refused to eat and lost a large amount of weight before slowly starting to get better. He also consulted a variety of doctors and began taking a variety of pills. Whether from one of these, the combination of all of them, or another cause, his hands started shaking. He imagined he had Parkinson's disease and worried he wouldn't be able to paint. Gala, who never fully recovered, became increasingly short of breath, dizzy, and confused. Her arteriosclerosis had likely affected the blood vessels in her brain. She began to exhibit symptoms of dementia.[1]

In March, at their friend Nanita's suggestion, Gala and Salvador checked into a private suite at the Incosol, an elegant health clinic in Marbella on Spain's Costa del Sol, where Nanita could visit them every day. By mid-April, they were well enough to charter a plane (Salvador took a tranquilizer to cope with the flight) to travel home to Portlligat, where they rested as best they could for the better part of that year. It wasn't until October that Salvador could even begin to think about painting again.

Althougth the historic Dalí retrospective in London was so popular that its run was extended for a further six weeks at the Tate, the Dalís spent a sad, lonely, and fretful spring by the shore in Portlligat. Then, unexpectedly, Gala received a telephone call from Jean-Claude Vérité, also known as the "Count du Barry," whose primary role in the Dalínean entourage was to supply them with models from his agency for Salvador's canvases. The count had a rapport with Gala, and when he exclaimed excitedly, "I have five million dollars for you!" Gala, thinking his message was an answered prayer, invited him to come over straightaway.

It turned out that du Barry had assembled a group of men with whom Peter Moore and Salvador had previously conducted business. These were the printmaker Gilbert Hamon, the French gallerist Jacques Carpentier, and a businessman named William Hellender. Hamon was willing to pay Gala a little under a million dollars in today's money for the rights to reproduce forty paintings as prints, and Carpentier wanted to buy the rights to remake a print edition of a Dalí series called "Horses," which had first been produced in the 1970s. Since Salvador was too weak to actually write his name, the new signature would be a stamp of his thumbprint that only Hamon could use.

The ensuing negotiation resulted in a series of confused and confusing legal documents. Gala, who signed her husband's name to all of them, said later that she thought the contracts merely represented fees to her personally for securing Salvador's agreement to let institutions like the Metropolitan Museum of Art in Manhattan issue a limited number of reproductions made by Gilbert Hamon of certain Dalí works in their possession. She had obviously done all the bargaining on her own, without the advice of a lawyer, and was totally unclear about what she had approved. Over the following months, the situation deteriorated.

As soon as the Dalís arrived in Paris and word got out that Gala was "signing," a feeding frenzy ensued. Dealers were walking in off the street to the Dalís' suite at Le Meurice with catalogs of Dalí paintings under their arms offering to pay what would be $200,000 in today's dollars for the reproduction rights to a painting.[2] Some gallery owners had even taken suites near the Dalís' so they could be on hand to negotiate. "One Spanish businessman, who holds a lucrative contract to make Dalí statuary, nearly came to blows with Mr. Vérité in the lobby of the Meurice," James Markham reported in the *New York Times*.[3]

In February, Gala, who was increasingly unable to handle all the pressure, had a serious fall in her hotel bedroom. She sustained multiple bruises, broke more than one rib, and was admitted to the American Hospital of Paris in Neuilly-sur-Seine.[4] At the same time, photomechanical reproductions apparently signed by Dalí and on sale for about $3,000 in today's money began circulating in the City of Light.[5] Enrique Sabater, who had lost control of the situation, resigned.

Finally, with Reynolds Morse's backing, Dalí released a short communiqué through the news agency Agence France-Presse, aimed at reassuring his public. It declared, "For several years and above all since my sickness, there were people who took advantage of my confidence, and my wishes were not respected." He promised that he was "doing everything to clarify the situation." "Gala and I," he announced, "are resuming our freedom."[6, 7]

As the *New York Times* explained, "An authentic lithograph presumes that the artist participated in its production, from the original drawing on stone to its reproduction in a limited, signed edition. According to art-world sources in Paris, the availability of the blank [Dalí] lithographs is closely related to a number of curious contracts that Dalí and his 87-year-old Russian-born wife, known as Gala, concluded last fall in a $1.3 million blitz of business at their home in Portlligat while the artist was recovering from a deep depression and a variety of ailments that have since been diagnosed as Parkinson's disease."

The article went on to say that after years of inconsistent management of Salvador Dalí's affairs, holders of Dalí contracts had finally been summoned to Paris, where a "wild tangle" of questionable documents, which were in several cases in open conflict with one another, had been discovered. In self-defense, Dalí had now assigned the worldwide protection of his copyright interests to the Paris-based Société de la Propriété Artistique et des Dessins et Modèles, which also represented the Picasso estate.

That September, a skeletal, porcelain-white, unsteady Gala, in scarlet lipstick and an ebony wig that would have been the delight of any Japanese Geisha, made a poetic last public appearance when she accompanied Salvador to the Teatro-Museo, where they placed *Lullian Wheels*, a brightly colored image of the wheel of fortune, on the Spanish national lottery poster.[8]

Meanwhile, the authentication controversies that had dogged the Dalís since Peter Moore's chicanery in the 1970s continued. Barely a month later, by which time her grip was so weak she could hardly hold her pen, Gala, who was still Chancellor of the Dalí Exchequer, was forced to sign a document swearing that Moore had no remaining blank sheets, presigned by Dalí, in his possession.[9]

Apparently, with Salvador's knowledge, Moore had previously sold 15,000 blank pages to his buddy Gilbert Hamon, who had also been part of the deal to issue reproductions put together by Vérité. Another 3,500 went to a friend named Klaus Cotta, and 9,500 to the dealer Carlos Galofre. Hamon later confessed to forgery; Klaus Cotta, who made his living importing films and television programs to Spain, was not a legitimate art dealer; and Carlos Galofre ran a gallery next to the Picasso Museum in Barcelona that specialized in selling Dalí prints with fake signatures. There is, however, no evidence that Salvador, who was aware of the sales, had any clear idea of who the purchasers really were.[10]

In January 1982, while King Juan Carlos was persenting Salvador with Spain's highest decoration, the Grand Cross of the Order of Charles III (the Golden Fleece) which cannot be held by more than one hundred Spanish citizens at any one time, Gala was recuperating at the Platón clinic in Barcelona from gallbladder surgery. On February 22, she slipped again in her Portlligat bathroom. This time she snapped a femur. Screaming with pain, Gala was rushed back to Barcelona, where she was operated on for a second time on March 22. There were serious complications. Skin irritations turned into bloody sores. Soon she began to lose any interest in food, and on May 15 Joaquim Goy, the parish priest from La Pera, came to administer Gala's last rites.

Cécile Éluard, who read about her mother's distress in the Paris newspapers, traveled to visit her in Portlligat, but Gala, who had seen Cécile just a few months previously, could only dimly remember her daughter. "She said that was a very long time ago," a maid who blocked entry and refused admission informed the disconsolate Cécile at the villa's front door.

On June 10, 1982, at approximately 6:00 a.m., Gala died. She was in her canopied bed at the villa in Portlligat, adjacent to the picture window she had designed to look out on her beloved Mediterranean coast: the landscape that had been the backdrop of so many of Salvador's paintings of her.

Her written wishes dictated that she be buried in her castle. Unfortunately, as a result of a fourteenth-century law enacted during the Black Death,[II] Gala's corpse could not be moved from one municipality to another without the permission of a judge. To sidestep endless delays, not to mention kilometers of red tape, the Dalí entourage decided to smuggle the corpse to its final resting place. Accordingly, Gala's body, wrapped in a blanket, was propped upright in the back of her Cadillac, with a nurse beside it as though she were still alive. In this way, if they were stopped, it could be explained that she had died on her way to the clinic.

At around eleven o'clock that morning, Arturo drove the Reine de Pauleùlgnn[12] on her last ride to her castle. "It was the first time Senõra traveled in the back seat and not in the front," the weeping driver told Nanita.[13] Gala's death certificate records the cause of her demise as heart failure in Púbol, at 2:15 p.m. on June 10, 1982.

According to Marie Albaretto, Gala had asked to be buried in a cherished red velvet dress by Christian Dior,[14] with Chanel's little black bow pinned to her hair. The intimate funeral took place at 6:00 in the evening in Púbol's elegant crypt,[15] which had been lovingly and playfully decorated by Dalí with two enormous chess pieces in the shape of horses to guard Gala's grave, and a tall giraffe and a marble sculpture of a beautiful Greek warrior to keep her company. The ceremony was conducted by Joaquim Goy and attended by Salvador's inner circle: Descharnes, Dalí's cousin Gonzalo Serraclara, Domènech, and the servants. Seeking privacy for his grief, Salvador stayed upstairs in his wife's bedroom with Antoni Pitxot, but, according to Serraclara, he mustered the courage to visit the tomb a few hours after the interment. "Look," he exclaimed, "I'm not crying." Serraclara looked. Salvador's face was streaming with tears.

Cécile Éluard hired a friend of the family as her lawyer and ultimately received the key to a safety-deposit box containing approximately $5 million from her mother's estate. She also inherited the famous 1929 Salvador Dalí portrait of her father, now in a private collection, which, according to Sotheby's records, last sold in 2011 for slightly over $27 million today, as well as other artworks that had belonged to Gala before her marriage to Salvador Dalí and some personal effects. Gala's jewelry, all of which seems to have disappeared, was nowhere to be found, but there was furniture, of which Gala was fond.[16] The rest of Gala's property was split equally between the Spanish state and Catalonia.[17]

Before his death in 1989, Salvador Dalí donated *The Three Glorious Enigmas of Gala Christ after "Pieta" and the Persian Sibyl by Michelangelo in the*

Sistine Chapel (1982), which was his final tribute to his wife, to the Kingdom of Spain.

Scent is the oldest memory. *Glorious Enigmas,* which is the image of three majestic profiles placed like pyramids on a vast imaginary desert with their noses facing the viewer, pays homage to Gala's powers of prediction and the beatific generosity of her love. The reference to Michelangelo's *Pietà* in the title underlines Gala's deific persona and according to notes on the Reina Sofia website, the three icons also represent the three stages of Salvador and Gala Dalí's joint life.[18]

THE LAST FAIRY TALE

When he was almost seven, Paul Éluard memorized the fables of La Fontaine. It was an experience he would never forget. Throughout his life he cherished the wonderful tales of the talking animals: naive crows, carefree crickets, conceited rabbits, wily foxes, and wise tortoises that inhabit La Fontaine's free-verse lessons of life. Appropriately, one of Éluard's last published works was a fairy tale with a message.

In *Grain-d'Aile* (1951), which means "wing-seed" in English and is a pun on the author's birth name, Grindel, a charming, much-loved little girl is born with a special talent. Grain-d'Aile is so light that, unlike anyone else in her family, she can jump high enough to pick the fruits and berries that grow at the very tops of the tallest trees in her garden. Like a tiny bird, she can rest on the thinnest branches without snapping them to chatter with her feathered friends. At home in the evening, she sings birdsongs to delight her parents and brothers, and at night she dreams of flying over her house in the moonlight. Sometimes in the morning she blows the down from her pillow out the window to watch it float up to the sunrise.

One sparkling day when all her feathered friends are off flying about in the sunshine, Grain-d'Aile begins to cry because she can't follow them. A few minutes later, she feels a soft little paw wiping away her tears. A small, bright-eyed squirrel with silky fire-red fur and a beautiful bushy tail is looking at her sympathetically. "Do you really want wings?" the little squirrel asks her seriously. "I can give them to you, but then you will lose your arms and you won't be a real little girl anymore."

Grain-d'Aile is so excited she doesn't care, so the squirrel grants her wish, and her arms became wings with wonderful white feathers. Soon she is flitting gaily from tree to tree in the neighboring forest. She travels so fast and so far that before long it is nighttime. She curls up cozily under her warm new wings and falls asleep at the top of a fragrant pine tree, where a friendly owl watches over her until the sky starts to pale.

When Grain-d'Aile awakes, she is ravenous. But all her bird friends have to offer for breakfast are some seeds and a worm. What Grain-d'Aile really wants are pancakes and syrup. She flies home as fast as she can and, entering through the kitchen window, she runs to hug her mother, who is very happy to see her. Oh, no! Grain-d'Aile's wings can't hug! They can't hold her fork. She has to be spoon-fed! Her wings can't hold her pencil at school or squeeze Pierre, her best friend's, hand when they go looking for buttercups during recess. Now Grain-d'Aile can't even play with her favorite doll, which, she is certain, is feeling neglected. Worse, her two brothers, who at first had been admiring of her special wings, are beginning to make fun of her.

Grain-d'Aile sits quietly by herself in her own little chair and thinks through her situation. She now understands the squirrel's warning. Flying back to the place where she met Mr. Squirrel as fast as she can, she is happy to find him there waiting for her and delighted when he does not say, "I told you so!" as so many grown-ups would. Instead, he kindly mumbles some magic words, and suddenly Grain-d'Aile is as joyful to discover that her arms have returned as she had been to grow wings.

And so the story ends: Grain-d'Aile goes back to live on the ground with "all the others": "those who are light and those who are less so; those who look at the sky when they are walking and those who see only the pebbles on the road; those who know that little girls can't fly," but especially "those who believe that one day—if they really want to—all children will be able to have both arms and wings."[1]

In keeping with Éluard's sensitivity, this small parable alludes to every child's quandary about discovering and embracing their personal abilities. It evokes what all talented people experience when they decide to follow their own calling: the fear of becoming isolated by their gift; the dread of falling, rather than flying, out of the nest. Unlike Grain-D'Aile, Gala was a trailblazer: forward-looking, sure-footed, and unusually brave. Her courage allowed her to become exceptional.

True partnerships can only be discovered, not imitated, but it is also probably true that Gala's innovative cocreations with Paul Éluard, Max Ernst, and Salvador Dalí paved the way for the acceptance of such famous contemporary collaborations as Coosje van Bruggen and her husband, Claes Oldenburg, who together received numerous awards, including the Distinction in Sculpture, SculptureCenter, New York (1994); and the Nathaniel S. Salton Partners in Education Award, Solomon R. Guggenheim Museum, New York (2002); for their vast surreal/Pop Art installations, including *Spoonbridge and Cherry* (1988), a giant (354 x 618 x 162 inches) fountain in the form of an aluminum spoon holding a cherry, which has become the iconic image of the city of Minneapolis.

Christo and Jeanne-Claude (Christo Vladimrov Javacheff and Jeanne-Claude Denat de Guillebon), who, for their first (1962) solo show in Paris, blocked an alley with 240 oil barrels in a performance-art piece called *Iron Curtain* to protest the Berlin Wall and later became famous for their trippy large-scale, site-specific environmental installations, which dramatically altered viewers' perceptions of well-known spaces, including *Wrapped Reichstag* (1993) and *The Gates* (2005), in New York City's Central Park, owe much to Gala's sensibilities too.

So does the Icelandic rock star Björk, who in conjunction with her former partner Matthew Barney cocreated the Surrealistic art film *Drawing Restraint 9* (2005), a dialogue-less exploration of Japanese culture in which Björk and Barney both appear as two occidental guests on a Japanese whaling vessel who ultimately transform into whales.

Gala, who was certainly never *just* a muse, was also always much more than a partner. She could not only spot promise[2] and coax it into bloom, she also knew how to present it so it would be best understood and most appreciated. Beyond the legacy of the great art and impactful literature that she cocreated with Éluard, Ernst, and Dalí, this inimitable tripartite talent was Gala's gift to cultural history.

Gala, in my opinion, was like the unicorn costume Salvador created for her "Night in a Surrealist Forest." She was sui generis. Through both her work and her persona, she is an example of self-realization. Her legacy is the possibility of accomplishment through uniqueness and originality. Gala knew how to have both arms and wings.

acknowledgments

Writing is always a special adventure. The experience of writing about Gala for the past four years was like opening a door to the vivid, imaginative, radical, and impactful realm of Surrealism that had previously been just hearsay to me. Michael Ward Stout, esq., the Dalís' American lawyer, who is and has been a friend to so many in the art world, was the person who not only showed me the way to that door but gave me the key. I can't thank Michael enough for his suggestion that I write about Gala Dalí. I could not, however, have used Michael's entrée to this wonderful world, where almost all the documents are in French, if my academic father hadn't warmed my childhood and taught me his native language by reading me all of Jules Verne's adventure novels in the original French before tucking me into bed. In all their dissimilarity, my father the professor and Michael the *avocat*, as the two guiding lights for this project, are a perfectly mismatched surreal pair.

I would also like to thank, in order of appearance:

My perspicacious agent Eve MacSweeney, who immediately saw both Gala's romantic charisma and the importance of her unacknowledged role in cultural history. Eve was the active enabler of all my efforts to discover and express Gala as the heroine she turned out to be.

Harper Collins's Jonathan Burnham and Gail Winston were unafraid of art-world controversy and brave enough to give Gala her chance.

Montse Aguer, director of the Fundació Gala–Salvador Dalí,

spent generous hours discussing Gala with me and introduced me to Esther Alvarez, an expert on *Hidden Faces*, the novel Gala wrote with Dalí in 1944. Both Montse and her assistant, Bea Crispo, went out of their way to answer my multitude of questions in person and by email over the years.

Claire Sarti, the granddaughter Gala and Paul Éluard, shared her home-baked teacake, her priceless stack of family albums, and previously untold childhood memories of her famously redoubtable and loving grandmother.

Sara Nelson, my brilliant editor, made it possible for me, with her clear-eyed view of the big picture, to puzzle together my carefully assembled mass of fascinating facts so as to structure the biography as a real story that flowed easily and was entertaining to read.

Sara's assistant, Edie Astley, deftly made the complicated easy, and Pich Chenda Sar, my meticulous, patient researcher, double-checked all my details and unearthed new ones.

Fashion authorities Dilys Blum at the Philadelphia Museum of Art and Francesco Pastore at Schiaparelli deepened my understanding of that great Italian Surrealist designer. Cécile Goddet Dirles at Chanel and Jona Tosta at Dior Heritage expanded my understanding of the Dalís' fashion interventions.

Ariane Batterberry and Elizabeth de Cuevas, who spent childhood summers with Gala and Salvador in Franconia, New Hampshire, recounted personal memories. Simon Coleman at West Dean House unearthed the contracts and (sometimes draft) correspondence between Edward James and Gala, who liked to call Edward *mon petit où* ("my little where") because they were both always traveling, as well as his letters to both the Dalís. Tiffany Dubin, the art jewelry expert at Sotheby's, critically appraised Salvador's famous jewel "the Royal Hart" for me. Dick Cavett, who in 1971 conducted one of the funniest television interviews I've ever seen with Salvador, told me that he had never met Dalí before they started taping but that he was thinking of issuing a rerun with subtitles. Alina Slonim translated the memoirs of the Brazilian poet Manuel Bandeira, Éluard's close friend from the Clavadel sanitarium, from the Portuguese; and Grazia D'Annunzio helped me understand Italian Futurist poetry in the twenties and thirties when I was writing about Gala's visit to the poet Casterense Civello in Sicily.

Thanks go equally to those who made my museum visits so fruitful: Emmanuelle Beuvin at the Musèee des Arts Décoratifs in Paris; Paul Cognard at the Bibliothèque Littéraire Jacques Doucet; and Beniamino Levi, the director of the Dalí Sculpture Collection in the same city. The late Pierre Apraxine, who organized her retrospective at the Metropolitan Museum of Art, offered his curatorial insight into the Comtesse de Castiglione, a fixation for both Gala and Dalí, who installed her bed in their museum.

Delightful details were added by the novelist Sofka Zinovieff, who told me all about George Berners's famous custom-made Rolls-Royce that the Dalís rode in Rome, which came equipped with its own harpsichord. Nita Renfrew, who modeled for Salvador, told me about his famous Pauper's Teas at the Plaza: "They were really audiences. We just sat around and waited for him to acknowledge us." Isabelle Maurin at Le Meurice recounted stories about Dalí's former assistant Peter Moore's pet ocelot, with which he would check into the hotel. And the delightful David Braunschvig corrected my French emails.

Special thanks go to William Rothlein, Gala's much younger lover in the seventies, who shared his memories of that exceptional experience; and to Rebecca Saletan, for putting us in touch.

And finally I am very grateful to the wonderful team at HarperCollins: my cover designer Milan Bozic, who made an image that says "buy me," my marketing expert Becca Putman, and my publicist Maya Baran.

PROLOGUE: PRINCESS OF THE FOREST

1.   Samuel F. B. Morse, Unpublished memoirs of Samuel F. B. Morse, Pebble, Beach Company Lagorio Archives, unpaginated.

2.   Herbert Cerwin, *In Search of Something: The Memoirs of a Public Relations Man* (Los Angeles: Sherbourne Press, Inc., 1966), 101.

3.   In 1941, Buick was the most popular car manufacturer in California.

4.   There is no documentation of how much money was received by MoMA as a final result of the Del Monte party. However, records at the Fundació Gala-Salvador Dalí indicate that throughout the war Gala sent donations to artists and writers who were trapped in Europe.

CHAPTER 1: FAIRY TALES AND SECRETS

1.   Omsk was also Russia's major point of dispatch for exiled citizens.

2.   Dominique Bona, *Gala* (Paris: Flammarion Grandes Biographies, 1995), 13.

3.   Gala Dalí, *Carnets Intimes* (Paris: Michel Laffont, 2012).

4.   Orlando Figes, *The Story of Russia* (New York: Henry Holt & Company, 2022), 1900.

5.   Marina Ivanovna Tsvetaeva (1892–1941) was a Russian poet whose work is some of the most highly regarded in twentieth-century Russian literature.

6.   Anastassia Tsvetaeva, *Souvenirs*, translated from Russian [to French] by Michèle Kahn (Arles, France: Solin Actes Sud, 2003), 357.

7.   Ibid., 359.

8.   Gala Dalí, *Carnets Intimes*, 155.

9.   Ibid, 154.

10. Ibid., 157.

11. Ibid., 164.

12. Karl Moor is the hero of Schiller's 1791 play *The Robbers*. Set in sixteenth-century Germany, the work is a protest against official corruption. It

condemns a society in which men of high purpose could be driven to live outside the law when justice was denied them.

13. Gala Dalí, *Carnets Intimes*, 133.

14. Tim McGirk, *Wicked Lady: Salvador Dalí's Muse* (Terra Alta, WV: Headline Books, 1989), 13.

15. Author interview with Gala's granddaughter, Claire Sarti, June 2022.

16. McGirk, *Wicked Lady*, 13.

17. Gala Dalí, *Carnets Intimes*, 149–152.

18. A painful gynecological disorder caused by stress and characterized by severe menstrual cramps. In Gala's case, this later also probably included pelvic infection and uterine fibroids.

CHAPTER 2: PAUL

1. Paul Eluard, "Le Temps qu'il faisait le 14 mars," published with three drawings by Man Ray in *Les Mains Libres* (Paris: Jeanne Bucher, 1937).

2. In this case, Triangulism—or "triangulation," which reappears as a leitmotif through Gala's life—is probably a reference to their new friend from Brazil, Manuel Bandeira, who met them at Clavadel after Paul and Gala had become friends. Bandeira would become one of his country's greatest poets—and a lifelong friend of Éluard. See Manuel Bandeira, *Itinerário de Pasárgada*, 4th ed., (Rio de Janeiro: Editora Nova Fronteira, 1992). Personal translation from the Portuguese.

3. Prince Klemens von Metternich, the Austrian Empire's Foreign Minister was the most influential leader of the Congress of Vienna (1814–1815), which sought to establish a long-term peace plan for Europe with participation of the great powers of Europe: Britain, Austria, Prussia, Russia, and eventually Metternich. He believed in reinstating a balance of power by restoring Europe's royal families to the throne so order could be created in the form of a monarchy.

4. A third Pierrot, off to the back of one of the photos in Claire Sarti's family album, probably their friend the Brazilian poet, Manuel Bandeira, also wore a white ruff, but his buttons were ivory.

CHAPTER 3: WAR EVERYWHERE

1. Vadim died in 1917 of unknown causes while he was completing a dissertation on philology.

CHAPTER 4: A BABY FOR PEACETIME AND A NEW BENEFACTOR

1. Author interview with Claire Sarti, May 2022.
2. [Poèmes de jeunesse]. 1911–1918: manuscrits et copies par Gala et moi. Bibliothèque Littéraire Jacques Doucet, Paris.

CHAPTER 5: LITTÉRATURE

1. Jean-Nicolas-Arthur Rimbaud (October 20, 1854–November 10, 1891) was a French poet famous for his transgressive and surreal verse and for his influence on modern literature and arts, which prefigured Surrealism. Born in Charleville-Mézières in the Ardennes near Luxembourg, he began writing poetry at age fifteen. Although he was an excellent student, he abandoned his education the following year during the Franco-Prussian War, when he ran away to Paris. Rimbaud's entire literary output was produced before his twentieth birthday, at which point he simply stopped writing. His last major work was *Illuminations* (1874— published in 1886). Jean-Nicolas-Arthur Rimbaud, who was handsome, dissolute, and magnetic, was idolized for his restless soul and his infamous, sometimes violent romantic relationship with fellow poet Paul Verlaine, which lasted nearly two years. After his sudden retirement as a writer, Rimbaud traveled extensively on three continents as an explorer and merchant until his death from cancer just after his thirty-seventh birthday. He is revered for his poetic contributions to Symbolism and, among other works, *A Season in Hell*, which is hailed as a precursor to Modernist literature.
2. Mark Polizzotti, *André Breton* (Paris: Gallimard, 1999), 56.
3. The Baccalaurate is the French national secondary school exit exam.
4. Translated as "House of Friends of Books" in English.
5. Approximately three hundred miles northeast of Paris, Nantes, the sixth-largest city in France, sits on the banks of the Loire River in upper Brittany. It has a long history as a port and industrial center and is home to the restored medieval Château des Ducs de Bretagne.
6. Philippe Soupault, *Vingt mille et un jours: Entretiens avec Serge Fauchereau* (Paris: P. Belfond, 1980), 46.
7. Giorgio de Chirico, *The Memoirs of Giorgio de Chirico* (Boston: Da Capo Press, 1994), 119.
8. Paul Trachtman, "A Brief History of Dada," *Smithsonian*, May 2006, https://www.smithsonianmag.com/arts-culture/dada-115169154/.

9. Francis Picabia born Francis-Marie Martinez de Picabia (January 22, 1879–November 30, 1953) was a French avant-garde painter, writer, filmmaker, magazine publisher, and poet closely associated with Dada (See *Oxford Dictionary of Modern and Contemporary Art* [Oxford, UK: Oxford University, 2009], 552).

CHAPTER 6: MAX

1. The Sans Pareil gallery was at 37 avenue Kleber in Paris's 16th arrondissement.

2. Violaine Vanoyeke, *Paul Éluard: Le Poète de la liberté* (Paris: Editions Juilliard, 1995), 115.

3. The literal translation is "Rose of Happiness." But Rosa Bonheur (March 16, 1822–May 25, 1899) was also a French artist known best as a painter of animals (animalière).

4. Max Ernst, "Some Data on the Youth of M.E. As Told By Himself," *View* 2nd ser. I (1942): 28–30.

5. Postcard from Max Ernst to Paul Éluard, 1921, *Max Ernst postcards and ephemera, 1921–1983*, Getty Research Institute.

6. Matthew Josephson, *Life Among the Surrealists* (New York: Holt, Rinehart, and Winston, 1962), 246.

CHAPTER 7: THE DOLL'S HOUSE

1. Diary of Paul Éluard, Bibliothèque Littéraire Jacques Doucet, Paris.

2. Henri Pastoureau, "Soirées chez Gala en 1933 et 1934," *Henri Pastoureau: Ma vie surréaliste* (Paris: Maurice Nadeau, 1998), 150.

3. Beatrix Blavier, *Max Ernst: Murals for the Home of Paul and Gala Éluard, Eaubonne 1923*, master's thesis, Rice University, 1985, 36.

4. "The Tour" refers to Gala, who was so guarded and guard-like that her friends described her as the "tower" of a medieval rampart.

5. Letter from de Chirico to Gala, February 10, 1924. Quoted in Jole De Sanna, "Giorgio de Chirico–André Breton Duel à Mort," *Metafisica* 1–2 (2002): 132, 134.

6. De Chirico, *The Memoirs*, 117.

CHAPTER 8: ESCAPE FROM "THE DOLL'S HOUSE"

1. This would be approximately $60,000 today.

2. Paul Éluard to his father, March 24, 1924, in Robert Valette, *Éluard, Livre d'identité* (Paris: Tchou, 1967), 49.

3. Simone Breton to Denise Levy, March 27, 1924, in Simone Breton, *Lettres à Denise Lévy 1929–1939* (Paris: Éditions Joëlle Losfeld, 2005), 169.

4. Dorothea Tanning, *Birthday* (San Francisco: Lapis Press, 1986), 40.

5. Letter I, May 12–20, 1924, Paul Éluard, *Lettres à Gala 1924–1948*, édition établie et annotée par Pierre Dreyfus (Paris: Gallimard, 1984), 17.

6. Robert McNab, *Ghost Ships: A Surrealist Love Triangle* (New Haven, CT: Yale University Press, 2004), 65.

7. Telegram from Paul Éluard to his father, 1924, as quoted in McNab, *Ghost Ships*, 83.

8. Letter from Simone Breton to Denise Levy, October 3, 1924, Simone Breton, *Lettres à Denise Lévy 1929–1939*, 202.

9. Ibid., 203.

CHAPTER 9: ENTR'ACTE

1. H. W. Janson, *History of Art*, Fifth Edition. Revised and Expanded by Anthony F. Janson (New York: Harry N. Abrams Inc., 1995), 766, 770–71, 775, 785.

2. André Breton, "*Lâchez tout*," *Littérature*, no. 2 (April 1922).

3. In 1925, writer and poet Jean Ballard launched the literary magazine *Les Cahiers du Sud* in Marseilles as a continuation of *Fortunio*, which had been founded by the cinematographer Marcel Pagnol in 1914. Under the direction of poet André Gaillard (1898–1929), the magazine published a wide range of up-and-coming, notable poets, including René Crevel and Paul Éluard.

4. By the time he died in 1931, Vachel Lindsay was one of the best-known poets in the United States. His most acclaimed work: "The Congo," with its onomatopoeic refrain "*Boomlay, boomlay, boomlay, BOOM*" exemplified his revolutionary aesthetic of sound for sound's sake.

5. Salvador Dalí, *The Secret Life of Salvador Dalí* (New York: Dial Press, 1942), 225.

CHAPTER 10: SALVADOR

1. "Dalí" is a derivative of "Dalil," from Arabic دَليل ("dalīl," meaning "portent, and guide").

2. Dalí, *The Secret Life*, 37.

3. Dalí, *The Secret Life*, 81.

4. Meryle Secrest, *Salvador Dalí: A Biography* (E. P. Dutton, 1986), 35.

5. Dalí, *The Secret Life*, 128–131.

6. Ibid., 203.

7. Ian Gibson, *The Shameful Life of Salvador Dalí* (London: Faber & Faber, 1997), xxviii.

8. Ramón Gómez de la Serna y Puig was a Spanish writer, dramatist, and avant-garde agitator. He strongly influenced filmmaker Luis Buñuel and was especially known for "greguería," a short form of poetry that because it offers new and often humorous perspectives roughly corresponds to the one-liner in comedy.

9. Quoted in Gibson, *The Shameful Life*, 192.

10. Dalí met Goemans through Joan Miró, Goemans's neighbor in Paris.

CHAPTER 11: GALA AND SALVADOR

1. First published in 1942.

2. Vaselino was the name of a 1920s slicked-back men's hairstyle popularized by the silent film star Rudolph Valentino.

3. Maurice Nadeau wrote in *A History of Surrealism* (1965) that Gradiva, the eponymous heroine of Wilhelm Jensen's 1902 novella *Gradiva*, who was also known as "the woman who walks through walls," was the emblematic muse of the Surrealists. As a character on the verge of mythology, dream, and psychoanalysis, she was a perfect fit for all those exploring the subconscious and especially sexual fantasy.

4. Buñuel wrote about how much he disliked her thin, muscled thighs that had a gap between them. See Luis Buñuel, *My Last Sigh* (New York: Vintage Books, 2013), 96.

5. In the 1920s, women wore so-called pajamas, which looked like jumpsuits or overalls, to fashionable seaside resorts.

6. Catalina, otherwise known as Tieta, would end her days in a psychiatric hospital.

7. Letter 205, March 1935, Paul Éluard, *Lettres à Gala*, 251. The translation reads: "Nusch . . . is for me, as Dali is for you: someone who wholly loves and is entirely devoted to me, perfect."

8. At five eight, Salvador was a full inch shorter and much slighter than Max Ernst.

9. Dalí's 1929 portrait of Paul Éluard was sold in 2011 for the equivalent of $27,648,000 in today's dollars.

10. Quoted in Gibson, *The Shameful Life*, 256.

CHAPTER 12: STARTING OVER

1. Polizzotti, *André Breton*, 437.

2. Theoria.art.zoom.com.

3. Gibson, *The Shameful Life*, 242.

4. Manuscript of the *Deuxieme Enquète sur la Sexualité*, 1928.

5. Max Ernst had made the frontispiece for the first *Manifesto*.

6. *The Invisible Man* is a trompe l'oeil image of a man who hides in the components of the painting. Yellow clouds appear to form his hair; the ruined architecture represents his face and upper body, while a waterfall creates the subtle outline of both his legs. Dalí took three years (1929–1932) to finish the work.

7. Gibson, *The Shameful Life*, 245.

8. Ibid., 257.

9. Fleur Cowles and A. Reynolds Morse, *The Case of Salvador Dalí* (Whitefish, MT: Literary Licensing LLC, 2011), 65.

10. Until 1933, when it became simply "Gala"; this signature included many variations of her name.

11. Dalí, *The Secret Life*, 272.

12. Gibson, *The Shameful Life*, 261.

13. Letter 78, April 1930, in Paul Éluard, *Lettres à Gala*, 107.

14. Char's previous published collaboration was the anthology *Ralentir Travaux* ("Slow! Under Construction") with Breton and Éluard (Paris: Editions Surréalistes, 1930).

15. In 1929, Dalí also made a famous painting titled *The Great Masturbator*, 1929.

16. Dalí, *The Secret Life*, 250.

CHAPTER 13: PARIS WHEN IT SIZZLES

1. *particule* refers to people with the word "de" in their last name. The "de" indicates that their family owns property and signifies "upperclassness."

2. Jean-Louis de Faucigny-Lucinge, *Un Gentilhomme Cosmopolite: Mémoires* (Paris: Perrin, 1990), 133.

3. Bona, *Gala*, 52.

4. Dalí, *The Secret Life*, 342.

5. Laurence Benaim, *Marie-Laure de Noailles, La vicomtesse du bizarre* (Paris: Grasset, 2001), 182.

6. Cowles and Morse, *The Case of Salvador Dalí*, 71.

7. Author telephone interview with Cécile Goddet-Dirles, head of education, Patrimoine Chanel, February 17, 2022.

8. Dalí, *The Secret Life*, 324.

9. Secrest, *Salvador Dalí: A Biography*, 141.

10. Robert de Saint-Jean, *Journal d'un Journaliste* (Paris: Editions du Seuil, 2009), 124.

11. Lifar was Nijinsky's principal dancer until 1929, when upon Nijinsky's death he was invited to take over the directorship of the Paris Opera Ballet.

12. Jean-François Millet (October 4, 1814–January 20, 1875) was a French artist and one of the founders of the Barbizon school, whose members would gather to paint in the forest of Fontainebleau forty miles southeast of Paris, near the village of Barbizon. Millet, who is renowned for his paintings of peasant farmers, can also be categorized as part of the Realism art movement.

13. An anamorphosis is a distorted projection or drawing that appears normal when viewed from a particular point or with a suitable mirror or lens.

14. Maxim Gorky (Russian: Максим Го́рький), a five-time Nobel Prize in Literature nominee, was a Soviet writer, socialist, and apologist for the Gulag.

15. Letter from Gala to Julien Levy, July 12, 1933, Philadelphia Museum of Art Archives, Julien Levy Gallery records.

16. Pastoureau, *Henri Pastoureau: Ma vie surréaliste*, 150.

CHAPTER 14: AMERICA

1. Gibson, *The Shameful Life*, 328.

2. Edward James, *Swans Reflecting Elephants: My Early Years* (London: Weindenfeld & Nicolson, 1982), 74.

3. Lewis Mumford, "The Frozen Nightmares of Señor Dalí," *New Yorker* IX, December 9, 1933.

4. Secrest, *Salvador Dalí: A Biography*, 146.

5. Rafael Santos Torroella, *Salvador Dalí, Corresponsal de J. V. Foix, 1932–1936* (Barcelona: Editorial Mediterrania, 1986), 63.

CHAPTER 15: LOSS AND FAME

1. Julien Levy, *Memoir of an Art Gallery*, (Boston: MFA Publications, 2003), 173.

2. Caresse Crosby, *The Passionate Years* (London: Alvin Redman, 1955), 138.

3. Barbara Woolworth Hutton (November 14, 1912–May 11, 1979) was an American debutante, socialite, and heiress who became famous for her notoriously troubled private life. New York's society press dubbed her the "Poor Little Rich Girl" when, amid the Great Depression, in 1930 she was given a lavish, widely publicized debutante ball.

4. "Alexis Mdivani dies in crash," *Urbana Daily Courier*, August 2, 1935. Illinois Digital Newspaper Collection, https://idnc.library.illinois.edu /?a=d&d=TUCI9350802&e=-------en-20--1--txt-txIN----------.

5. Kihm, "Polo Widows," *Faithful Reader*, December 10, 2013.

6. Postcard from Salvador Dalí to Edward James, undated, The Edward James Archive, West Dean.

7. Gibson, *The Shameful Life*, 351.

8. Ibid.

9. Letter drafts from Edward James to Pavel Tchelitchew, undated, The Edward James Archive, West Dean.

10. Letter 213, September 1935, in Paul Éluard, *Lettres à Gala*, 259.

11. Levy, *Memoir of an Art Gallery*, 175, and Meredith Etherington-Smith, *The Persistence of Memory: A Biography of Dalí* (New York: Random House, 1992), 203.

12. The sketch was published in *American Weekly*. The magazine had commissioned drawings based on the painter's experiences in New York to appear in their periodical from February through July 1935.

13. Draft letter, August 1936, The Edward James Archive, West Dean.

14. Ibid. and author interview with West Dean archivist Simon Coleman, September 2022.

15. "Reali$m in Surrealism. Modernists are not Priceless Asses," *Star* (London), July 2, 1936.

16. Secrest, *Salvador Dalí: A Biography*, 165.

17. Gibson, *The Shameful Life*, 360.

18. Ibid., 367.

19. Draft letter from Edward James, undated, The Edward James Archive, West Dean.

20. Sofka Zinovieff, *The Mad Boy, Lord Berners, My Grandmother and Me* (New York: Harper, 2015), 1.

21. Ibid., 137.

22. Dalí, *The Secret Life*, 361.

23. In 1958, Peter Watson underwrote *Horizon* magazine and became, with Cyril Connolly, its de facto art editor.

24. Exhibition catalog *Fantastic Art, Dada, and Surrealism*, ed. Alfred H. Barr (New York: Museum of Modern Art, 1937).

25. Salvador Dalí was channeling the bride from his painting *Necrophilic Spring*, 1936.

26. Gibson, *The Shameful Life*, 366.

27. Polizzotti, *André Breton*, 488.

28. *Giraffes on Horseback Salad* was never produced.

29. When the Art Institute of Chicago acquired the painting in 1948 Dalí sent his congratulations and noted "According to Nostradamus the apparition of monsters presages the outbreak of war." He described *Inventions of the Monsters* as "predictive." https://www.artic.edu/artworks /151424/inventions-of-the-monsters.

30. The contents of this book are: a poem intended to "illustrate" Narcissus, some explanatory notes, and a reproduction of the work *A Couple with Their Heads Full of Clouds*: the image of a man and a woman whose bodies are made of clouds.

CHAPTER 16: EVERYDAY MARVELS

1. Secrest, *Salvador Dalí: A Biography*, 166.

2. Elsa Schiaparelli's daughter Maria, aka Gogo, had polio.

3. The Schiaparelli newspaper print sometimes attributed as an early collaboration with Dalí was a collage of all of her newspaper clippings reproduced in 1935 by Concolombier, a fabled French fabric manufacturer of that time.

4. Secrest, *Salvador Dalí: A Biography*, 161.

5. Author interview with Dilys Blum, October 2022.

6. Author interview with Francesco Pastore, June 2022.

7. Jonathan Keats, "Sorry Dalí," *Forbes*, July 11, 2022.

8. Portrait of Gala's naked body with drawers in it (the property of Edward James).

9. Made by Italian shoemaker Andrée Perugia.

10. *Hat* (Designer Elsa Schiaparelli), https://www.metmuseum.org/art /collection/search/83437.

11. This is an idea the Dalís took up again for the entrance hall of their house in Portlligat.

12. Letter from Bettina Bergery to Schiaparelli in Dilys E. Blum, *Shocking! The Art and Fashion of Elsa Schiaparelli* (New Haven, CT: Yale University Press, 2003), 124.

13. Blum, *Shocking!*, 139.

CHAPTER 17: END OF THE ERA

1. Calvin Tomkins, *The Lives of Artists* (New York: Phaidon Press, 2019), 145.

2. George Wildenstein was an Alsatian/French gallery owner, international art dealer, art collector, editor, and art historian who had represented both Picasso and Matisse. After the war, he opened a gallery at 685 Fifth Avenue in New York.

3. Letter 246, late November–early December 1938, Paul Éluard, *Lettres à Gala*, 291–292. This close, mercurial, and long-lived association ended when Breton tried to stop Éluard from publishing poetry in Aragon's new daily *Ce soir* (*This Evening*).

4. *Dictionnaire Abrégé du Surréalisme* (Paris: Galerie des Beaux-Arts, 1938), 13.

5. In this double portrait, Dalí (who in real life was right-handed) sits at his easel, seemingly fending off the unknown and imminent with his right/conscious hand. He is gazing in the mirror, and uses his left/ subconscious hand to paint himself and Gala, who like an ancient spirit haunting his imagination appears in the background as a haze emerging from Rome's evocative ruins.

6. Letter 236, April 1938, letter 237, July–August 1938, and letter 238, August 238, Paul Éluard, *Lettres à Gala*, 284–85.

7. Bettina Ballard, *In My Fashion* (New York: D. McKay, 1969), 49.

8. Isabelle Fiemeyer, *Intimate Chanel* (Paris: Flammarion, 2011), 55.

9. The Munich Agreement, signed on September 30, 1938, by Germany, Italy, France, and Great Britain to—in Neville Chamberlain's famous words—preserve "peace in our time," effectively allowed the Nazis to overrun Czechoslovakia.

10. Jonathan Jones, "Dalí's Enigma, Picasso's Protest: The Most Important Art Works of the 1930s," *Guardian*, March 4, 2017.

11. Despite his grace and intelligence, Cocteau was viewed with suspicion by both Dalís, who mistrusted him as an opium-addicted socialite. In an undated letter to the poet Joë Bousquet, now conserved in Carcassonne Municipal Library, Gala referred to Cocteau, who took opium for pain, as *"Une petit ordure"* (a little turd).

12. Fiemeyer, *Intimate Chanel*, 109.

13. Letter from Gala to Julien Levy, November 12, 1938, Philadelphia Museum of Art Archives, Julien Levy Gallery records.

14. Polizzotti, *André Breton*, 536.

15. The last edition of the *Minotaure* was published May 13, 1939.

16. Éluard wrote to Breton "please remove my name from the masthead— which is the last vestige of our mutual entente" in a letter to Breton dated October 12, 1938. *André Breton, Paul Éluard Correspondance 1919–1938* (Paris: Gallimard, 2019).

17. Simon Legree, a famous fictional character, is a vicious slave owner and the principal villain in Harriet Beecher Stowe's antislavery novel *Uncle Tom's Cabin* (1851–52).

18. Secrest, *Salvador Dalí: A Biography*, 169.

19. "Dalí's Display," *Time*, March 27, 1939, 31.

20. "Store Window Fails to Stop Raging Artist," *Daily News*, March 17, 1939.

21. "Salvador Dalí: New Yorkers Stand in Line to See His Six-in-One Surrealist Painting," *Time*, April 17, 1939, 45.

22. Draft letter, The Edward James Archives, West Dean.

23. "World: As You Enter," *Time*, June 26, 1939.

24. Gala Dalí, *Carnets Intimes*, 176.

25. Parisian-born André Pieyre de Mandiargues (March 14, 1909– December 13, 1991) was an associate of the Surrealists and a particularly close friend of the painter Leonor Fini. His novel *La Marge* (1967; *The Margin*), which won the Prix Goncourt, was made into an eponymous film by Walerian Borowczyk in 1976. He also wrote the introduction to Anne Desclos's *Story of O*.

26. Peggy Guggenheim was famous for her plethora of lovers, an eminent group that included Yves Tanguy, Roland Penrose, and Samuel Beckett. In 1939, she was Max Ernst's latest bedmate.

27. Peggy Guggenheim, *Out of This Century: Confessions of an Art Addict* (New York: Universe Publishing, 1987), 214.

28. Claude Delay, *Chanel Solitaire* (Paris: Gallimard, 1983), 273.

29. Lilou Marquand, *Chanel m'a dit* (Paris: Jean-Claude Lattes, 1990), 46.

30. Rafael Santos Torroella (ed.), "Salvador Dalí escribe a Federico García Lorca [1925–1936]," *Poesia, Revista Ilustrada de informacion poetica, Madrid*, nos. 27–28 (April 1987).

31. Nini Arlette Theilade (June 15, 1915–February 13, 2018) was a Danish ballet dancer, choreographer, and teacher.

32. "Portrait de Gala Écrit Par Léonor Fini," Chantal Vieuille, *Gala* (Paris: Favre, 1988), 181.

CHAPTER 18: EXILE

1. In 1940, Soupault was the director of Tunis Radio in Tunisia.

2. "Salvador Dalí Returns With Plans for November Exhibit and an Autobiography," *New York Times*, August 17, 1940.

3. "After Uneventful Trip," *Daily News*, August 17, 1940.

4. George Ross, "He'll Be Good," *Pittsburgh Press*, August 28, 1940.

5. Gala Dalí, *Carnets Intimes*, 177.

6. Anaïs Nin, *The Diary of Anaïs Nin: 1939–1944*, vol. 3 (Boston: Mariner Books Classics, 1971), 144.

7. Gala Dalí, *Carnets Intimes*, 182.

8. The photograph appeared in the April 7, 1941, issue of *Life*.

9. Undated draft, The Edward James Archives, West Dean.

10. Parke Rouse, Jr., "Spiders: That's What Fascinates Dali Most About Virginia," *Richmond News Leader*, April 6, 1941.

11. Nicolas Calas, "Anti-Surrealist Dalí," *View*, June 1941.

12. Levy, *Memoir of an Art Gallery*, 250.

13. Ibid., 255.

14. India Moffett, "Dalí Attracts Record Crowds to Arts Club," *Chicago Daily Tribune*, May 24, 1941, 13.

15. Harold Fowler McCormick was the head of the International Harvester Company.

16. Levy, *Memoir of an Art Gallery*, 255.

17. Unpublished draft letter, 1944, Fundació Gala-Salvador Dalí, archives.

CHAPTER 19: METAMORPHOSIS

1. John Martin, "Season Is Opened by Ballets Russes," *New York Times*, October 9, 1941.

2. Levy, *Memoir of an Art Gallery*, 253.

3. Miró's show debuted just before Dalí's.

4. James Thrall Soby, *Salvador Dalí* (New York: Museum of Modern Art, 1941), 7–8.

5. Peyton Boswell Jr., "Dalí Goes to Town," *Art Digest*, December 1, 1941.

6. Gibson, *The Shameful Life*, 416.

7. Now known as Black Star Publishing Company, this photographic agency was established in 1935 by German/Jewish refugees.

8. Salvador's name for the portrait was *The Medusa of Dream*.

9. "Introducing us to a new visual code, photographs alter and enlarge our notions of what is worth looking at and what we have the right to observe." Susan Sontag, "In Plato's Cave," from *On Photography* (New York: Delta Books, 1977), 3–24; ebook location 15 of 2528.

10. *Click* was subtitled "The National Magazine Devoted to Pictures."

11. Bea Crespo and Clara Silvestre, "Gala: the Chronology," Fundació Gala-Salvador Dalí, Centre d'Estudis Dalínians, 226.

12. Caresse Crosby, who received an endpaper acknowledgment, was instrumental in the design of the book.

13. Author interview with Montse Aguer, head of Fundació Gala-Salvador Dalí, June 2022.

14. Gibson, *The Shameful Life*, 407.

15. Secrest, *Salvador Dalí: A Biography*, 183.

16. $120 today.

17. Eleanor Lambert's highly publicized "Best Dressed List" was published by her husband, Bill Berkson, who was the editor in chief of the popular newspaper *New York Journal American*.

18. "Done the Dalí Way," *Art Digest*, April 15, 1943.

19. Secrest, *Salvador Dalí: A Biography*, 186.

20. Martin Schieder, "Surrealistic Socialite: Dalí's Portrait Exhibition at the Knoedler Galleries in 1943" in Julia Drost, Fabrice Flahutez, Anne Helmreich, and Martin Schieder, *Networking Surrealism in the USA* (Heidelberg, Germany: arthistoricum.net-ART-Books, 2019), 194–219.

CHAPTER 20: EXPRESSIONS OF TALENT

1. Franconia, a tiny township (982 people in 2022) near the Canadian border, was a wartime refuge to a diverse group that included Boston Brahmins and a Bolivian tin millionaire. Its remoteness made it feel safe. According to Ariane Batterberry, who grew up next door to the de Cuevases in New York and summered near them in New Hampshire, "There were no fancy mansions, just plain white farm houses, but people brought their butlers, and dinner at the hotel was always black tie." Author interview with Ariane Batterberry, March 10, 2023.

2. *Le Bal du Comte d'Orgel* was Raymond Radiguet's second and last work of fiction, which, heavily edited by Jean Cocteau, became a bestseller when it was published almost immediately after its twenty-year-old author's tragic death from typhoid fever in 1923.

3. The French critic Marion Galichon-Brasart in her "commentaries" called *Le Bal du Comte d'Orgel* "a novel in which it's the psychology that's romantic." Marion Galichon Brasart, in *Le Bal du Comte d'Orgel* (Paris: Grasset, 1990), 167–86.

4. Author interview with Esther Álvarez, March 2023.

5. "Dalí's Love and Death," *Newsweek*, July 1944.

6. Edmund Wilson, "Salvador Dalí as a Novelist," *New Yorker*, July 1, 1944.

7. Author interview with Esther Alvarez, February 2, 2023.

8. Fundació Gala-Salvador Dalí archives.

9. Salvador Dalí, "The Gala Names," *The Dalí News*, 1945 (Getty Research Library Special Collections).

10. One example of design as an art form is Gala's 1935 *Ladder of Love*, which is an artwork but also the maquette of a Surrealist apartment and therefore a bridge between art and design.

11. These tie patterns were not taken from Salvador Dalí canvases. Instead, Dalí drew the patterns on cardboard and then cut out the shapes. The tie maker was supplied with not only the design but its placement and the exact dimensions of the tie in question—courtesy Museum at FIT archives.

12. Sonya Dutta Choudhury, "Dalí's Ashtray in Mumbai," *Hindustan Times*, June 19, 2023.

13. Secrest, *Salvador Dalí: A Biography*, 247.

14. Warner Brothers documentary: *The Brothers Warner*, 2008, directed by Cass Warner.

15. Irene Brin, "Complicità con Dalí," *Come vi piace (As You Like It) di William Shakespeare*, 1948, unpaginated.

16. *Script* magazine, August 1947.

17. While it was not named a war crime at the time, historians in the twenty-first century have, because of the German armies' systematic starvation and destruction of the city's population, classified the siege of Leningrad as genocide.

18. Christian Esquevin, *Adrian: Silver Screen to Custom Label* (New York: Monacelli Press, 2008), 153–54.

19. Miguel de Cervantes, *Don Quichotte de la Manche* (Paris: Joseph Foret, 1957).

20. Jimmy Ernst, *A Not-So-Still Life* (New York: St. Martin's Press, 1984), 153–54.

21. Although we don't have Gala's response to this letter because Paul destroyed it, it is safe to say that she must have been pleased but probably didn't take any money from him.

22. Carlyle Burrows, "Art of the Week," *New York Herald Tribune*, November 24, 1945.

23. The list of books illustrated by Dalí in the '40s includes: *The Maze* by Maurice Sandoz, published by Doubleday, 1944; *Fantastic Memories* by Maurice Sandoz, published by Doubleday, 1946; *Macbeth* by William Shakespeare, reprint of the play published by Doubleday, 1947; *Don Quixote de la Mancha* by Miguel de Cervantes, English edition, published by Random House; *The Autobiography of Benvenuto Cellini*, published by Doubleday, 1947; *Essays* by Michel de Montaigne, published by Doubleday, 1948; *Wine Women and Words* by Billy Rose, published by Simon & Schuster, 1948.

24. Dalí notes, Fundació Gala-Salvador Dalí archives.

25. Edward Alden Jewell, "Dalí, An Enigma? Only His Exegesis," *New York Times*, November 21, 1945.

26. Francine Prose, *The Lives of the Muses* (New York: HarperCollins, 2019), 217. It is not at all sure, however, that Salvador and James (who liked to promote the rumor of their love affair) were ever actually lovers.

27. Irving Hoffman "Tale of Hoffman," *Hollywood Reporter*, December 14, 1945, 3.

28. Letter 267, November 25, 1946, Paul Éluard, *Lettres à Gala*, 316.

29. Letter 266, August 6, 1946; Letter 267, November 25, 1946; Letter 268 (from Cécile and Paul), March 10, 1947, Paul Éluard, *Lettres à Gala*, 314, 316, 318.

30. The Rosicrucians were a mystical community of philosophers who studied what they termed "Natural Laws" in order to live in harmony

with the world's ecological order. Rosicrucianism, which would have been considered a heresy by the Orthodox Church, is symbolized by the Rosy Cross or Rose Cross.

31. Marina Zetlina's collection is now housed in the Ramat Gan Museum in Israel.

32. Christie's catalog entry for *Portrait of Maria Zetlina*, 1910, by Valentin Serov, Christie's, November 24, 2014, lot 15. (Price realized GBP 9,266,500), https://www.christies.com/en/lot/lot-5849203.

33. Alonzo Lansford, "New Exhibition Reveals a Modified Dalí," *Art Digest*, December 1, 1947, 13.

34. Salvador Dalí, *50 Secrets of Magic Craftsmanship* (Mineola, NY: Dover Publications, 1992), 90.

CHAPTER 21: HOME

1. Ian Gibson, interview with Doña Roser Villar, Figueres, June 28, 1996, in Gibson, *The Shameful Life*, 440.

2. Irene Brin, "*Complicita con Dalí*," 1948.

3. Gala Dalí, *Carnets Intimes*, 187.

4. Unoffical English translation of Anna Maria Dalí, *Salvador Dalí, visto por su hermana* (Barcelona: Ediciones Del Cotal, 1983), provided by the Dalí Museum, St. Petersburg, Florida.

CHAPTER 22: A MADONNA IN PORTLLIGAT

1. *The Madonna of Port Lligat*, 1950, by Salvador Dali, dalipaintings.com, https://www.dalipaintings.com/the-madonna-of-port-lligat.jsp.

2. "Dalí Exhibit opens Monday," *New York Herald Tribune*, November 24, 1950.

3. As quoted in Montse Aguer, *Salvador Dalí: An Illustrated Life* (London: Tate Publishing, 2007), 200–201.

4. The *Almanach de Gotha* is a directory of Europe's royalty and highest nobility.

5. Bea Crespo, "The Ball of the Century," in Montse Aguer, Joana Bonet, Bea Crespo, and Clara Silvestre, *Gala/Dalí/Dior: Of Art and Fashion* (Figueres: Fundació Gala-Salvador Dalí, 2020), 57.

6. Ibid.

7. Dominick Dunne, "All that Glittered," *Vanity Fair*, August 1998.

8. "The Big Party," *Time*, September 11, 1951.

9. "Art: A Mystic Feeling," *Time*, November 17, 1952.

10. Aguer, *Salvador Dalí: An Illustrated Life*, 104.

11. "Letter From London," *New Yorker*, December 12, 1952.

CHAPTER 23: TURNING A PAGE

1. Violaine Vanoyeke, *Paul Éluard* (Paris: Éditions Julliard), 377.

2. As quoted by Hugh Atkins, "Paul Éluard, Picasso, Poésie, Poésy et Paris," March 12, 2021. See https://www.purefrance.com/en/blog /paul-eluard-picasso-poesie-poesy-et-paris.

3. Author interview with Claire Sarti, May 2022.

4. Translated by G. E. Manca from Salvador Dalí, *Manifiesto Místico* (Figueres/La Bisbal d'Empordà: Ediciones extraordinarias de El Empurdanés, 1952), 3, 146.

5. Tiffany Dubin, art jewelry expert at Sotheby's auction house, commented, "Salvador Dalí often flirted with kitsch in a manner that brings a smile and piques curiosity. However, in the case of *The Royal Heart*, he seems to have done almost the opposite. The purity and deep hue of rubies in Christian tradition symbolize the ultimate sacrifice of Christ. In this piece; however, the rubies do not evoke reverence or admiration. Instead, their pulsating presence is unsettling, reminiscent of horror film special effects. Thus, despite its delicate beauty, *The Royal Heart* throws the viewer into an uncomfortable world of chaos and contradiction." Author interview with Tiffany Dubin, June 1, 2024.

6. M. Del Arco, "Salvador Dalí visto por del Arco," *Revista: Semanario de información. Artes y Letras*, Barcelona, May 27, 1954, 11.

7. Aguer, *Salvador Dalí: An Illustrated Life*, 207.

8. Lledia is the province of Catalonia that lies to the west of Girona.

9. Dalí's painting *Portrait of Laurence Olivier in the Role of Richard III* (1955) was most recently exhibited at the Tate Modern in London in 2007.

10. "Plans Speed for December 2 Ball," *New York Times*, November 12, 1955.

11. Walt Disney visited Portlligat in October 1957.

12. "Spain: Dalí's Villa on the Costa Brava: Salvador Dalí's Villa," *Harper's Bazaar*, February 1956, 118–21.

13. Gibson interview with Drs. Giuseppe and Anna Maria Albaretto, London, March 2, 1994, in Gibson, *The Shameful Life*, 487.

14. Leonard Lyons, "The Lyons Den," syndicated column, April 19, 1959.

15. *America*'s debut had been at a private viewing in one of the world's largest art dealerships, French & Company on Manhattan's East Sixty-Fifth Street, where it was seen by more than one thousand visitors.

16. Draft letter, February 1960, Fundació Gala-Salvador Dalí archives.

17. The exhibition was called "Surrealist Intrusion in the Enchanter's Domain" and ran from November 28, 1960, to January 14, 1961.

CHAPTER 24: NEW FRONTIERS

1. The Princesse de Faucigny-Lucinge died at home of an unexpected heart attack in 1945.

2. Secrest, *Salvador Dalí: A Biography*, 195.

3. Television interview with Dick Cavett, *The Dick Cavett Show*, February 10, 1971, and author interview with Dick Cavett, August 2023. This is an exceptionally funny improv interview in which Dalí's accent is so thick that Dick Cavett now promises he will soon have it subtitled.

4. Marcel Duchamp bought a house on the Costa Brava near the Dalís in 1958 and lived there until his death in 1968.

5. Published by Joseph Fort in 1946.

6. Samuel F. B. Morse, Unpublished memoirs of Samuel F. B. Morse, unpaginated.

7. Authors William Strauss and Neil Howe, in their 1991 book *Generations*, define the social generation of boomers as "that cohort born from 1943 to 1960, who were too young to have any personal memory of World War II, but old enough to remember the postwar American High before John F. Kennedy's assassination."

8. Carlton Lake, *In Quest of Dalí* (New York: G. P. Putnam's Sons, 1969), 25.

9. Ian Gibson interview with Peter Moore, Gibson, *The Shameful Life*, 494–95.

10. *Soft Watches Hard Times, the unpublished memoirs of Peter Moore*, as quoted by Ian Gibson in *The Shameful Life*, 495.

11. Author interview with Michael Ward Stout, July 2021.

12. James Watson and Frances Crick were the Nobel Prize–winning scientists whose discovery of the double helix twisted-ladder structure of deoxyribonucleic acid (DNA, the material that carries the genetic code that determines the development of all living things) gave rise to modern molecular biology and its investigations of the power of genetic influence.

13. Lake, *In Quest of Dalí*, 27.

14. Although $150,270 in 1961 translates into a mere $1,514,000 in today's dollars, artwork in the 1950s and 1960s was not priced the way it is now. As a comparative example: In 1956 costume-jewelry manufacturer Victor Ganz bought the entire fifteen-canvas *Les Femmes d'Alger* series from Picasso, who was already considered one of the world's greatest art geniuses, for $212,500, or approximately $2.45 million now. In 1995, Ganz sold just one of the canvases in the group, a work titled *Version 'O'* for $31.9 million, and in 2015 the same painting was auctioned at Christie's for $179.4 million, which was a record for a painting at auction at that time. See "Victor and Sally Ganz, Picasso Connoisseurs: 'A Brand That People Were Proud to Own,'" *ARTnews*, April 14, 2021, https://www.artnews.com/feature/who-are-victor-sally-ganz-collectors-1234589587/.

15. Mary Clarke and Clement Crisp, *The History of Dance* (London: Orbis, 1961), 60.

16. Francisco Hidalgo, "Carmen Amaya, Biographical Epilogue," in Ana María Moix, *Carmen Amaya 1963* (Barcelona: Focal Ediciones: Institut d'Edicions Diputació de Barcelona, 1999), unpaginated.

CHAPTER 25: NEW LOVE

1. John Giorno, *Great Demon Kings* (New York: Farrar, Straus and Giroux, 2020), 94–96.

2. Ibid.

3. St. Regis, Salvador Dalí press release. Note: In 1986, one year before his death, Andy Warhol made a silk screen called *War Bonnet*.

4. Giorno, *Great Demon Kings*, 94–96.

5. According to Nita Renfrew, who modeled for Dalí in the late '60s, these teas were more like royal audiences than social events. None of the guests actually spoke to one another. They just sat around waiting for Dalí to pay attention to them. Although Gala was never there, according to Nita, Mme Dalí's disapproval of these gatherings was evident. Gala, whom Nita described as Salvador's "handler," only cared about Salvador. She disdained his jet-set groupies.

6. Ada Louise Huxtable, "A&P heir Huntington Hartford's Palatial New Museum," *New York Times*, February 25, 1964.

7. "Hartford's Gallery Has 4,277 Visitors," *New York Times*, March 23, 1964.

8. Salvador had no memory of having made *Homage to Immanuel Kant*.

9. Lake, *In Quest of Dalí*, 100–159.

10. V. Samaniego, "Gala," *Revista Garbo*, Barcelona/Madrid, September 5, 1964, 18, 44.

11. Salvador Dalí, *Diary of a Genius* (New York: Doubleday, 1965), first page.

12. Author interview with William Rothlein, April 26, 2023.

13. Lake, *In Quest of Dalí*, 211–12.

14. See Bonham's catalog entry, https://bonhams.com/auctions/14038 /lot/6115/. The "W" or French "double v" in "LOWE" means "love two ways."

15. Lake, *In Quest of Dalí*, 223.

16. Arabella Árbenz committed suicide on October 6, 1965, in Bogotá, Colombia.

17. Author interview with William Rothlein, June 2021.

18. From May 16 to June 16, this yearly exhibition of works by living artists including Dalí, Picasso, and René Magritte was held at the Musée d'Art Moderne de la Ville de Paris, 11 avenue de Président Wilson.

19. Lake, *In Quest of Dalí*, 245.

20. Amanda Lear, *My Life with Dalí* (London: Virgin Books, 1985), 84.

21. Lake, *In Quest of Dalí*, 250.

22. Castrense's most famous work is *Aria Madre: Glorificazione dell'aviazione italiana in versi liberi e parole in libertà*, Edizioni Futuriste di Poesia, Rome 1941. (Mother Air: A Glorification of the Flight of Italian Free Words and Free Verse).

23. Previously known as Alan Tapp, a performer at the legendary transvestite Cabaret Carousel, 30 avenue d'Italie near the Place Pigalle in Paris as well as an art student and model Amanda had always identified as she/ her. See Gibson, *The Shameful Life*, 527.

24. Lear, *My Life with Dalí*, 13.

25. Ibid., 24–26.

26. 1910 was the year when a six-and-a-half-year-old Dalí scratched his famous first drawings of swans and ducks on his parents' terrace table in Barcelona.

27. Ruth Robinson, "Dalí and His Art Attract Throng to Preview," *New York Times*, December 18, 1965.

28. As quoted in "Salvador Dalí, the Sewer-Realist," *Tudor City Confidential*, September 25, 2022, https://tudorcityconfidential.com/2022/09 /salvador-dali-sewer-realist.html.

29. Grace Glueck, "Dalí Concocts a Happening of Sorts," *New York Times*, February 24, 1966.

30. Carlton Lake, *In Quest of Dalí*, 305. Although Lake's book was not published until 1969, the accuracy of his summation was apparent well before that.

CHAPTER 26: PETER MOORE'S SCANDAL

1. Manuel Pertegaz dressed Ava Gardner, Jackie Kennedy, and Audrey Hepburn. He designed the wedding dress for Letizia Ortiz's marriage to Felipe VI, the future king of Spain. After Christian Dior's death, he turned down an offer to become Dior's successor in Paris. He lived and worked in Barcelona and was considered Spain's leading couturier.

2. Lear, *My Life with Dalí*, 51.

3. Interview with Amanda Lear, Alice Cooper, et al. about Dalí— temporarily removed from YouTube.com.

4. Ian Gibson interview with Emilio Puignau, in Gibson, *The Shameful Life*, 548.

5. *Soft Watches Hard Times, the unpublished memoirs of Peter Moore*, as quoted in Gibson, *The Shameful Life*, 495.

6. Gibson, *The Shameful Life*, 548.

7. Mark Rogerson, *The Dalí Scandal: An Investigation* (London: Gollancz, 1987), 10.

8. James M. Markham, "Dalí Trying to Repair Business Affairs and Resolve Scandals," *New York Times*, March 26, 1981.

9. This quote is an approximation based on the author interview with Michael Stout in June 2023. Moore may have worded it slightly differently.

10. Rogerson, *The Dalí Scandal*, 13.

11. Elizabeth Nash, "Peter Moore," *Independent*, December 30, 2005.

CHAPTER 27: AMANDA BECOMES A ROCK STAR, GALA IS ISHTAR

1. His Christian name was Alexis, but the name he was called by was Alex.

2. Spanish Fashion designer Francisco Rabaneda Cuervo, known as Paco Rabanne, was Salvador Dalí's friend and an *enfant terrible* of the fashion world. He dressed Jane Fonda for the 1968 Roger Vadim film *Barbarella* and is famous for his 1991 perfume XS.

3. Ossie Clark was a British designer and major figure in the Swinging Sixties scene in London and the fashion industry of that era.

4. The British specialty store Biba was known for its cutting-edge fashion designed by Bárbara Hulanicki, which attracted up to a million customers weekly, making it one of the most visited tourist attractions in London in the late '60s.

5. Lear, *My Life with Dalí*, 255.

6. Lidia Jarolymek, "Lettre à mon frère," 1987, in Vieuille, *Gala*, 179.

7. *"Macou,"* which means "mob" in French slang, is an invented term of endearment.

8. By "a brain," Gala meant "a scientific genius."

9. Antonio Pitxot and Josep Playà, *Gala Dalí's Castle: The Road to Púbol* (Figueres: Fundació Gala-Salvador Dalí, 1997).

10. Excerpted, translated, and adapted from Michel Pastore in "Lettre à mon frère," in Vieuille, *Gala*, 195–98.

11. Reynolds Morse, *Ode à Gala Incognita* (Cleveland, OH: Editions Chagrin, 1968)

12. Recorded circa 2001 BC, "Gilgamesh and the Bull of Heaven" is one of the poems that make up what remains of *The Epic of Gilgamesh*.

13. N. K. Sandars, trans., *The Epic of Gilgamesh*, Kindle version by Penguin Classics.

CHAPTER 28: A CASTLE IN SPAIN

1. Ian Gibson interview with Enrique Sabater, June 30, 1996, in Gibson, *The Shameful Life*, 598.

2. Lear, *My Life with Dalí*, 166.

3. Ibid., 212–13.

4. Emilio Puignau, *Vivènces amb Salvador Dalí* (Barcelona: Juventude, 1995), 821, 822.

5. Originally bred in Portugal as warhorses, Lusitanos are now chiefly used for bullfights.

6. Pitxot and Playà, *The Road to Púbol*, 27.

7. Taken from an early photograph of Gala, which she inscribed "Tête à Château."

8. Author interview with Michael Stout, June 2022.

9. Ibid.

10. The *L'Angélus* imagery is about spiritual nourishment. In Gala's domain it is about physical nourishment as well.

11. *Dalí in Rotterdam*, by Hans Wessels, YouTube video, https://www
.youtube.com/watch?v=q7GfOWEzSOQ.

12. Arthur Annesley Ronald Firbank (January 17, 1886–May 21, 1926) was
an English novelist who was inspired by the London aesthetes of the
1890s, especially Oscar Wilde. His work consists largely of dialogue,
with references to religion, social climbing, and sexuality.

CHAPTER 29: DARKNESS AND LIGHT

1. *Jesus Christ Superstar* is a sung-through rock opera with music by Andrew
Lloyd Webber and lyrics by Tim Rice. Loosely based on the Gospels'
accounts of the Passion, the work interprets the psychology of Jesus and
other characters. It premiered October 12, 1971.

2. Alex Greenberg, "7 Key MoMA Shows from the 1970s and What
ARTnews Said at the Time," *ARTnews*, October 9, 2019, https://www
.artnews.com/art-news/retrospective/moma-1970s-frank-stella-robert
-rauschenberg-13325/.

3. Jeff Fenholt, *From Darkness to Light* (Tulsa, OK: Harrison House, 1994), 13.

4. Ibid.

5. "Jesus Christ Superstar Rocks Broadway," *Time*, October 25, 1971. It
premiered in New York on October 12, 1971.

6. Fenholt, *From Darkness to Light*, 48.

7. Ibid., 57.

8. Author interview with Michael Stout, 2023.

9. The Trinity Broadcasting Network is an international Christian-based
broadcast television network that is also the world's largest religious
television network.

10. Twitter, September 11, 2019, 4:47 PM Pacific time.

11. Vérité furnished most of the models for Salvador's paintings.

12. John Richardson, "Dalí's Demon Bride," *Vanity Fair*, December 1988.

13. Aguer, *Salvador Dalí: An Illustrated Life*, 431.

14. James was beheaded by Herod Agrippa, king of Judea in 44 AD.

CHAPTER 30: JACOB'S LADDER

1. Totem poles are monuments created by First Nations of the Pacific
Northwest to represent and commemorate ancestry, histories, people,
or events. Most totem poles display beings, or crest animals, marking

a family's lineage and validating the powerful rights and privileges that the family held. Totem poles would not necessarily *tell* a story so much as they would serve to document stories and histories familiar to community members or particular family or clan members. https://indigenousfoundations.arts.ubc.ca/home/.

2. In the biblical book named after her, Esther is a young Jewish woman living in the Persian diaspora who marries Xerxes I, king of Persia, becomes queen, and risks her life to save her people from destruction when the court official Haman persuades Xerxes to authorize a pogrom against all the Jews of the empire. https://jwa.org/encyclopedia/article/esther-bible.

3. "People in the News," *Pittsburgh Press*, September 30, 1974.

4. The bay of Rosas is the most northeastern bay in Catalonia.

5. Narcís Monturiol (1819–1885) was a Spanish artist, writer, and inventor born in Figueres. He made the first autonomously propelled manned submarine, called the Ictíneo.

6. The brothel operated at 12 rue Chabanais from 1878 until 1946, when brothels were outlawed in France. It was founded by the Irish-born Madame Kelly, who was closely acquainted with members of Paris' most exclusive men's club: the Jockey.

7. Author conversation with Pierre Apraxine, May 2007.

8. Retired from court life and engrossed by her own beauty, the countess attempted to capture it in all its facets for the camera of photographer Pierre-Louis Pierson who she employed to endlessly imprint her image. Far from being merely a passive subject, it was she who decided the expressive content of the pictures and assumed the art director's role, even to the point of choosing the camera angle. She also gave precise directions on the enlargement and repainting of her photographs in order to transform the simple documents into imaginary visions—taking up the paintbrush herself at times. Her painted photographs are among the most beautiful examples of the genre. See Malcolm Daniel, "The Countess da Castiglione," Heilbrunn Timeline of Art History, The Met, July 2007, http://www.metmuseum.org/toah/hd/coca/hd_coca.htm.

9. Stereoscopy is a technique used to enable a three-dimensional effect, adding an illusion of depth to a flat image.

10. A stereoscope is a machine for viewing a pair of separate images, depicting left-eye and right-eye views of the same scene, as a single three-dimensional image.

11. Estrella de Diego, *Gala Salvador Dalí: A Room of One's Own at Púbol* (Barcelona: Museu Nacional d'Art de Catalunya, 2018), 147.

12. Jesus Christ was anointed with spikenard oil before the Crucifixion.

13. Lear, *My Life with Dalí*, 252.

14. Figueres is the capital of Alt Empordà in the province of Girona.

CHAPTER 31: A TIME TO REAP

1. *Wine with a Curator: Dalí's Visions of the Dark Grape*, Dalí Museum, YouTube video, April 12, 2021 https://www.youtube.com/watch?v=r_98P4GMGrg.

2. Andy Warhol, *Andy Warhol's Exposures* (New York: Andy Warhol Books / Grosset & Dunlap, 1979).

3. Ibid., 128.

4. Ibid.

5. Author interview with Beniamino Levi, June 22, 2022.

6. Gibson, *The Shameful Life*, 567.

7. "Los Reyes de España almorzaron con Salvador Dalí," *El País*, August 5, 1979.

8. *La Gare de Perpignan*, 1965, is a large-scale oil on canvas painting by Salvador Dalí, of the railway station of the French city of Perpignan, near the border with Spain. It held special significance for Dalí, who in the '20s boarded the train to Paris in that station and proclaimed it to be the "Center of the Universe" after experiencing a cosmic vision there in 1963.

CHAPTER 32: A TIME TO REST

1. Author interview with Michael Stout, July 16, 2023.

2. Rogerson, *The Dalí Scandal*, 29.

3. Markham, "Dalí Trying to Repair Business Affairs and Resolve Scandals."

4. Secrest, *Salvador Dalí: A Biography*, 243.

5. Rogerson, *The Dalí Scandal*, 30.

6. Ibid.

7. Markham, "Dalí Trying to Repair Business Affairs and Resolve Scandals."

8. *Lullian Wheels* is dedicated to the memory of Ramon Llull (1232–1316), who was an artist and alchemist from Paloma, Catalonia. He was among the first to write in his native Catalan.

9. Gala was considered the "money man" to the end. Michael Stout tells the story of a check he received from Dalí after Gala's death. When Stout took the check to the bank, they would not cash it because it hadn't been countersigned by Gala.

10. Lee Catterall, *The Great Dalí Art Fraud and Other Deceptions* (Fort Lee, NJ: Barricade Books Inc., 1992), 60–61.

11. In the Iberian Peninsula, the Black Death is estimated to have killed 60 to 65 percent of the population, reducing its total population from six million to 2.5 million between 1347 and 1353.

12. Reference to Gala and Paul Éluard's collaborative 1913 collection of poems: *Dialogues des Inutiles* where Gala signed her essay "*la Reine de Pauleùlgnn.*"

13. Gibson, *The Shameful Life*, 597.

14. Gibson, *The Shameful Life*, 597.

15. Formerly the part of *delme*.

16. Author interview with Claire Sarti, May 2022.

17. Gibson, *The Shameful Life*, 648.

18. The full name of the work is *The Three Glorious Enigmas of Gala Christ after "Pietà" and the Persian Sibyl by Michelangelo in the Sistine Chapel.*

EPILOGUE: THE LAST FAIRY TALE

1. Translated and summarized by the author from *Grain-d'Aile* by Paul Éluard.

2. One of the most important childhood memories for sculptor Elizabeth (Bessie) de Cuevas, who was a little girl when the Dalís spent summers with her parents in New Hampshire during the war, was how overjoyed she was when Gala told her mother that she had artistic abilities. For an aspiring creator, a nod from Gala was considered the ultimate endorsement. Author's interview with Elizabeth de Cuevas, May 2020.

BIBLIOGRAPHY

Ades, Dawn. *Dalí (World of Art)*. London: Thames & Hudson, 1995.

Aguer Teixidor, Montse, Antoni Pitxot Soler, and Jordi Puig Castellano. *Theater-Museum Dalí of Figueres: Theater-Museum Dalí of Figueres*, Barcelona: Triangle Postals, 2005.

———. *Château Gala Dalí Púbol*. Barcelona: Triangle Postals, 2019 (French edition).

Aguer Teixidor, Montse, Joana Bonet, Bea Crespo, and Clara Silvestre. *Gala/Dalí/Dior: Of Art and Fashion*. Figueres: Fundació Gala-Salvador Dalí, 2020.

Aguer Teixidor, Montse. *Salvador Dalí: An Illustrated Life*. Translated by Chris Miller. London: Tate Publishing, 2007.

Ballard, Bettina. *In My Fashion*. New York: D. McKay, 1969.

Becker, Lucille Frackman. *Louis Aragon*. New York: Twayne Publishers, 1971.

Benaim, Laurence. *Marie-Laure de Noailles, La vicomtesse du bizarre*. Paris: Grasset, 2001.

Blavier, Beatrix. *Max Ernst: Murals For the Home of Paul and Gala Éluard, Eaubonne 1923*. Master's thesis, Rice University, 1985.

Blum, Dilys. *Shocking! The Art and Fashion of Elsa Schiaparelli*. Philadelphia: Philadelphia Museum of Art, 2003.

Bocquet, José-Louis, and Catel Muller. *Kiki de Montparnasse*. New York: Harry N. Abrams, 2012.

Bona, Dominique. *Gala: La muse redoutable*. Grandes Biographies. Paris: Flammarion, 1995.

Boothe, Clare. *Europe in the Spring* New York: Alfred A. Knopf, 1940.

Breton, André. *Lettres à Jacques Doucet*. Paris: Gallimard, 2016.

———. *Manifestoes of Surrealism*. Translated by Richard Seaver and Helen R. Lane. Ann Harbor, MI: University of Michigan Press, 1972. Available online: https://archive.org/details/andrebretonmanifestoesofsurrealism/mode/2up.

————. *Nadja*. Paris: Gallimard, 1972.

Breton, André, and Paul Éluard. *Correspondance 1919–1938*. Paris: Gallimard, 2019.

————. *Dictionnaire Abrégé du Surréalisme*. Paris: Galerie des Beaux-Arts, 1938.

Breton, Simone. *Lettres à Denise Lévy 1929–1939*. Paris: Éditions Joëlle Losfeld, 2005.

Briggs-Anderson, Barbara. *Salvador Dalí's "A Surrealistic Night in an Enchanted Forest."* Bookbaby, 2012. Kindle.

Brown, Dr. Christopher Heath. *The Dalí Legacy: How an Eccentric Genius Changed the Art World and Created a Lasting Legacy*. New York: Apollo Publishers, 2021.

Buñuel, Luis. *My Last Sigh: The Autobiography of Luis Buñuel*. New York: Vintage Books, 2013.

Bushkovitch, Paul. *A Concise History of Russia* (Cambridge Concise Histories). Cambridge: Cambridge University Press, 2011.

Carron de la Carrière, Marie-Sophie. *Shocking: The Surreal World of Elsa Schiaparelli*. London: Thames & Hudson, 2022.

Caws, Mary Ann. *The Surrealist Look: An Erotics of Encounter*. Cambridge, MA: The MIT Press, 1999.

Cerwin, Herbert. *In Search of Something: The Memoirs of a Public Relations Man*. Los Angeles: Sherbourne Press, 1966.

Clark, Adrian, and Jeremy Dronfield. *Queer Saint: The Cultured Life of Peter Watson*. London: Lume Books, 2022.

Cowles, Fleur, and A. Reynolds Morse, *The Case of Salvador Dalí*. Whitefish, MT: Literary Licensing LLC, 2011.

Crosland, Margaret. *The Enigma of Giorgio de Chirico*. London: Peter Owen Ltd., 2000.

Crosby, Caresse. *The Passionate Years*. London: Alvin Redman, 1955.

Daguerre, Pierre. *Le Marquis de Cuevas*. Paris: Denoel, 1954.

Dalí. Tarot. Deck of seventy-eight tarot cards with booklet by Johannes Fiebig. Cologne: Taschen, 2024.

Dalí, Gala. *Carnets Intimes*. Paris: Michel Lafon, 2012.

Dalí, Salvador. *50 Secrets of Magic Craftsmanship*. Translated by Haakon M. Chevalier. New York: Dove Publications, 1992.

————. *Dalí Jewels: The Collection of the Gala-Salvador Dalí Foundation*. London: Umberto Allemandi & Co., 2006.

————. *Dalí: Les Diners de Gala*. Translated by Captain J. Peter Moore. Cologne: Taschen, 2016.

————. *Dalí: Les Vins de Gala*. Cologne: Taschen, 2017.

————. *Hidden Faces*. Translated by Haakon Chevalier. London: Pushkin Press Classics, 2024.

————. *Ode à Gala Incognita*. Cleveland, Ohio: Editions Chagrin, 1968.

————. *The Secret Life of Salvador Dalí*. Translated by Haakon Chevalier. New York: Burton C. Hoffman Dial Press, 1942.

Dalí, Salvador, and Federico García Lorca. *Sebastian's Arrows: Letters and Mementos of Salvador Dalí and Federico García Lorca*. Translated by Christopher Maurer. Chicago: Swan Isle Press, 2005.

de Burca, Jackie. *Salvador Dalí at Home*. London: Frances Lincoln Publishers, 2012.

de Chirico, Giorgio. *The Memoirs of Giorgio de Chirico*. Boston: Da Capo Press, 1994.

de Courcy, Anne. *Chanel's Riviera: Glamour, Decadence, and Survival in Peace and War, 1930–1944*. New York: St. Martin's Press, 2020.

de Diego, Estrella. *Gala Salvador Dalí: A Room of One's Own at Púbol*. Barcelona: Museu Nacional d'Art de Catalunya, 2018.

de Faucigny-Lucinge, Jean-Louis. *Un Gentilhomme Cosmopolite: Mémoires*. Paris: Perrin, 1990.

de La Fontaine, Jean. *The Complete Fables of Jean de La Fontaine*. Translated by Norman R. Shapiro. Champagne, IL: University of Illinois Press, 2007.

de Saint Jean, Robert. *Journal d'un Journaliste*. Paris: Grasset, 2009.

Delay, Claude. *Chanel Solitaire*. Paris: Gallimard, 1983.

Descharnes, Robert. *The World of Salvador Dalí*. Translated by Albert Field. New York: Atide Books, 1962.

————. *Dalí: The Work. The Man*. New York: Harry N. Abrams, 1984.

Domingo, Carmen. *Gala-Dalí: Le Roman d'un amour surréaliste*. Traduit par Guillaume Contré et Margot Nguyen-Béraud. Paris: Presses de la Cité, 2018.

Éluard, Paul. *Grain-d'Aile*. Paris: Nathan Jeunesse, 1995.

————. *Lettres à Gala: 1924–1948*. Edition établie et annotée par Pierre Dreyfus. Paris: Gallimard, 1984.

————. *Œuvres Complètes*. Edition établie par Marcelle Dumas et Lucien Scheler. Bibliothèque de la Pleiade. Paris: Gallimard, 1968.

————. *[Poèmes de jeunesse]. 1911–1918: manuscrits et copies par Gala et moi*. Bibliothèque Littéraire Jacques Doucet, Paris.

The Edward James Archive, West Dean.

The Epic of Gilgamesh. Translated by Andrew George. New York: Penguin Classics, 2003.

Ernst, Jimmy. *A Not-So-Still Life: A Memoir by Jimmy Ernst.* New York: St. Martin's/Marek, 1984.

Ernst, Max. *Max Ernst: Fotografische Porträts und Dokumente.* Brühl, Germany: Stadt Brühl, 1991.

Etherington-Smith, Meredith. *The Persistence of Memory: A Biography of Dalí.* New York: Random House, 1992.

Fanés, Felix. *Dalí and Mass Culture.* Figueres: Fundacion "La Caixa" / Fundació Gala-Salvador Dalí / Salvador Dalí Museum, 2004.

Fenholt, Jeff, *From Darkness to Light.* Tulsa, OK: Harrison House, 1994.

Fiemeyer, Isabelle. *Intimate Chanel.* Paris: Flammarion, 2011.

Figes, Orlando. *The History of Russia.* New York: Metropolitan Books, 2022.

Fini, Leonor with Jose Alvarez. *Le Livre de Leonor Fini. Peintures, dessin, écrits, notes.* Paris: Editions Clairefontaine–Vilo, 1975.

Fizdale, Robert, and Arthur Gold. *Misia: The Life of Misia Sert.* New York: HarperCollins, 1981.

Gibson, Ian. *The Shameful Life of Salvador Dalí.* London: Faber & Faber, 1997.

Giorno, John. *Great Demon Kings. A Memoir of Poetry, Sex, Art, Death and Enlightenment.* New York: Farrar, Straus and Giroux, 2020.

Guggenheim, Peggy. *Out of This Century: Confessions of an Art Addict.* New York: Universe Publishing, 1987.

Hooks, Margaret. *Surreal Lovers: Eight Women Integral to the Life of Max Ernst.* Madrid: La Fabrica, 2018.

James, Edward. *Swans Reflecting Elephants. My Early Years.* London: Weindenfeld & Nicolson, 1982.

Janson, H.W. *History of Art. Fifth Edition. Revised and Expanded by Anthony F. Janson.* New York: Harry N. Abrams Inc., 1995.

Josephson, Matthew. *Life Among the Surrealists.* New York: Holt, Rinehart, and Winston, 1962.

Kusunoki, Sharon-Michi. *Surreal Life: Edward James 1907–1984.* East Sussex, England: Brighton & Hove Museums, 1998.

Lake, Carlton. *In Quest of Dalí.* New York: Putnam, 1969.

Lear, Amanda. *My Life with Dalí.* London: Virgin Books, 1985.

————. *Persistence of Memory: A Personal Biography of Salvador Dalí.* Bethesda, MD: National Press, 1987.

Leith, Sam. *Lord Berners: The Last Eccentric.* London: Faber & Faber, 2012.

Levy, Julien. *Memoir of an Art Gallery.* Boston: MFA Publications, 2003.

Mallett, Renee. *Wicked New Hampshire.* Cheltenham, Gloucestershire, England: The History Press, 2020.

Marquand, Lilou. *Chanel m'a dit.* Paris: Jean-Claude Lattes, 1990.

Massine, Léonide, and Phyllis Hatnoll (ed.), Robert Rubens (ed.). *My Life in Ballet.* London: Macmillan; New York: St. Martin's Press, 1968.

McGirk, Tim. *Wicked Lady: Salvador Dalí's Muse.* Terra Alta, West Virginia: Headline Books, 1989.

McNab, Robert. *Ghost Ships: A Surrealist Love Triangle.* New Haven, CT: Yale University Press, 2004.

Meyer-Stabley, Bertrand. *La Véritable Gala Dalí.* Paris: Pygmalion, 2006.

Morse, Reynolds. *The Decade, 1971–1961: Updating supplement to A New Introduction to Salvador Dalí.* St. Petersburg, Florida: The Salvador Dalí Museum, 1971.

Morse, Samuel F. B. Unpublished memoirs of Samuel F. B. Morse.

Mousli, Béatrice. *Philippe Soupault.* Grandes Biographies. Paris: Flammarion, 2011.

Nadeau, Maurice. *The History of Surrealism.* Translated by Richard Howard. London: Jonathan Cape, 1968.

Nin, Anaïs. *The Diary of Anaïs Nin: 1939–1944*, vol. 3. Boston: Mariner Books Classics, 1971.

Pastoureau, Henri. *Ma vie surréaliste.* Paris: Maurice Nadeau, 1998.

Picardie, Justine. *Coco Chanel: The Legend and the Life.* New York: HarperCollins, 2011.

Pitxot, Antonio, and Josep Playà. *The Road to Púbol.* Figueres: Fundació Gala-Salvador Dalí, 1997.

Polizzotti, Mark. *Revolution of the Mind: The Life of André Breton.* Boston: Da Capo Press, 1997.

———. *André Breton.* Biographies. Traduit de l'américain par Jean-François Sené. Paris: Gallimard, 1999.

Prose, Francine. *The Lives of the Muses: Nine Women & the Artists They Inspired.* New York: HarperCollins, 2003.

Puignau, Emilio. *Vivencias con Salvador Dali.* Barcelona: Juventude, 1995.

Roe, Sue. *In Montparnasse: The Emergence of Surrealism in Paris, from Duchamp to Dalí.* New York: Penguin Press, 2019.

Rogerson, Mark. *The Dalí Scandal: An Investigation.* London: Victor Gollancz, 1989.

Russell, John. *Max Ernst: Life and Work.* New York: Harry N. Abrams, 1967.

Secrest, Meryle. *Elsa Schiaparelli: A Biography*. New York: Knopf, 2014.

———. *Salvador Dalí: A Biography*. New York: E. P. Dutton, 1986.

Sontag, Susan. *On Photography*. London: Picador, 2001.

Soupault, Philippe. *Histoire d'un blanc 1897–1927: Mémoires de l'Oubli*. Paris: Gallimard, 2002.

Spies, Werner. *Max Ernst: Life and Work*. London: Thames & Hudson, 2006.

Straus-Ernst, Louise. *The First Wife's Tale: A Memoir by Louise Straus-Ernst*. Translated by Marylin Richter and Marietta Schmitz-Esser. New York: Midmarch Arts Press, 2004.

Tanning, Dorothea. *Between Lives: An Artist and Her World*. New York: W. W. Norton & Company, 2001.

———. *Birthday*. San Francisco: Lapis Press, 1986.

Tomkins, Calvin. *Duchamp: A Biography*. New York: Henry Holt & Company, 1996.

———. *The Lives of Artists*. New York: Phaidon Press, 2019.

Trachtman, Paul. "A Brief History of Dada," *Smithsonian*, May 2006, https://www.smithsonianmag.com/arts-culture/dada-115169154/.

Tsvétaeva, Anastassia. *Souvenirs*. Traduit du russe par Michèle Kahn. Arles, France: Solin Actes Sud, 2003.

Valette, Robert D. *Éluard, Livre d'identité*. Paris: Tchou, 1967.

Vallin, Marjolaine. *Louis Aragon, la théâtralité de l'œuvre dernière*. Paris: L'Harmattan, 2005.

Vanoyeke, Violaine. *Paul Éluard: Le Poète de la liberté*. Paris: Flammarion, 1995.

Vieuille, Chantal. *Gala*. Paris: Favre, 1988.

Warhol, Andy, and Bob Colacello. *Andy Warhol's Exposures*. New York: The Putnam Publishing Group, 1980.

Weld, Jacqueline Bograd. *Peggy: The Wayward Guggenheim*. New York: Dutton, 1986.

Whitney, D. Quincy. *Hidden History of New Hampshire*. Cheltenham, Gloucestershire, England: The History Press, 2008.

Yersin, Véronique. *Minotaure – Chants exploratoires – La Revue d'Albert Skira, 1933–1939*. Geneva: JPR, 2008.

Zinovieff, Sofka. *The Mad Boy, Lord Berners, My Grandmother and Me*. New York: Harper, 2015.

MICHÈLE GERBER KLEIN is an author and journalist who writes frequently about art and fashion. Her first book, *Charles James: Portrait of an Unreasonable Man*, was named a *Financial Times* Best Book of 2018. A columnist for Mann Publications, she has contributed to numerous publications, including the *Brooklyn Rail*, *Cottages and Gardens*, and *Quest*, where her subjects have included Elsa Schiaparelli, Christian Lacroix, Tina Barney, Maurizio Cattelan, and Diane Arbus. She serves as the vice president of the Bertha and Isaac Liberman Foundation and is involved with many arts institutions, including the Museum of Modern Art, the Whitney Museum, the Metropolitan Museum of Art, and the Drawing Center. She is the founder of joan vass U.S.A., a popularly priced collection of elegant knitwear and was head of Lanvin S.A. women's licenses in the America. She holds a bachelor's degree in English literature from Bryn Mawr College. She lives in New York.